Essays and Sketches in Biography

ESSAYS
AND SKETCHES
IN BIOGRAPHY

Including the complete text of
ESSAYS IN BIOGRAPHY and TWO MEMOIRS

by John Maynard Keynes

 MERIDIAN BOOKS   *New York, 1956*

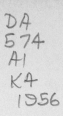

DA
574
A1
K4
1956

Publisher's Note

The present Meridian Books edition has been drawn from two separate volumes by Lord Keynes, *Essays in Biography* and *Two Memoirs*. All the essays included in both volumes appear in their entirety, although their order of appearance has been slightly altered.

With a few minor corrections made by Lord Keynes in 1933, and additional corrections in the footnotes made for the present text by Geoffrey Keynes, Sections I, II, and IV are reprinted as originally published.

Section III, *Two Memoirs,* appears with introductory notes by the editor, David Garnett. Since these memoirs were addressed to gatherings of Lord Keynes' most intimate friends, they are supplemented by Mr. Garnett with background information necessary to their proper appreciation. A key to persons mentioned in the *Two Memoirs* by other than their full names has been retained. The footnotes to the text of *Two Memoirs* were prepared by Mr. Garnett.

John Maynard Keynes

One of the world's great economists, Lord Keynes was that rare combination: an authority in a technical discipline and a brilliant literary artist. When he died in 1946 in his sixty-third year he left, in addition to his many published works, *Two Memoirs* to be released only after his death. Reprinted in the present volume together with *Essays in Biography*, they embody Keynes' own statement of his philosophy and beliefs.

Contents

Part I: Lives of Economists

ROBERT MALTHUS [1]

1766-1835

Bacchus—when an Englishman is called Bacchus—derives from Bakehouse. Similarly the original form of the rare and curious name of Malthus was Malthouse. The pronunciation of English proper names has been more constant one century with another than their spelling, which fluctuates between phonetic and etymological influences, and can generally be inferred with some confidence from an examination of the written variations. On this test (Malthus, Mawtus, Malthous, Malthouse, Mauthus, Maltus, Maultous) there can be little doubt that *Maultus,* with the first vowel as in brewer's malt and the *h* doubtfully sounded, is what we ought to say.

We need not trace the heredity of Robert Malthus[2] further back than to the Reverend Robert Malthus who became Vicar of Northolt under Cromwell and was evicted at the Restoration. Calamy calls him "an ancient divine, a man of strong reason, and mighty in the Scriptures, of great eloquence and fervour, though defective in elocution." But his parishioners thought him "a very unprofitable and fruitless minister," perhaps because he was strict in the exaction of tithes, and in a petition for his removal complained of him as having "uttered

11

invective expressions against our army while they were in Scotland," and also that "Mr. Malthus is one who hath not only a low voice but a very great impediment in his utterance"; from which it seems probable that he shared with his great-great-grandson not only the appellation of the Reverend Robert Malthus, but also the defect of a cleft palate. His son Daniel was appointed apothecary to King William by favour of the celebrated Dr. Sydenham and afterwards to Queen Anne,[3] and became a man of sufficient substance for his widow to own a coach and horses. Daniel's son Sydenham further improved the family fortunes, being a clerk in Chancery, a director of the South Sea Company, rich enough to give his daughter a dowry of £5000, and the proprietor of several landed properties in the Home Counties and Cambridgeshire.[4]

The golden mediocrity of a successful English middle-class family being now attained, Sydenham's son Daniel, our hero's father, found himself in a position of what is known in England as "independence" and decided to take advantage of it. He was educated at Queen's College, Oxford, but took no degree, "travelled much in Europe and in every part of this island," settled down in a pleasant neighbourhood, led the life of a small English country gentleman, cultivated intellectual tastes and friendships, wrote a few anonymous pieces,[5] and allowed diffidence to overmaster ambition. It is recorded that he "possessed the most pleasing manners with the most benevolent heart, which was experienced by all the poor wherever he lived." [6] When he died the *Gentleman's Magazine* (February 1800, p. 177) was able to record that he was "an eccentric character in the strictest sense of the term."

In 1759 Daniel Malthus had purchased a "small elegant mansion" near Dorking "known by the name of Chert-gate Farm, and taking advantage of its beauties, hill and dale, wood and water, displaying them in their naked simplicity, converted it into a gentleman's seat, giving it the name of The Rookery." [7] Here on February 13,[8] 1766, was born Thomas Robert Malthus, his second son, the author of the *Essay on the Principle of Population*. When the babe was three weeks old, on March 9, 1766, two fairy godmothers, Jean-Jacques Rousseau and David

Hume, called together at The Rookery,[9] and may be presumed to have assigned to the infant with a kiss diverse intellectual gifts.

For Daniel Malthus was not only a friend of Hume,[10] but a devoted, not to say passionate, admirer of Rousseau. When Rousseau first came to England, Hume endeavoured to settle him in Surrey in the near neighbourhood of Daniel Malthus, who, "desirous of doing him every kind of service," would have provided congenial company and kept upon him a benevolent eye.[11] Like most of Hume's good intentions towards his uneasy visitant, the project broke down. The cottage at the foot of Leith Hill pointed out to Fanny Burney in later years as *l'asile de Jean-Jacques*[12] was never occupied by him, but was, doubtless, the retreat which Daniel Malthus had fixed upon as suitable and Jean-Jacques had inspected[13] on March 8, 1766, but afterwards rejected. A fortnight later Rousseau had begun his disastrous sojourn at Wootton[14] in the Peak of Derbyshire, where, cold and bored and lonely, he brewed within a few weeks his extraordinary quarrel with Hume.[15]

This most famous of literary *causes* might never have occurred, I think, if only Jean-Jacques had accepted Daniel Malthus's most pressing invitation. For he would have had affection poured out upon him, and have been amused and within reach. Daniel Malthus's passionate declarations of devotion to Jean-Jacques were, probably, the only occasion in his life in which his reserves were fully broken down.[16] I think that they met three times only,—when Malthus paid a tourist's visit to Môtiers in the spring of 1764, when Hume brought Rousseau to the Rookery in March 1766, and when Malthus travelled up to see him at Wootton in June of the same year. But to judge from thirteen letters from Malthus to Rousseau, which have been preserved, and one from Rousseau to Malthus,[17] the meetings were a great success. Malthus worshipped Jean-Jacques, and Jean-Jacques was cordial and friendly in return, speaking of "les sentiments d'estime et d'attachement que vous m'avez inspirés," and of Malthus's "hospitalité si douce." Malthus was even able to defend the character of Hume without becoming embroiled in the quarrel. There are many references to their botanising together, and Rousseau complains what a nuisance it is that he cannot identify the names of what he sees on his walks in Derbyshire; for he needs, he says, "une occupation qui demande de l'exercice; car rien ne me fait tant de mal que de rester assis, ou d'écrire ou lire." Later on (in 1768) we find Daniel Malthus taking great pains to complete Rousseau's botanical library for him, at a time when Rousseau was probably contemplating his *Letters to a Lady on the Elements of Botany,* which were dated 1771; and two years later Rousseau, who had a craze for dispossessing himself of his books from time to time, sold the whole library back to Malthus, adding to it the gift of a part of his herbarium.[18] These books reappear in Daniel Malthus's will, where we find the following provision: "To Mrs. Jane Dalton[19] I give all my botanical books in which the name of Rousseau is written and a box of plants given me by Mons. Rousseau." Two of these books are still to be found in the library of Dalton Hill, Albury, now owned by Mr. Robert Malthus,[20] namely, Ray's *Synopsis Methodica Stirpium Britannicarum* and de Sauvage's *Méthode pour connoître les plantes par les feuilles,* both inscribed with the name of Rousseau and heavily scored.[21]

Otter relates that Daniel Malthus was a literary executor of Rousseau. This seems improbable.[22] But Daniel Malthus's loyalty lasted to the end, and he subscribed for six copies, at a cost of thirty guineas, of Rousseau's posthumous *Consolations des misères de ma vie.* And now in these few pages I piously fulfil his wish: "Si jamais je suis connu, ce seroit sous le nom de l'ami de Rousseau."

There is a charming account of Daniel's way of life in his letter to Rousseau of January 24, 1768.[23] In the summer botanising walks.

ma chère Henriette et ses enfants en prenoient leur part, et nous fûmes quelque fois une famille herborisante, couchée sur la pente de cette colline que peut-être vous vous rappelez. . . . L'hiver un peu de lecture (je sens déjà l'effet de votre lettre, car je me suis saisi de l'*Émile*). Je fais des grandes promenades avec mes enfants. Je passe plus de temps dans les chaumières que dans les châteaux du voisinage. Il y a toujours à s'employer dans une ferme et à faire des petites expériences. Je chasse le renard, ce qui je fais en partie par habitude, et en partie de ce que cela amuse mon imagination de quelque idée de vie sauvage.

With this delightful thought our gentle fox-hunting squire could picture himself as Rousseau's Noble Savage.

As a friend of the author of the *Émile*, Daniel Malthus was disposed to experiments in education; and Robert, showing a promise which awakened his father's love and ambition, was educated privately, partly by Daniel himself and partly by tutors. The first of these was Richard Graves, "a gentleman of considerable learning and humour," a friend of Shenstone and author of *The Spiritual Quixote*, a satire on the Methodists. At sixteen he was transferred to Gilbert Wakefield, an heretical clergyman, "wild, restless and paradoxical in many of his opinions, a prompt and hardy disputant," a correspondent of Charles Fox and a disciple of Rousseau, who stated his principles of education thus:

The greatest service of tuition to any youth is to teach him the exercise of his own powers, to conduct him to the limits of knowledge by that gradual process in which he sees and secures his own way, and rejoices in a consciousness of his own faculties and his own proficiency.[24]

In 1799, Wakefield was imprisoned in Dorchester gaol for expressing a wish that the French revolutionaries would invade and conquer England.

Some schoolboy letters of Robert Malthus still extant[25] show that he was much attached to Wakefield. Wakefield had been a Fellow of Jesus College, Cambridge; and as a consequence of this connection Robert Malthus, the first of the Cambridge economists, came up to Jesus as a pensioner in the winter term of 1784, being eighteen years of age. On November 14, 1784, he wrote home as follows:

I am now pretty well settled in my rooms. The lectures begin to-morrow; and, as I had time last week to look over my mathematics a little, I was, upon examination yesterday, found prepared to read with the year above me. We begin with mechanics and Maclaurin, Newton, and Keill's *Physics*. We shall also have lectures on Mondays and Fridays in Duncan's *Logick,* and in Tacitus's *Life of Agricola* on Wednesdays and Saturdays. I have subscribed to a bookseller who has supplied me with all the books necessary. We have some clever men at college, and I think it seems rather the fashion to read. The chief study is mathematics, for all honour in taking a degree depends upon that science, and the great aim of most of the men is to take an honourable degree. At the same time I believe we have some good classics. I am acquainted with two, one of them in this year, who is indeed an exceedingly clever man and will stand a very good chance for the classical prize if he does not neglect himself. I have read in chapel twice.

His expenses came to £100 a year. If it rose higher, Daniel Malthus wrote, the clergy could not go on sending their sons to college; abroad at Leipzig it could be done for £25.[26]

At this time the University was just stirring from a long sleep, and Jesus, which had been among the sleepiest, was becoming a centre of intellectual ferment. Malthus probably owes as much to the intellectual company he kept during his years at Jesus as to the influence and sympathy of his father. His tutor, William Frend, who had been a pupil of Paley's and was an intimate of Priestley's, became in Malthus's third year (1787) the centre of one of the most famous of University controversies, through his secession from the Church of England and his advocacy of Unitarianism, freedom of thought, and pacifism. Paley[27] himself had left Cambridge in 1775, but his *Principles of Moral and Political Philosophy,* or, as it was originally called, the *Principles of Morality and Politics,* was published in Malthus's first year (1785) at Cambridge, and must be placed high,[28] I think, amongst the intellectual influences on the author of the *Essay on Population.*[29] Moreover, he found himself in a small group of brilliant undergraduates of whom Bishop Otter, his biographer, and E. D. Clarke, traveller, Cambridge eccentric, and professor, may be chiefly named. After Malthus had taken his B.A. degree Coleridge entered the College (in 1791). When the young Coleridge occupied the ground-floor room on the right hand of the staircase facing the great gate, Jesus cannot have been a dull place—unending conversation rolling out across the Court:

As erst when from the Muses' calm abode
I came, with Learning's meed not unbestow'd:
When as she twin'd a laurel round my brow,
And met my kiss, and half returned my vow.[30]

"What evenings have I spent in those rooms!" wrote a contemporary.[31] "What little suppers, or sizings, as they were called, have I enjoyed, when Aeschylus and Plato and Thucydides were pushed aside with a pile of lexicons, to discuss the pamphlets of the day. Ever and anon a pamphlet issued from the pen of Burke. There was no need of having the book before us. Coleridge had read it in the morning, and in the evening he would repeat whole pages *verbatim*. Frend's trial was then in progress. Pamphlets swarmed from the Press. Coleridge had read them all; and in the evening, with our negus, we had them *vivâ-voce* gloriously."

As Malthus succeeded to a fellowship in June 1793 he was one of those who passed the following order on December 19, 1793:

Agreed, that if Coleridge, who has left College without leave, should not return within a month from this day, and pay his debts to his tutor, or give reasonable security that they should be paid, his name be taken off the Boards.

Coleridge, it seems, had enlisted in the 15th Dragoons in the assumed name of Silas Tomkins Comberbach. I must not be further drawn into the career of Coleridge at Jesus,[32] but on his return from this escapade he was sentenced to a month's confinement to the precincts of the College, and to translate the works of Demetrius Phalereus into English. Coleridge's later violence against the *Essay on Population* is well known:

Finally, behold this mighty nation, its rulers and its wise men listening—to Paley and—to Malthus! It is mournful, mournful [*Literary Remains of Samuel Taylor Coleridge, p. 328*].
I solemnly declare that I do not believe that all the heresies and sects and factions, which the ignorance and the weakness and the wickedness of man have ever given birth to, were altogether so disgraceful to man as a Christian, a philosopher, a statesman, or citizen, as this abominable tenet [*Table Talk, p. 88*] [33]

At College Robert Malthus is said to have been fond of cricket and skating, obtained prizes for Latin and English

Declamations, was elected Brunsell Exhibitioner in the College in 1786, and graduated as Ninth Wrangler in 1788. In an undergraduate letter home, just before achieving his Wranglership, he writes of himself as reading Gibbon and looking forward to the last three volumes, which were to come out a few months later:

I have been lately reading Gibbon's *Decline of the Roman Empire*. He gives one some useful information concerning the origin and progress of those nations of barbarians which now form the polished states of Europe, and throws some light upon the beginning of that dark period which so long overwhelmed the world, and which cannot, I think, but excite one's curiosity. He is a very entertaining writer in my opinion; his style is sometimes really sublime, everywhere interesting and agreeable, though perhaps it may in general be call'd rather too florid for history. I shall like much to see his next volumes [April 17, 1788].[34]

In later life Malthus's mildness and gentleness of temper and of demeanour may have been excessive,[35] but at Cambridge he was a gay companion. His humorous quality, says Otter,

was prevalent throughout his youth, and even survived a portion of his manhood, and at Cambridge in particular, set off as it used to be by a very comic expression of features, and a most peculiar intonation of voice when he was in the vein, was often a source of infinite delight and pleasantry to his companions.

But even as an undergraduate he was particularly distinguished, according to Otter, by

a degree of temperance and prudence, very rare at that period, and carried by him even into his academical pursuits. In these he was always more remarkable for the steadiness than for the ardour of his application, preferring to exert his mind equally in the various departments of literature then cultivated in the College rather than to devote it exclusively or eminently to any one.

On June 10, 1793, when the movement for the expulsion of Frend[36] from the College was at its height, he was admitted to a fellowship, and resided irregularly until he vacated it by marriage in 1804. He had taken orders about 1788,[37] and after 1796 he divided his time between Cambridge and a curacy at Albury, near his father's house. He was instituted to the rectory of Walesby, Lincs, on Nov. 21, 1803, on the presentation of Henry Dalton, doubtless a relative, and held it as a non-resident incumbent for the rest of his life, leaving the parish in charge of a succession of curates.[38]

A few letters written by Daniel Malthus to his son, when the latter was an undergraduate at Jesus, were printed by Otter in his *Memoir.* The following from a letter written by his father to Robert Malthus on his election to a fellowship must be quoted in full for the light it casts on their relationship:

I heartily congratulate you upon your success; it gives me a sort of pleasure which arises from my own regrets. The things which I have missed in life, I should the more sensibly wish for you.

Alas! my dear Bob, I have no right to talk to you of idleness, but when I wrote that letter to you with which you were displeased, I was deeply impressed with my own broken purposes and imperfect pursuits; I thought I foresaw in you, from the memory of my own youth, the same tendency to lose the steps you had gained, with the same disposition to self-reproach, and I wished to make my unfortunate experience of some use to you. It was, indeed, but little that you wanted it, which made me the more eager to give it you, and I wrote to you with more tenderness of heart than I would in general pretend to, and committed myself in a certain manner which made your answer a rough disappointment to me, and it drove me back into myself. You have, as you say, worn out that impression, and you have a good right to have done it; for I have seen in you the most unexceptionable character, the sweetest manners, the most sensible and the kindest conduct, always above *throwing little stones into my garden,* which you know I don't easily forgive, and uniformly making everybody easy and amused about you. Nothing can have been wanting to what, if I were the most fretful and fastidious, I could have required in a companion; and nothing even to my wishes for your happiness, but where they were either whimsical, or unreasonable, or most likely mistaken. I have often been on the point of taking hold of your hand and bursting into tears at the time that I was refusing you my affections: my approbation I was precipitate to give you.

Write to me, if I could do anything about your church, and you want any thing to be done for you, such as I am, believe me, dear Bob, yours most affectionately,

DANIEL MALTHUS

Malthus's first essay in authorship, *The Crisis, a View of the Recent Interesting State of Great Britain by a Friend to the Constitution,* written in 1796, in his thirtieth year, in criticism of Pitt's administration, failed to find a publisher. Extracts quoted by Otter and by Empson indicate that his interest was already aroused in the social problems of Political Economy, and even in the question of Population itself:

On the subject of population [he wrote] I cannot agree with Archdeacon Paley, who says, that the quantity of happiness in any country is best measured by the number of people. Increasing population is the most certain possible sign of the happiness and prosperity of a state; but the actual population may be only a sign of the happiness that is past.

In 1798, when Malthus was thirty-two years old, there was published anonymously *An Essay on the Principle of Population, as it affects the future improvement of Society: with remarks on the speculations of Mr. Godwin, M. Condorcet, and other writers.*

It was in conversation with Daniel Malthus that there occurred to Robert Malthus the generalisation which has made him famous. The story is well known on the authority of Bishop Otter, who had it from Malthus himself. In 1793 Godwin's *Political Justice* had appeared. In frequent discussion the father defended, and the son attacked, the doctrine of a future age of perfect equality and happiness.

And when the question had been often the subject of animated discussion between them, and the son had rested his cause, principally upon the obstacles which the tendency of population, to increase faster than the means of subsistence, would always throw in the way; he was desired to put down in writing, for maturer consideration, the substance of his argument, the consequence of which was the Essay on Population. Whether the father was converted or not we do not know, but certain it is that he was strongly impressed with the importance of the views and the ingenuity of the argument contained in the MS., and recommended his son to submit his labours to the public.

The first edition, an octavo volume of about 50,000 words, is an almost completely different book from, and for posterity superior to, the second edition of five years later in quarto. By the fifth edition the book had swollen to some 250,000 words in three volumes. The first edition, written, as Malthus explains in the second edition, "on the impulse of the occasion, and from the few materials which were then within my reach in a country situation," is mainly an *a priori* work, concerned on the one hand with the refutation of the perfectibilists and on the other with the justification of the methods of the Creator, in spite of appearance to the contrary.

The first essay is not only *a priori* and philosophical in method, but it is bold and rhetorical in style with much *bravura* of language and sentiment; whereas in the later editions political philosophy gives way to political economy, general principles are overlaid by the inductive verifications of a pioneer in sociological history, and the brilliance and high spirits of a young man writing in the last years of the Directory disappear. "Verbiage and senseless repetition" is Coleridge's marginal comment in his copy of the second edition:

Are we now to have a quarto to teach us that great misery and great vice arise from poverty, and that there must be poverty in its worst shape wherever there are more mouths than loaves and more Heads than Brains?

To judge from the rarity of the book, the first edition must have been a very small one (Malthus stated in 1820 that he had not made out of his writings above £1000 altogether[39]), and we know that it went out of print almost immediately, though five years passed before it was followed by a second. But it attracted immediate attention, and the warfare of pamphlets instantly commenced (more than a score, according to Dr. Bonar, even in the five years before the second edition) which for 135 years has never ceased. The voice of objective reason had been raised against a deep instinct which the evolutionary struggle had been implanting from the commencement of life; and man's mind, in the conscious pursuit of happiness, was daring to demand the reins of government from out of the hands of the unconscious urge for mere predominant survival.

Paley himself was converted, [40] who had once argued that
"the decay of population is the greatest evil a State can suffer,
and the improvement of it the object which ought in all countries to be aimed at, in preference to every other political purpose whatsoever." Even the politicians took note, and Otter
records a meeting between Pitt and Malthus in December
1801:

It happened that Mr. Pitt was at this time upon a sort of
canvassing visit at the University. . . . At a supper at Jesus
lodge in the company of some young travellers, particularly Mr.
Malthus, etc., he was induced to unbend in a very easy conversation respecting Sir Sidney Smith, the massacre at Jaffa, the
Pasha of Acre, Clarke, Carlisle, etc.

A year before, in dropping his new Poor Bill, Pitt, who in 1796
thought that a man had "enriched his country" by producing a
number of children, even if the whole family were paupers,[41]
had stated in the House of Commons that he did so in defer-
ence to the objections of "those whose opinions he was bound
to respect," meaning, it is said, Bentham and Malthus.

Malthus's *Essay* is a work of youthful genius. The author
was fully conscious of the significance of the ideas he was expressing. He believed that he had found the clue to human
misery. The importance of the *Essay* consisted not in the novelty of his facts but in the smashing emphasis he placed on a
simple generalisation arising out of them. Indeed his leading
idea had been largely anticipated in a clumsier way by other
eighteenth-century writers without attracting attention.

The book can claim a place amongst those which have had
great influence on the progress of thought. It is profoundly in
the English tradition of humane science—in that tradition of
Scotch and English thought, in which there has been, I think,
an extraordinary continuity of *feeling*, if I may so express it,
from the eighteenth century to the present time—the tradition
which is suggested by the names of Locke, Hume, Adam
Smith, Paley, Bentham, Darwin, and Mill, a tradition marked
by a love of truth and a most noble lucidity, by a prosaic sanity
free from sentiment or metaphysic, and by an immense disinterestedness and public spirit. There is a continuity in these

writings, not only of feeling, but of actual matter. It is in this company that Malthus belongs.

Malthus's transition from the *a priori* methods of Cambridge —whether Paley, the Mathematical Tripos, or the Unitarians—to the inductive argument of the later editions was assisted by a tour which he undertook in search of materials in 1799 "through Sweden, Norway, Finland, and a part of Russia, these being the only countries at the time open to English travellers," and another in France and Switzerland during the short peace of 1802.[42] The northern tour was in the company of a party of Jesus friends, Otter, Clarke, and Cripps, of whom Malthus and Otter, exhausted perhaps by the terrific and eccentric energy of E. D. Clarke, by nature a traveller and collector, performed a part only of the journey. Clarke and Cripps continued for a period of two or three years, returning by Constantinople, having accumulated a number of objects of every description, many of which now rest in the Fitzwilliam Museum.[43] Clarke's letters, many of which are printed in his *Life and Travels,* were read out by his stay-at-home friends in the Combination Room at Jesus amidst the greatest curiosity and interest.[44] Clarke later became Senior Tutor of Jesus (1805), first Professor of Mineralogy (1808), and finally University Librarian (1817).

Meanwhile Malthus had continued his economic studies with a pamphlet, published anonymously (like the first edition of the *Essay*) in 1800, entitled *An Investigation of the Cause of the Present High Price of Provisions.* This pamphlet has importance both in itself and as showing that Malthus was already disposed to a certain line of approach in handling practical economic problems which he was to develop later on in his correspondence with Ricardo,—a method which to me is most sympathetic, and, as I think, more likely to lead to right conclusions than the alternative approach of Ricardo. But it was Ricardo's more fascinating intellectual construction which was victorious, and Ricardo who, by turning his back so completely on Malthus's ideas, constrained the subject for a full hundred years in an artificial groove.

According to Malthus's good common-sense notion prices

and profits are primarily determined by something which he described, though none too clearly, as "effective demand." Ricardo favoured a much more rigid approach, went behind "effective demand" to the underlying conditions of money on the one hand and real costs and the real division of the product on the other hand, conceived these fundamental factors as automatically working themselves out in a unique and unequivocal way, and looked on Malthus's method as very superficial. But Ricardo, in the course of simplifying the many successive stages of his highly abstract argument, departed, necessarily and more than he himself was aware, away from the actual facts; whereas Malthus, by taking up the tale much nearer its conclusion, had a firmer hold on what may be expected to happen in the real world. Ricardo is the father of such things as the Quantity Theory of Money and the Purchasing Power Parity of the Exchanges. When one has painfully escaped from the intellectual domination of these pseudo-arithmetical doctrines, one is able, perhaps for the first time for a hundred years, to comprehend the real significance of the vaguer intuitions of Malthus.

Malthus's conception of "effective demand" is brilliantly illustrated in this early pamphlet by "an idea which struck him so strongly as he rode on horseback from Hastings to Town" that he stopped two days in his "garret in town," "sitting up till two o'clock to finish it that it might come out before the meeting of parliament." [45] He was pondering why the price of provisions should have risen by so much more than could be accounted for by any deficiency in the harvest. He did not, like Ricardo a few years later, invoke the quantity of money.[46] He found the cause in the increase in working-class *incomes* as a consequence of parish allowances being raised in proportion to the cost of living.

I am most strongly inclined to suspect, that the attempt in most parts of the kingdom to increase the parish allowances in proportion to the price of corn, combined with the riches of the country, which have enabled it to proceed as far as it has done in this attempt, is, comparatively speaking, the sole cause which has occasioned the price of provisions in this country to rise so much higher than the degree of scarcity would seem to warrant, so much higher than it would do in any other country where this cause did not operate. . . .

Let us suppose a commodity in great request by fifty people, but of which, from some failure in its production, there is only sufficient to supply forty. If the fortieth man from the top have two shillings which he can spend in this commodity, and the thirty-nine above him, more, in various proportions, and the ten below, all less, the actual price of the article, according to the genuine principles of trade, will be two shillings. . . . Let us suppose, now, that somebody give the ten poor men, who were excluded, a shilling apiece. The whole fifty can now offer two shillings, the price which was before asked. According to every genuine principle of fair trading, the commodity must immediately rise. If it do not, I would ask, upon what principle are ten, out of the fifty who are all able to offer two shillings, to be rejected? For still, according to the supposition, there is only enough for forty. The two shillings of a poor man are just as good as the two shillings of a rich man; and, if we interfere to prevent the commodity from rising out of the reach of the poorest ten, whoever they may be, we must toss up, draw lots, raffle, or fight, to determine who are to be excluded. It would be beyond my present purpose to enter into the question whether any of these modes would be more eligible, for the distribution of the commodities of a country, than the sordid distinction of money; but certainly, according to the customs of all civilised and enlightened nations, and according to every principle of commercial dealing, the price must be allowed to rise to that point which will put it beyond the power of ten out of the fifty to purchase. This point will, perhaps, be half a crown or more, which will now become the price of the commodity. Let another shilling apiece be given to the excluded ten: all will now be able to offer half a crown. The price must in consequence immediately rise to three shillings or more, and so on *toties quoties*.

The words and the ideas are simple. But here is the beginning of systematic economic thinking. There is much else in the pamphlet—almost the whole of it—which would bear quotation. This *Investigation*[47] is one of the best things Malthus ever wrote, though there are great passages in the *Essay;* and, now well launched on quotation, I cannot forbear to follow on with that famous passage from the second edition (p. 571), in which a partly similar idea is introduced, more magnificently clothed, in a different context (in criticism of Paine's *Rights of Man*):

A man who is born into a world already possessed, if he cannot get subsistence from his parents on whom he has a just demand, and if the society do not want his labour, has no claim of *right* to the smallest portion of food, and, in fact, has no business to be where he is. At nature's mighty feast there is no vacant cover for him. She tells him to be gone, and will quickly execute her own orders, if he do not work upon the compassion of some of her guests. If these guests get up and make room for him, other intruders immediately appear demanding the same favour. The report of a provision for all that come, fills the hall with numerous claimants. The order and harmony of the feast is disturbed, the plenty that before reigned is changed into scarcity; and the happiness of the guests is destroyed by the spectacle of misery and dependence in every part of the hall, and by the clamorous importunity of those, who are justly enraged at not finding the provision which they had been taught to expect. The guests learn too late their error, in counteracting those strict orders to all intruders, issued by the great mistress of the feast, who, wishing that all her guests should have plenty, and knowing that she could not provide for unlimited numbers, humanely refused to admit fresh comers when her table was already full.

Malthus's next pamphlet, *A Letter to Samuel Whitbread, Esq., M.P., on his Proposed Bill of the Amendment of the Poor Laws,* published in 1807, is not so happy. It is an extreme application of the principle of the *Essay on Population*. Mr. Whitbread had proposed "to empower parishes to build cottages," in short, a housing scheme, partly to remedy the appalling shortage, partly to create employment. But Malthus eagerly points out that "the difficulty of procuring habitations" must on no account be alleviated, since this is the cause why "the poor laws do not encourage early marriages so much as might naturally be expected." The poor laws raise the rates, the high level of rates prevents the building of cottages, and the deficiency of cottages mitigates the otherwise disastrous effect of the poor laws in increasing population.

Such is the tendency to form early connections, that with the encouragement of a sufficient number of tenements, I have very little doubt that the population might be so pushed and such a quantity of labour in time thrown into the market, as to render the condition of the independent labourer absolutely hopeless.

Economics is a very dangerous science.

In 1803 the new version of the *Essay on Population* appeared in a fine quarto of 600 pages priced at a guinea and a half. Up to this time Malthus had had no specific duties and was entirely free to pursue his economic inquiries. In 1804 he married.[48] In 1805, at thirty-nine years of age, he took up his appointment, made in the previous year, to the Professorship of Modern History and Political Economy at the newly founded East India College, first at Hertford and soon after at Haileybury. This was the earliest chair of Political Economy[49] to be established in England.

Malthus had now entered upon the placid existence of a scholar and teacher. He remained at Haileybury for thirty years until his death in 1834, occupying the house under the clock-turret afterwards occupied by Sir James Stephen,[50] who was the last holder of Malthus's chair. He had three children, of whom one daughter died before her maturity, and the other, Mrs. Pringle, lived on till 1885, whilst his son, the Reverend Henry Malthus, died without issue in 1882.

The *Essay* was amplified in successive editions. In 1814 and 1815 he published pamphlets on the Corn Laws, in 1815 his celebrated essay on *Rent,* and in 1820 his second book, *The Principles of Political Economy considered with a View to their Practical Application.*[51]

"The tradition of Mrs. Malthus's delightful evening parties, at which the élite of the London scientific world were often present, lingered at Haileybury as long as the College lasted." [52] "His servants lived with him till their marriage or settlement in life." [53] His students called him "Pop." He was a Whig; he preached sermons which dwelt especially on the goodness of the Deity; he thought Haileybury a satisfactory institution and Political Economy a suitable study for the young who "could not only understand it, but they did not even think it dull"; his sentiments were benevolent, his temper mild and

easy, his nature loyal and affectionate; and he was cheerful—
thus corroborating his conclusions of 1798 when he had written in the first edition of the *Essay* that "life is, generally
speaking, a blessing independent of a future state . . . and
we have every reason to think, that there is no more evil in the
world than what is absolutely necessary as one of the ingredients in the mighty process."

The contrast between this picture and the cruel and vicious
monster of pamphleteering controversy, of which Malthus
seems to have taken the least possible notice, made some of
his friends indignant, but was better handled by Sydney Smith,
who wrote to a correspondent in July 1821:

> Philosopher Malthus came here last week. I got an agreeable
> party for him of unmarried people. There was only one lady
> who had had a child; but he is a good-natured man, and, if
> there are no appearances of approaching fertility, is civil to
> every lady. . . . Malthus is a real moral philosopher, and I
> would almost consent to speak as inarticulately, if I could think
> and act as wisely.

The *Gentleman's Magazine* (1835, p. 325) tells us in obituary language that:

> In person Mr. Malthus was tall and elegantly formed; and his
> appearance, no less than his conduct, was that of a perfect gen-
> tleman.

The admirable portrait painted by John Linnell in 1833, now
in the possession of Mr. Robert Malthus,[54] familiar through
Linnell's well-known engraving of it, shows him to have been
of a ruddy complexion with curling reddish or auburn hair,
a strikingly handsome and distinguished figure. Miss Martineau wrote of him in her *Autobiography:*

> A more simple-minded, virtuous man, full of domestic affec-
> tions, than Mr. Malthus could not be found in all England. . . .
> Of all people in the world, Malthus was the one whom I heard
> quite easily without my trumpet;—Malthus, whose speech was
> hopelessly imperfect, from defect in the palate. I dreaded meet-
> ing him when invited by a friend of his who made my ac-
> quaintance on purpose. . . . When I considered my own deaf-
> ness, and his inability to pronounce half the consonants, in the

alphabet, and his hare-lip which must prevent my offering him my tube, I feared we should make a terrible business of it. I was delightfully wrong. His first sentence—slow and gentle with the vowels sonorous, whatever might become of the consonants—set me at ease completely. I soon found that the vowels are in fact all that I ever hear. His worst letter was *l,* and when I had no difficulty with his question,—"Would not you like to have a look at the lakes of Killarney?" I had nothing more to fear.

How this delightful scene brings us within reach of our own memories, separated by a gulf of aeons from Rousseau and Hume! Influenced too much by impressions of Dr. Johnson and Gibbon and Burke, we easily forget both the importance of the young radical England of the last quarter of the eighteenth century in which Malthus was brought up, and the destructive effect on it of the crushing disappointment of the outcome of the French Revolution (comparable to that which the outcome of the Russian Revolution may soon bring to their fellows of to-day)—though we know it in the evolution of Wordsworth and Coleridge and in the invincible ardour of Shelley—in making the passage from the eighteenth to the nineteenth century. Malthus, at any rate, had now passed over completely in surroundings and intellectual outlook from the one century to the other. Rousseau, his father Daniel, Gilbert Wakefield, the Cambridge of 1784, Paley, Pitt, the first edition of the *Essay* belonged to a different world and a different civilisation. His links with ourselves grow close. He was an original member of the Political Economy Club[55] which still dines on the first Wednesday of the month.[56] He was also an original Fellow of the Royal Statistical Society, founded just before his death. He attended the Cambridge meeting of the British Association in 1833. Some readers of this essay may have known some of his pupils.

The most important influence of his later years was his intimacy with Ricardo, of whom he said:

I never loved anybody out of my own family so much. Our interchange of opinions was so unreserved, and the object after which we were both enquiring was so entirely the truth, and nothing else, that I cannot but think we sooner or later must have agreed.

As Maria Edgeworth, who knew both well, wrote of them:

They hunted together in search of Truth, and huzzaed when they found her, without caring who found her first; and indeed I have seen them both put their able hands to the windlass to drag her up from the bottom of that well in which she so strangely loves to dwell.

The friendship between Malthus and David Ricardo began in June 1811,[57] when Malthus "took the liberty of introducing himself" in the hope "that as we are *mainly* on the same side of the question, we might supersede the necessity of a long controversy in print respecting the points in which we differ, by an amicable discussion in private." It led to a long intimacy which was never broken. Ricardo paid repeated week-end visits to Haileybury; Malthus seldom came to London without staying, or at least breakfasting, with Ricardo, and in later years was accustomed to stay with his family at Gatcomb Park. It is evident that they had the deepest affection and respect for one another. The contrasts between the intellectual gifts of the two were obvious and delightful. In economic discussions Ricardo was the abstract and *a priori* theorist, Malthus the inductive and intuitive investigator who hated to stray too far from what he could test by reference to the facts and his own intuitions. But when it came to practical finance, the rôles of the Jewish stockbroker and the aristocratic clergyman were, as they should be, reversed, as is illustrated by a trifling incident which it is amusing to record. During the Napoleonic War, Ricardo was, as is well known, a principal member of a Syndicate which took part in operations in Government stocks corresponding to what is now effected by "underwriting." His Syndicate would take up by tender from the Treasury a mixed bag of stocks of varying terms known as the *Omnium,* which they would gradually dispose of to the public as favourable opportunities offered. On these occasions Ricardo was in the habit of doing Malthus a friendly turn by putting him down for a small participation without requiring

him to put up any money,[58] which meant the certainty of a
modest profit if Malthus did not hold on too long, since ini-
tially the Syndicate terms would always be comfortably below
the current market price. Thus, as it happened, Malthus found
himself a small "bull" of Government stock a few days before
the battle of Waterloo. This was, unfortunately, too much for
his nerves, and he instructed Ricardo, unless "it is either wrong
or inconvenient to you," "to take an early opportunity of realis-
ing a small profit on the share you have been so good as to
promise me." Ricardo carried out the instructions, though he
himself by no means shared that view, since it appears that he
carried over the week of Waterloo the maximum bull position
of which his resources were capable. In a letter to Malthus of
June 27, 1815, he modestly reports: "This is as great an advantage as ever I expect or wish to make by a rise. I have been
a considerable gainer by the loan." "Now for a little of our old
subject," he continues, and plunges back into the theory of the
possible causes of a rise in the price of commodities.[59] Poor
Malthus could not help being a little annoyed.

I confess [he writes on July 16, 1815] I thought that the
chances of the first battle were in favour of Buonaparte, who
had the choice of attack; and it appears indeed from the Duke
of Wellington's despatches that he was at one time very near
succeeding. From what has happened since, however, it seems
certain that the French were not so well prepared as they ought
to have been. If there had been the energy and enthusiasm
which might have been expected in the defence of their independence, one battle, however sanguinary and complete, could
not have decided the fate of France.

This friendship will live in history on account of its having
given rise to the most important literary correspondence in
the whole development of Political Economy. In 1887 Dr.
Bonar discovered Ricardo's side of the correspondence in the
possession of Colonel Malthus, and published his well-known
edition. But the search for Malthus's letters, which should have
been in the possession of the Ricardo family, was made in vain.
In 1907 Professor Foxwell published in the *Economic Journal*
a single letter from the series, which David Ricardo hap-

pened to have given to Mrs. Smith of Easton Grey for her collection of autographs, and declared—with great prescience as it has turned out—that "the loss of Malthus's share in this correspondence may be ranked by economists next to that other literary disaster, the destruction of David Hume's comments on *The Wealth of Nations*." [60] But Mr. Piero Sraffa, from whom nothing is hid, has discovered the missing letters in his researches for the forthcoming complete and definitive edition of the Works of David Ricardo, which he is preparing for the Royal Economic Society (to be published in the course of the present year[61]). It will be found that the publication of both sides of the correspondence enhances its interest very greatly. Here indeed, are to be found the seeds of economic theory, and also the divergent lines—so divergent at the outset that the destination can scarcely be recognised as the same until it is reached—along which the subject can be developed. Ricardo is investigating the theory of the *distribution* of the product in conditions of equilibrium, and Malthus is concerned with what determines the *volume* of output day by day in the real world. Malthus is dealing with the monetary economy in which we happen to live; Ricardo with the abstraction of a neutral money economy.[62] They largely recognised the real source of their differences. In a letter of January 24, 1817 Ricardo wrote:

It appears to me that one great cause of our difference in opinion on the subjects which we have so often discussed is that you have always in your mind the immediate and temporary effects of particular changes, whereas I put these immediate and temporary effects quite aside, and fix my whole attention on the permanent state of things which will result from them. Perhaps you estimate these temporary effects too highly, whilst I am too much disposed to undervalue them. To manage the subject quite right, they should be carefully distinguished and mentioned, and the due effects ascribed to each.

To which Malthus replied with considerable effect on January 26, 1817:

I agree with you that one cause of our difference in opinion is that which you mention. I certainly am disposed to refer frequently to things as they are, as the only way of making one's writings practically useful to society, and I think also the only way of being secure from falling into the errors of the tay-lors of Laputa, and by a slight mistake at the outset arrive at conclusions the most distant from the truth. Besides I really think that the progress of society consists of irregular move-ments, and that to omit the consideration of causes which for eight or ten years will give a great *stimulus* to production and population, or a great *check* to them, is to omit the causes of the wealth and poverty of nations—the grand object of all en-quiries in Political Economy. A writer may, to be sure, make any hypothesis he pleases; but if he supposes what is not at all true practically, he precludes himself from drawing any practi-cal inferences from his hypotheses. In your essay on profits you suppose the real wages of labour constant; but as they vary with every alteration in the prices of commodities (while they remain nominally the same) and are in reality as variable as profits, there is no chance of your inferences being just as applied to the actual state of things.[63] We see in all the countries around us, and in our own particularly, periods of greater and less pros-perity and sometimes of adversity, but *never* the uniform prog-ress which you seem alone to contemplate.

But to come to a still more specific and fundamental cause of our difference, I think it is this. You seem to think that the wants and tastes of mankind are always ready for the supply; while I am most decidedly of opinion that few things are more difficult than to inspire new tastes and wants, particularly out of old materials; that one of the great elements of demand is the value that people set upon commodities, and that the more com-pletely the supply is suited to the demand the higher will this value be, and the more days' labour will it exchange for, or give the power of commanding. . . . I am quite of opinion that *practically* the actual check to produce and population arises more from want of stimulus than want of power to produce.

One cannot rise from a perusal of this correspondence with-out a feeling that the almost total obliteration of Malthus's line of approach and the complete domination of Ricardo's for a period of a hundred years has been a disaster to the progress of economics. Time after time in these letters Malthus is talking plain sense, the force of which Ricardo with his head in the clouds wholly fails to comprehend. Time after time a crushing refutation by Malthus is met by a mind so completely closed that Ricardo does not even see what Malthus is saying. I must

not, however, further anticipate the importance of the forthcoming publication of Mr. Piero Sraffa, to whose generosity
I owe the opportunity of making these excerpts, except to show
Malthus's complete comprehension of the effects of excessive
saving on output *via* its effects on profit.

As early as October 9, 1814, in the letter printed by Prof.
Foxwell in the *Economic Journal* (1907, p. 274), Malthus was
writing:

> I cannot by any means agree with you in your observation
> that "the desire of accumulation will occasion demand just as
> *effectually* as a desire to consume" and that "consumption and
> accumulation equally promote demand." I confess indeed that
> I know no other cause for the fall of profits which I believe
> you will allow generally takes place from accumulation than
> that the price of produce falls compared with the expense of
> production, or in other words that the *effective* demand is
> diminished.

But the following extracts from two letters written by
Malthus in July 1821 show that by that date the matter was
still clearer in his mind and foggier still in Ricardo's:

[July 7, 1821]

We see in almost every part of the world vast powers of production which are not put into action, and I explain this phenomenon by saying that from the want of a proper distribution
of the actual produce adequate motives are not furnished to
continued production. By inquiring into the immediate causes
of the progress of wealth, I clearly mean to inquire mainly into
motives. I don't at all wish to deny that some persons or others
are entitled to consume all that is produced; but the grand
question is whether it is distributed in such a manner between
the different parties concerned as to occasion the most effective
demand for future produce: and I distinctly maintain that an
attempt to accumulate very rapidly which necessarily implies
a considerable diminution of unproductive consumption, by
greatly impairing the usual motives to production must prematurely check the progress of wealth. This surely is the great
practical question, and not whether we ought to call the sort of
stagnation which would be thus occasioned a glut. That I hold
to be a matter of very subordinate importance. But if it be true
that an attempt to accumulate very rapidly will occasion such a
division between labour and profits as almost to destroy both the
motive and the power of future accumulation and consequently

the power of maintaining and employing an increasing population, must it not be acknowledged that such an attempt to accumulate, or that saving too much, may be really prejudicial to a country.

[July 16, 1821]

With regard to our present subject of discussion, it seems as if we should never thoroughly understand each other, and I almost despair of being ever able to explain myself, if you could read the two first paragraphs of the first section of my last chapter, and yet "understand me to say that vast powers of production are put into action, and the result is unfavourable to the interests of mankind." I expressly say that it is my object to show what are the causes which call forth the powers of production; and if I recommend a certain proportion of unproductive consumption, it is obviously and expressly with the sole view of furnishing the necessary motive to the greatest continued production. And I think still that this certain proportion of unproductive consumption varying according to the fertility of the soil, etc., is absolutely and indispensably necessary to call forth the resources of a country. . . . Now among the motives to produce, one of the most essential certainly is that an adequate share of what is produced should belong to those who set all industry in motion. But you yourself allow that a great temporary saving, commencing when profits were sufficient to encourage it, might occasion such a division of the produce as would leave no motive to a further increase of production. And if a state of things in which for a time there is no motive to a further increase of production be not properly denominated a stagnation, I do not know what can be so called; particularly as this stagnation must inevitably throw the rising generation out of employment. We know from repeated experience that the money price of labour never falls till many workmen have been for some time out of work. And the question is, whether this stagnation of capital, and subsequent stagnation in the demand for labour arising from increased production without an adequate proportion of unproductive consumption on the part of the landlords and capitalists, could take place without prejudice to the country, without occasioning a less degree both of happiness and wealth than would have occurred if the unproductive consumption of the landlords and capitalists had been so proportioned to the natural surplus of the society as to have continued uninterrupted the motives to production, and prevented first an unnatural demand for labour, and then a necessary and sudden diminution of such demand. But if this be so, how can it be said with truth that parsimony, though it may be prejudicial to the producers cannot be prejudicial to the state; or that an increase of unproductive consumption among landlords and capitalists may not sometimes be the proper remedy for a state of things in which the motives to production fail.

If only Malthus, instead of Ricardo, had been the parent stem from which nineteenth-century economics proceeded, what a much wiser and richer place the world would be today! We have laboriously to rediscover and force through the obscuring envelopes of our misguided education what should never have ceased to be obvious. I have long claimed Robert Malthus as the first of the Cambridge economists; and we can do so, after the publication of these letters, with increased sympathy and admiration.

In these letters Malthus was indeed only re-stating from his *Principles of Political Economy,* published in 1820, the argument of Chapter VII. Section IX. "Of the Distribution occasioned by unproductive consumers, considered as a Means of increasing the exchangeable Value of the whole Produce," which had wholly failed to enter the comprehension of Ricardo just as it has failed to influence the ideas of posterity. But he makes it much clearer. If we go back, however, to the *Political Economy* with our attention awakened, it is evident that the essence of the argument is there set forth.[64] In Section X. of the same chapter Malthus proceeded to apply these principles "to the Distresses of the Labouring Classes since 1815." He points out that the trouble was due to the diversion of resources, previously devoted to war, to the accumulation of savings; that in such circumstances deficiency of savings could not possibly be the cause, and saving, though a private virtue, had ceased to be a public duty; and that public works and expenditure by landlords and persons of property was the appropriate remedy. The two passages following may be quoted as illustrations from the best economic analysis ever written of the events of 1815-20:

When profits are low and uncertain, when capitalists are quite at a loss where they can safely employ their capitals, and when on these accounts capital is flowing out of the country; in short, when all the evidence which the nature of the subject admits, distinctly proves that there is no effective demand for capital at home, is it not contrary to the general principles of political economy, is it not a vain and fruitless opposition to that first, greatest, and most universal of all its principles, the principle of supply and demand, to recommend saving, and the conversion of more revenue into capital? Is it not just the same sort of thing as to recommend marriage when people are starving and emigrating? [65]

Altogether I should say, that the employment of the poor in roads and public works, and a tendency among landlords and persons of property to build, to improve and beautify their grounds, and to employ workmen and menial servants, are the means most within our power and most directly calculated to remedy the evils arising from that disturbance in the balance of produce and consumption, which has been occasioned by the sudden conversion of soldiers, sailors, and various other classes which the war employed, into productive labourers. [66]

The whole problem of the balance between Saving and Investment had been posed in the *Preface* to the book, as follows:

Adam Smith has stated, that capitals are increased by parsimony, that every frugal man is a public benefactor, and that the increase of wealth depends upon the balance of produce above consumption. That these propositions are true to a great extent is perfectly unquestionable. . . . But it is quite obvious that they are not true to an indefinite extent, and that the principles of saving, pushed to excess, would destroy the motive to production. If every person were satisfied with the simplest food, the poorest clothing, and the meanest houses, it is certain that no other sort of food, clothing, and lodging would be in existence. . . . The two extremes are obvious; and it follows that there must be some intermediate point, though the resources of political economy may not be able to ascertain it, where, taking into consideration both the power to produce and the will to consume, the encouragement to the increase of wealth is the greatest. [67]

Surely it was a great fault in Ricardo to fail entirely to see any significance in this line of thought. But Malthus's defect lay in his overlooking entirely the part played by the rate of interest. Twenty years ago I should have retorted to Malthus that the state of affairs he envisages could not occur unless the rate of interest had first fallen to zero. Malthus perceived, as often, what was true; but it is essential to a complete comprehension of why it is true, to explain how an excess of frugality does not bring with it a decline to zero in the rate of interest.

Adam Smith and Malthus and Ricardo! There is something about these three figures to evoke more than ordinary sentiments from us their children in the spirit. Malthus and Ricardo were not hindered by the contrary qualities of their minds from conversing together in peace and amity all their days. The last sentence in Ricardo's last letter to Malthus before his death runs:

And now, my dear Malthus, I have done. Like other disputants, after much discussion, we each retain our own opinions. These discussions, however, never influence our friendship; I should not like you more than I do if you agreed in opinion with me.

Malthus survived his friend by ten years, and then he too had done.

My views are before the public [he wrote shortly before his death]. If I am to alter anything, I can do little more than alter the language: and I don't know that I should alter it for the better.

In 1833, the year before his death, Miss Martineau visited him at Haileybury. She was pleased with "the well-planted county of Herts. Almost daily we went forth when work was done—a pleasant riding party of five or six, and explored all the green lanes, and enjoyed all the fine views in the neighbourhood. The families of the other professors made up a very pleasant society—to say nothing of the interest of seeing in the students the future administrators of India. The subdued jests and external homage and occasional insurrections of the young men; the archery of the young ladies; the curious politeness of the Persian professor; the fine learning and eager scholarship of Principal Le Bas, and the somewhat old-fashioned courtesies of the summer evening parties are all over now."

ALFRED MARSHALL [1]

1842-1924

Alfred Marshall was born at Clapham on July 26, 1842, the son of William Marshall, a cashier in the Bank of England, by his marriage with Rebecca Oliver. The Marshalls were a clerical family of the West, sprung from William Marshall, incumbent of Saltash, Cornwall, at the end of the seventeenth century. Alfred was the great-great-grandson of the Reverend William Marshall,[2] the half-legendary herculean parson of Devonshire, who, by twisting horseshoes with his hands, frightened local blacksmiths into fearing that they blew their bellows for the devil.[3] His great-grandfather was the Reverend John Marshall, Headmaster of Exeter Grammar School, who married Mary Hawtrey, daughter of the Reverend Charles Hawtrey, Sub-Dean and Canon of Exeter, and aunt of the Provost of Eton.[4]

His father, the cashier in the Bank of England, was a tough old character, of great resolution and perception, cast in the mould of the strictest Evangelicals, bony neck, bristly projecting chin, author of an Evangelical epic in a sort of Anglo-Saxon language of his own invention which found some favour in its appropriate circles, surviving despotically minded into his ninety-second year. The nearest objects of his masterful instincts were his family, and their easiest victim his wife; but their empire extended in theory over the whole of womankind, the old gentleman writing a tract entitled *Man's Rights and Woman's Duties*. Heredity is mighty, and Alfred Marshall did not altogether escape the influence of the parental mould. An implanted masterfulness towards womankind warred in him with the deep affection and admiration which he bore to his own wife, and with an environment which threw him in closest touch with the education and liberation of women.

II

At nine years of age Alfred was sent to Merchant Taylors' School, for which his father, perceiving the child's ability, had begged a nomination from a Director of the Bank.[5] In mingled affection and severity his father recalls James Mill. He used to make the boy work with him for school, often at Hebrew, until eleven at night. Indeed, Alfred was so much overworked by his father that, he used to say, his life was saved by his Aunt Louisa, with whom he spent long summer holidays near Dawlish. She gave him a boat and a gun and a pony, and by the end of the summer he would return home, brown and well. E. C. Dermer, his fellow-monitor at Merchant Taylors', tells that at school he was small and pale, badly dressed, looked overworked, and was called "tallow candles"; that he cared little for games, was fond of propounding chess problems,[6] and did not readily make friends.[7]

Rising to be Third Monitor, he became entitled in 1861, under old statutes, to a scholarship at St. John's College, Oxford, which would have led in three years to a Fellowship, and would have furnished him with the same permanence of security as belonged in those days to Eton scholars at King's or Winchester scholars at New College. It was the first step to ordination in the Evangelical ministry for which his father designed him. But this was not the main point for Alfred—it meant a continued servitude to the Classics.[8] He had painful recollections in later days of his tyrant father keeping him awake into the night for the better study of Hebrew, whilst at the same time forbidding him the fascinating paths of mathematics. His father hated the sight of a mathematical book, but Alfred would conceal Potts' Euclid in his pocket as he walked to and from school. He read a proposition and then worked it out in his mind as he walked along, standing still at intervals, with his toes turned in. The fact that the curriculum of the Sixth Form at Merchant Taylors' reached so far as the differential calculus had excited native proclivities. Airy, the mathematical master, said that "he had a genius for mathematics." Mathematics represented for Alfred emancipation, and he used to rejoice greatly that his father could not understand them. No! he would not be buried at Oxford under dead languages; he would run away—to be a cabin-boy at Cambridge and climb the rigging of geometry and spy out the heavens.

At this point there comes on the scene a well-disposed uncle, willing to lend him a little money (for his father was too poor to help further when the Oxford Scholarship was abandoned) —repaid by Alfred soon after taking his degree from what he earned by teaching—which, with a Parkin's Exhibition[9] of £40 a year from St. John's College, Cambridge,[10] opened to him the doors of Mathematics and of Cambridge. Since it was a legacy of £250 from this same uncle which enabled him, fourteen years later, to pay his visit to the United States, the story of the sources of this uncle's wealth, which Alfred often told, deserve a record here. Having sought his fortunes in Australia and being established there at the date of the gold discoveries, a little family eccentricity disposed him to seek his benefit indirectly. So he remained a pastoralist, but, to the mirth of his neighbours, refused to employ anyone about his place who did not suffer from some physical defect, staffing himself entirely with the halt, the blind, and the maimed. When the gold boom reached its height his reward came. All the able-bodied labourers migrated to the goldfields and Charles Marshall was the only man in the place able to carry on. A few years later he returned to England with a fortune, ready to take an interest in a clever, rebellious nephew.

In 1917 Marshall put into writing the following account of his methods of work at this time and later:

An epoch in my life occurred when I was, I think, about seventeen years old. I was in Regent Street, and saw a workman standing idle before a shop-window: but his face indicated alert energy, so I stood still and watched. He was preparing to sketch on the window of a shop guiding lines for a short statement of the business concerned, which was to be shown by white letters fixed to the glass. Each stroke of arm and hand needed to be made with a single free sweep, so as to give a graceful result; it occupied perhaps two seconds of keen excitement. He stayed still for a few minutes after each stroke, so that his pulse might grow quiet. If he had saved the ten minutes thus lost, his employers would have been injured by more than the value of his wages for a whole day. That set up a train of thought which led me to the resolve never to use my mind when it was not fresh, and to regard the intervals between successive strains as sacred to absolute repose. When I went to Cambridge and became full master of myself, I resolved never to read a mathematical book for more than a quarter of an hour at a time without a break. I had some light literature always by my side, and in the breaks I read through more than once nearly the whole of Shakespeare, Boswell's *Life of Johnson*, the *Agamemnon* of Æschylus (the only Greek play which I could read without effort), a great part of Lucretius and so on. Of course I often got excited by my mathematics, and read for half an hour or more without stopping; but that meant that my mind was intense, and no harm was done.

A power of intense concentration for brief periods, combined with a lack of power of continuous concentration, was characteristic of him all his life. He was seldom able to execute at white heat any considerable piece of work. He was also bothered by the lack of a retentive memory: even as an undergraduate his mathematical book-work troubled him as much as the problems did. As a boy he had a strong arithmetical faculty, which he afterwards lost.

Meanwhile at St. John's College, Cambridge, Alfred Marshall fulfilled his ambitions. In 1865 he was Second Wrangler,[11] the year when Lord Rayleigh was Senior, and he was immediately elected to a Fellowship. He proposed to devote himself to the study of molecular physics. Meanwhile he earned his living (and repaid Uncle Charles) by becoming for a brief period a mathematical master at Clifton, under Percival, for whom he had a great veneration. A little later he returned to Cambridge and took up coaching for the Mathematical Tripos for a short time. In this way "Mathematics," he said, "had paid my arrears. I was free for my own inclinations."

The main importance of Marshall's time at Clifton was that he made friends with H. G. Dakyns, who had gone there as an assistant master on the foundation of Clifton College in 1862, and, through him, with J. R. Mozley. These friendships opened to him the door into the intellectual circle of which Henry Sidgwick was the centre. Up to this time there is no evidence of Marshall's having been in touch with the more eminent of his contemporaries, but soon after his return to Cambridge he became a member of the small informal Discussion Society known as the "Grote Club."

The Grote Club came into existence with discussions after dinner in the Trumpington Vicarage of the Reverend John Grote, who was Knightbridge Professor of Moral Philosophy from 1855 till his death in 1866. The original members, besides Grote, were Henry Sidgwick, Aldis Wright, J. B. Mayor, and John Venn.[12] J. R. Mozley of King's and J. B. Pearson of St. John's joined a little later. Marshall wrote[13] the following account of his own connection with the Society:

When I was admitted in 1867, the active members were Professor F. D. Maurice (Grote's successor), Sidgwick, Venn, J. R. Mozley and J. B. Pearson. . . . After 1867 or 1868 the club languished a little; but new vigour was soon imparted to it by the advent of W. K. Clifford and J. F. Moulton. For a year or two Sidgwick, Mozley, Clifford, Moulton, and myself were the active members; and we all attended regularly. Clifford and Moulton had at that time read but little philosophy; so they kept quiet for the first half-hour of the discussion, and listened eagerly to what others, and especially Sidgwick, said. Then they let their tongues loose, and the pace was tremendous. If I might have verbatim reports of a dozen of the best conversations I have heard, I should choose two or three from among those evenings in which Sidgwick and Clifford were the chief speakers. Another would certainly be a conversation at tea before a Grote Club meeting, of which I have unfortunately no record

(I think it was early in 1868), in which practically no one spoke but Maurice and Sidgwick. Sidgwick devoted himself to drawing out Maurice's recollections of English social and political life in the thirties, forties, and fifties. Maurice's face shone out bright, with its singular holy radiance, as he responded to Sidgwick's inquiries and suggestions; and we others said afterwards that we owed all the delight of that evening to him. . . .

It was at this time and under these influences that there came the crisis in his mental development of which in later years he often spoke. His design to study physics was (in his own words) "cut short by the sudden rise of a deep interest in the philosophical foundation of knowledge, especially in relation to theology."

In Marshall's undergraduate days at Cambridge a preference for Mathematics over Classics had not interfered with the integrity of his early religious beliefs. He still looked forward to ordination, and his zeal directed itself at times towards the field of Foreign Missions. A missionary he remained all his life, but after a quick struggle religious beliefs dropped away and he became, for the rest of his life, what used to be called an agnostic. Of his relationship to Sidgwick at this time, Marshall spoke as follows (at the meeting for a Sidgwick Memorial, Trinity Lodge, November 26, 1900):

Though not his pupil in name, I was in substance his pupil in Moral Science, and I am the oldest of them in residence. I was fashioned by him. He was, so to speak, my spiritual father and mother: for I went to him for aid when perplexed, and for comfort when troubled; and I never returned empty away. The minutes that I spent with him were not ordinary minutes; they helped me to live. I had to pass through troubles and doubts somewhat similar to those with which he, with broader knowledge and greater strength, had fought his way; and perhaps of all the people who have cause to be grateful to him, none has more than I.

Marshall's Cambridge career came just at the date which will, I think, be regarded by the historians of opinion as the critical moment at which Christian dogma fell away from the serious philosophical world of England, or at any rate of Cambridge. In 1863 Henry Sidgwick, aged twenty-four, had subscribed to the Thirty-Nine Articles as a condition of tenure of his Fellowship,[14] and was occupied in reading Deuteronomy in Hebrew and preparing lectures on the Acts of the Apostles. Mill, the greatest intellectual influence on the youth of the age, had written nothing which clearly indicated any divergence from received religious opinions up to his *Examination of Hamilton* in 1865.[15] At about this time Leslie Stephen was an Anglican clergyman, James Ward a Nonconformist minister, Alfred Marshall a candidate for holy orders, W. K. Clifford a High Churchman. In 1869 Sidgwick resigned his Trinity Fellowship, "to free myself from dogmatic obligations." A little later none of these could have been called Christians. Nevertheless, Marshall, like Sidgwick,[16] was as far as possible from adopting an "anti-religious" attitude. He sympathised with Christian morals and Christian ideals and Christian incentives. There is nothing in his writings depreciating religion in any form; few of his pupils could have spoken definitely about his religious opinions. At the end of his life he said, "Religion seems to me an attitude," and that, though he had given up Theology, he believed more and more in Religion.

The great change-over of the later sixties was an intellectual change, not the ethical or emotional change which belongs to a later generation, and it was a wholly intellectual debate which brought it about. Marshall was wont to attribute the beginning of his own transition of mind to the controversy arising out of H. L. Mansel's *Bampton Lectures,* which was first put into his hands by J. R. Mozley. Mansel means nothing to the present generation. But, as the protagonist of the last attempt to found Christian dogma on an intellectual basis, he was of the greatest importance in the sixties. In 1858, Mansel, an Oxford don and afterwards Dean of St. Paul's, "adopted from Hamilton[17] the peculiar theory which was to enlist Kant in the service of the Church of England" [18]—an odd tergiversation of the human mind, the influence of which was great in Oxford for a full fifty years. Mansel's *Bampton Lectures* of 1858 brought him to the front as an intellectual champion of orthodoxy. In 1865, the year in which Marshall took his degree and had begun to turn his mind to the four quarters of heaven, there appeared Mill's *Examination of Sir William Hamilton's Philosophy*, which included a criticism of Mansel's extension of Hamilton to Christian Theology. Mansel replied. Mansel's defence of orthodoxy "showed me," Marshall said, "how much there was to be defended." The great controversy dominated Marshall's thoughts and drove him for a time to metaphysical studies, and then onward to the social sciences.

Meanwhile in 1859, the year following the *Bampton Lectures*, the *Origin of Species* had appeared, to point away from heaven or the clouds to an open road on earth; and in 1860-1862 Herbert Spencer's *First Principles* (unreadable as it now is), also born out of the Hamilton-Mansel controversy, took a new direction, dissolved metaphysics in agnosticism, and warned all but ingrained metaphysical minds away from a blind alley. Metaphysical agnosticism, Evolutionary progress, and—the one remnant still left of the intellectual inheritance of the previous generation—Utilitarian ethics joined to propel the youthful mind in a new direction.

From Metaphysics, therefore, Marshall turned his mind to Ethics. It would be true, I suppose, to say that Marshall never departed explicitly from the Utilitarian ideas which dominated the generation of economists which preceded him. But it is remarkable with what caution—in which respect he goes far beyond Sidgwick and is at the opposite pole from Jevons— he handled all such matters. There is, I think, no passage in his works in which he links economic studies to any ethical doctrine in particular. The solution of economic problems was for Marshall not an application of the hedonistic calculus, but a prior condition of the exercise of man's higher faculties, irrespective, almost, of what we mean by "higher." The economist can claim, and this claim is sufficient for his purposes, that "the study of the causes of poverty is the study of the causes of the degradation of a large part of mankind." [19] Correspondingly, the possibility of progress "depends in a great measure upon facts and inferences, which are within the province of economics; and this it is which gives to economic studies their chief and their highest interest." [20] This remains true even though the question also "depends partly on the moral and political capabilities of human nature; and on these matters the economist has no special means of information; he must do as others do, and guess as best he can." [21]

This was his final position. Nevertheless, it was only through Ethics that he first reached Economics. In a retrospect of his mental history, drawn from him towards the end of his life, he said:

From Metaphysics I went to Ethics, and thought that the justification of the existing condition of society was not easy. A friend, who had read a great deal of what are now called the Moral Sciences, constantly said: "Ah! if you understood Political Economy you would not say that." So I read Mill's *Political Economy* and got much excited about it. I had doubts as to the propriety of inequalities of *opportunity*, rather than of material comfort. Then, in my vacations I visited the poorest quarters of several cities and walked through one street after another, looking at the faces of the poorest people. Next, I resolved to make as thorough a study as I could of Political Economy.

His passage into Economics is also described in his own words in some pages,[22] written about 1917 and designed for the Preface to *Money, Credit and Commerce:*

About the year 1867 (while mainly occupied with teaching Mathematics at Cambridge), Mansel's *Bampton Lectures* came into my hands and caused me to think that man's own possibilities were the most important subject for his study. So I gave myself for a time to the study of Metaphysics; but soon passed to what seemed to be the more progressive study of Psychology. Its fascinating inquiries into the possibilities of the higher and more rapid development of human faculties brought me into touch with the question: how far do the conditions of life of the British (and other) working classes generally suffice for full-ness of life? Older and wiser men told me that the resources of production do not suffice for affording to the great body of the people the leisure and the opportunity for study; and they told me that I needed to study Political Economy. I followed their advice, and regarded myself as a wanderer in the land of dry facts; looking forward to a speedy return to the luxuriance of pure thought. But the more I studied economic science, the smaller appeared the knowledge which I had of it, in pro-portion to the knowledge that I needed; and now, at the end of nearly half a century of almost exclusive study of it, I am conscious of more ignorance of it than I was at the beginning of the study.

In 1868, when he was still in his metaphysical stage, a desire to read Kant in the original led him to Germany. "Kant my guide," he once said, "the only man I ever worshipped: but I could not get further: beyond seemed misty, and social problems came imperceptibly to the front. Are the opportunities of real life to be confined to a few?" He lived at Dresden with a German professor who had previously coached Henry Sidgwick.[23] Hegel's *Philosophy of History* greatly influenced him. He also came in contact with the work of the German economists, particularly Roscher. Finally Dr. Bateson, the Master of St. John's, was instrumental in giving him a career in life by persuading the College to establish for him a special lectureship in Moral Science.[24] He soon settled down to Economics, though for a time he gave short courses on other branches of Moral Science—on Logic and on Bentham.[25]

His dedication to economic study—for so he always considered it, not less ordained in spirit than if he had fulfilled his father's desire—was now effected. His two years of doubt and disturbance of mind left on his imagination a deep impression, to which in later years he would often recur with pupils whom he deemed worthy of the high calling—for so he reckoned it—of studying with scientific disinterestedness the modes and principles of the daily business of life, by which human happiness and the opportunities for good life are, in great measure, determined.

Before we leave the early phase, when he was not yet an economist, we may pause a moment to consider the colour of his outlook on life as, at that time, it was already fixed in him.

Like his two colleagues, Henry Sidgwick and James Ward, in the Chairs of the Moral Sciences at Cambridge during the last decades of the nineteenth century, Alfred Marshall belonged to the tribe of sages and pastors; yet, like them also, endowed with a double nature, he was a scientist too. As a preacher and pastor of men he was not particularly superior to other similar natures. As a scientist he was, within his own field, the greatest in the world for a hundred years. Nevertheless, it was to the first side of his nature that he himself preferred to give the pre-eminence. This self should be master, he thought; the second self, servant. The second self sought knowledge for its own sake; the first self subordinated abstract aims to the need for practical advancement. The piercing eyes and ranging wings of an eagle were often called back to earth to do the bidding of a moraliser.

This double nature was the clue to Marshall's mingled strength and weakness; to his own conflicting purposes and waste of strength; to the two views which could always be taken about him; to the sympathies and antipathies he inspired.

In another respect the diversity of his nature was pure advantage. The study of economics does not seem to require any specialised gifts of an unusually high order. Is it not, intellectually regarded, a very easy subject compared with the higher branches of philosophy and pure science? Yet good, or even competent, economists are the rarest of birds. An easy subject, at which very few excel! The paradox finds its explanation, perhaps, in that the master-economist must possess a rare *combination* of gifts. He must reach a high standard in several different directions and must combine talents not often found together. He must be mathematician, historian, statesman, philosopher—in some degree. He must understand symbols and speak in words. He must contemplate the particular in terms of the general, and touch abstract and concrete in the same flight of thought. He must study the present in the light of the past for the purposes of the future. No part of man's nature or his institutions must lie entirely outside his regard. He must be purposeful and disinterested in a simultaneous mood; as aloof and incorruptible as an artist, yet sometimes as near the earth as a politician. Much, but not all, of this ideal many-sidedness Marshall possessed. But chiefly his mixed training and divided nature furnished him with the most essential and fundamental of the economist's necessary gifts—he was conspicuously historian and mathematician, a dealer in the particular and the general, the temporal and the eternal, at the same time.

III

The task of expounding the development of Marshall's Economics is rendered difficult by the long intervals which generally separated the initial discovery and its oral communication to pupils from the final publication in a book to the world outside. Before attempting this it will be convenient to trace briefly the outward course of his life from his appointment to a lectureship at St. John's College, Cambridge in 1868, to his succession to the Chair of Political Economy in Cambridge in 1885.

For nine years Marshall remained Fellow and Lecturer of St. John's, laying the foundations of his subject but publishing nothing.[26] After his introduction to the Grote Club he was particularly intimate with W. K. Clifford [27] and Fletcher Moulton. Clifford was chief favourite, though "he was too fond of astonishing people." As a member, a little later on, of the "Eranus" he was in touch with Sidgwick, Venn, Fawcett, Henry Jackson, and other leaders of that first age of the emancipation of Cambridge. At this time he used to go abroad almost every long vacation. Mrs. Marshall writes:

He took with him £60[28] and a knapsack, and spent most of the time walking in the high Alps. This walking, summer after summer, turned him from a weak into a strong man. He left Cambridge early in June jaded and overworked and returned in October brown and strong and upright. Carrying the knapsack pulled him upright, and until he was over eighty he remained so. He even then exerted himself almost painfully to hold himself straight. When walking in the Alps his practice was to get up at six and to be well on his way before eight. He would walk with knapsack on his back for two or three hours. He would then sit down, sometimes on a glacier, and have a long pull at some book—Goethe or Hegel or Kant or Herbert Spencer—and then walk on to his next halting-place for the night. This was in his philosophic stage. Later on he worked out his theories of Domestic and Foreign Trade in these walks. A large box of books, etc., was sent on from one stage to another, but he would go for a week or more just with a knapsack. He would wash his shirt by holding it in a fast-running stream and dry it by carrying it on his alpenstock over his shoulder. He did most of his hardest thinking in these solitary Alpine walks.

These *Wanderjahre* gave him a love for the Alps which he always retained, and even in 1920 (for the last time) we went to the South Tyrol, where he sat and worked in the high air.

Alfred always did his best work in the open air. When he became Fellow of St. John's he did his chief thinking between 10 A.M. and 2 P.M. and between 10 P.M. and 2 A.M. He had a monopoly of the Wilderness in the daytime and of the New Court Cloisters at night. At Palermo in the early eighties he worked on the roof of a quiet hotel, using the cover of the bath as an awning. At Oxford he made a "Den" in the garden in which he wrote. At Cambridge he worked in the balcony, and later in a large revolving shelter, fitted up as a study, called "The Ark," and in the Tyrol he arranged a heap of stones, a camp stool and an air cushion into what he called a "throne," and in later years we always carried a tent shelter with us, in which he spent the day.

In 1875 Marshall visited the United States for four months. He toured the whole of the East, and travelled as far as San Francisco. At Harvard and Yale he had long talks with the academic economists, and he had many introductions everywhere to leading citizens. But his chief purpose was the "study of the Problem of Protection in a New Country." About this he inquired on all hands, and towards the end of his trip was able to write in a letter home:

In Philadelphia I spent many hours in conversation with the leading protectionists. And now I think, as soon as I have read some books they have recommended me to read, I shall really know the whole of their case; and I do not believe there is or ever has been another Englishman who could say the same.

On his return to England he read a paper at the Cambridge Moral Science Club on American Industry, November 17, 1875, and later on he lectured at Bristol, in 1878, on "The Economic Condition of America." The American trip made on him a great impression, which coloured all his future work. He used to say that it was not so much what he actually learnt, as that he got to know what things he wanted to learn; that he was taught to see things in proportion; and that he was enabled to expect the coming supremacy of the United States, to know its causes and the directions it would take.

Meanwhile he had been helping Fawcett, who was professor, and Henry Sidgwick, to establish Political Economy as a serious study in the University of Cambridge. Two of his earliest pupils, H. S. Foxwell and, later on, my father, John Neville Keynes, who took the Moral Sciences Tripos in 1875, joined these three as lecturers on Political Economy in the University.

In 1876 Alfred Marshall became engaged to Miss Mary Paley, a great-granddaughter of the famous Archdeacon. Miss Paley was a former pupil of his and was a lecturer in Economics at Newnham.[29] His first book, *Economics of Industry*, published in 1879, was written in collaboration with her; indeed it had been, at the start, her book and not his, having been undertaken by her at the request of a group of Cambridge University Extension lecturers. They were married in 1877. During forty-seven years of married life his dependence upon her devotion was complete. Her life was given to him and to his work with a degree of unselfishness and understanding that makes it difficult for friends and old pupils to think of them separately or to withhold from her shining gifts of character a big share in what his intellect accomplished.

Marriage, by involving the loss of his Fellowship, meant leaving Cambridge for a time,[30] and Marshall went to Bristol as the first Principal of University College, and as Professor of Political Economy.

Just at that time [Marshall has recorded] Balliol and New Colleges at Oxford were setting up at Bristol the first "University College": that is, a College designed to bring higher educational opportunities within the reach of the inhabitants of a large city, which had no University of its own. I was elected its first Principal: my wife lectured on Political Economy to a class consisting chiefly of ladies in the morning, and I lectured in the evening to a class composed chiefly of young business men.

Apart from his regular classes he gave a number of public evening lectures,[31] including a series on Henry George's *Progress and Poverty*. The work of the Marshalls at Bristol was much appreciated there, and the town kept up an interest in his career long after he had left it. But the administrative work, especially the business of begging money, which in view of the meagre endowments of the college was one of the main duties of the Principal, proved irksome and uncongenial. Soon after his marriage his health and nerves began to break down, chiefly as a result of stone in the kidney. He was anxious to resign the position of Principal, but there was no convenient opportunity until 1881, when the appointment of Professor Ramsay to the Department of Chemistry provided a suitable successor. He went with his wife to Italy for nearly a year, working quietly on the roof of a small hotel at Palermo for five months and then moving to Florence and to Venice. He came back to Bristol, where he was still Professor of Political Economy, in 1882 with his health much restored; but he remained for the rest of his life somewhat hypochondriacal and inclined to consider himself on the verge of invalidism. In fact, his constitution was extremely tough and he remained in harness as a writer up to a very advanced age. But his nervous equilibrium was easily upset by unusual exertion or excitement or by controversy and difference of opinion; his power of continuous concentration on difficult mental work was inferior to his wishes, and he became dependent on a routine of life adapted even to his whims and fancies. In truth, he was haunted by a feeling that his physical strength and power of continuous concentration were inferior to the fields of work which he saw stretching ahead, and to the actual constructions he had conceived but not yet given to the world. By 1877, when he was thirty-five years of age, he had worked out within him the foundations of little less than a new science, of great consequence to mankind; and a collapse of health and strength during the five years following, when he should have been giving all this to the world, partly broke his courage, though not his determination.

Amongst the Governors of University College, Bristol, were Dr. Jowett, the Master of Balliol, and Professor Henry Smith, and these two were accustomed to stay with the Marshalls on their periodic visits to Bristol. Jowett's interest in Economics was always lively. While Tutor of Balliol he had given courses of set lectures on Political Economy, and he continued to direct individual undergraduates in the subject up to the end of his life.[32] Jowett's interest and belief in Alfred Marshall were keenly aroused by the long evening talks which followed the meetings of the Governing Body, and on the premature death of Arnold Toynbee in 1883 he invited Marshall to take his place as Fellow of Balliol and Lecturer in Political Economy to the selected candidates for the Indian Civil Service.[33]

Marshall's Oxford career was brief but successful. He attracted able pupils, and his public lectures were attended by larger and more enthusiastic classes than at any other period of his life. He encountered with credit, on different occasions, Henry George and Hyndman in public debate, and was taking a prominent position in the University. In November 1884, however, Fawcett died, and in January 1885 Marshall returned to Cambridge as Professor of Political Economy.

IV

Marshall's serious study of Economic Theory began in 1867; his characteristic doctrines were far developed by 1875, and by 1883 they were taking their final form. Nevertheless, no part of his work was given to the world at large in adequate shape until 1890 (*Principles of Economics*), and that part of the subject at which he had worked earliest and which was most complete by 1875, was not treated in a published book until nearly fifty years later, in 1923 (*Money, Credit and Commerce*). Meanwhile he had not kept his ideas to himself, but had shared them without reserve in lecture and in talk with friends and pupils. They leaked out to wider circles in privately printed pamphlets and through the writings of his pupils, and were extracted in cross-examination by Royal Commissions. Inevitably, when the books themselves appeared, they lacked the novelty and path-breaking powers which would have been acclaimed in them a generation earlier, and those economists all over the world who know Marshall only by his published work may find it difficult to understand the extraordinary position claimed for him by his English contemporaries and successors. It is proper, therefore, that I should make an attempt, necessarily imperfect from lack of full data, to trace the progress of his ideas, and then to set forth the reasons or the excuses for the unhappy delay in their publication.

Marshall's serious study of Economics began in 1867. To fix our ideas of date: Mill's *Political Economy*[34] had appeared in 1848; the seventh edition, in 1871, was the last to receive Mill's own corrections; and Mill died in 1873. *Das Kapital* of Marx appeared in 1868; Jevons' *Theory of Political Economy*[35] in 1871; Menger's *Grundsätze der Volkswirtschaftslehre* also in 1871; Cairnes' *Leading Principles* in 1874.

Thus when Marshall began, Mill and Ricardo still reigned supreme and unchallenged. Roscher, of whom Marshall often spoke, was the only other influence of importance. The notion of applying mathematical methods was in the air. But it had not yet yielded anything substantial. Cournot's *Principes mathématiques de la Théorie des Richesses* (1835) is mentioned by Marshall in the Preface to the first edition of the *Principles of Economics* as having particularly influenced him; but I do not know at what date this book first came into his hands.[36] This, and the natural reaction of Ricardo on a Cambridge mathematician of that date,[37] with perhaps some hints of algebraical treatment in the arithmetical examples of Mill's Book III. chap. xviii.[38] on "International Values," were all that Marshall had to go upon in the first instance. An account of the progress of his thought from 1867 to his American trip in 1875, which Marshall himself put into writing,[39] is appropriate at this point:

While still giving private lessons in mathematics,[40] he translated as many as possible of Ricardo's reasonings into mathematics; and he endeavoured to make them more general. Meanwhile he was attracted towards the new views of economics taken by Roscher and other German economists; and by Marx, Lassalle and other Socialists. But it seemed to him that the analytical methods of the historical economists were not always sufficiently thorough to justify their confidence that the causes which they assigned to economic events were the true causes. He thought indeed that the interpretation of the economic past was almost as difficult as the prediction of the future. The Socialists also seemed to him to underrate the difficulty of their problems, and to be too quick to assume that the abolition of private property would purge away the faults and deficiencies of human nature. . . . He set himself to get into closer contact with practical business and with the life of the working classes. On the one side he aimed at learning the broad features of the technique of every chief industry; and on the other he sought the society of trade unionists, co-operators and other working-class leaders. Seeing, however, that direct studies of life and work would not yield much fruit for many years, he decided to fill the interval by writing a separate monograph or special treatise on Foreign Trade; for the chief facts relating to it can be obtained from printed documents. He proposed that this should be the first of a group of monographs on special economic problems; and he hoped ultimately to compress these monographs into a general treatise of a similar scope to Mill's. After writing that larger treatise, but not before, he thought he might be ready to write a short popular treatise. He has never changed his opinion that this is the best order of work; but his plans were overruled, and almost inverted, by the force of circumstances. He did indeed write the first draft of a monograph on Foreign Trade; and in 1875 he visited the chief seats of industry in America with the purpose of studying the problem of Protection in a new country. But this work was suspended by his marriage; and while engaged, in conjunction with his wife, in writing a short account of the Economics of Industry, forcibly simplified for working-class readers, he contracted an illness so serious that for some time he appeared unlikely to be able to do any more hard work. A little later he thought his strength might hold out for recasting his diagrammatic illustrations of economic problems. Though urged by the late Professor Walras about 1873 to publish these, he had declined to do so; because he feared that if separated from all concrete study of actual conditions, they might seem to claim a more direct bearing on real problems than they in fact had. He began, therefore, to supply some of the requisite limitations and conditions, and thus was written the kernel of the fifth book of his *Principles*. From that kernel the present volume was extended gradually backwards and forwards, till it reached the form in which it was published in 1890.

The fateful decision was the abandonment of the project to write "a group of monographs on special economic problems" in favour of a comprehensive treatise which should be born complete and fully armed from the head of an economic Jove—particularly when the special problems on which Marshall had worked first, Money and Foreign Trade, were held to occupy, logically, the latest sections of this treatise, with the result that they did not see the light for fifty years.

The evidence as to the order of his studies is as follows: In

1867 he began with the development of diagrammatic methods, with special regard to the problems of foreign trade,
mainly under the influence of Ricardo and Mill. To this was
added the influence of Cournot, and in a less degree that of
von Thünen, by which he

was led to attach great importance to the fact that our observations of nature, in the moral as in the physical world, relate not
so much to aggregate quantities, as to increments of quantities,
and that in particular the demand for a thing is a continuous
function, of which the "marginal" increment is, in stable equilibrium, balanced against the corresponding increment of its
cost of production. It is not easy to get a clear full view of Continuity in this aspect without the aid either of mathematical
symbols or of diagrams.[41]

By 1871 his progress along these lines was considerably advanced. He was expounding the new ideas to pupils and the
foundations of his diagrammatic economics had been truly
laid. In that year there appeared, as the result of independent
work, Jevons' *Theory of Political Economy*. The publication
of this book must have been an occasion of some disappointment and annoyance to Marshall. It took the cream of novelty
off the new ideas which Marshall was slowly working up without giving them—in Marshall's judgement—adequate or accurate treatment. Nevertheless, it undoubtedly gave Jevons
priority of publication as regards the group of ideas connected
with "marginal" (or, as Jevons called it, "final") utility. Marshall's references to the question of priority are extremely reserved. He is careful to leave Jevons' claim undisputed, whilst
pointing out, indirectly, but quite clearly and definitely, that
his own work owed little or nothing to Jevons.[42]

In 1872 Marshall reviewed[43] Jevons' *Political Economy* in
The Academy. This review,[44] while not unfavourable, is somewhat cool and it points out several definite errors:

The main value of the book [it concludes] does not lie in its
more prominent theories, but in its original treatment of a number of minor points, its suggestive remarks and careful analyses.
We continually meet with old friends in new dresses. . . . Thus
it is a familiar truth that the total utility of any commodity is

not proportional to its final degree of utility. . . . But Prof. Jevons has made this the leading idea of the costume in which he has displayed a large number of economic facts.

When, however, Marshall came, in later years, to write the *Principles,* his desire to be scrupulously fair to Jevons and to avoid the least sign of jealousy is very marked. It is true that in one passage[45] he writes: "It is unfortunate that here as elsewhere Jevons' delight in stating his case strongly has led him to a conclusion, which not only is inaccurate, but does mischief. . . ." But he says elsewhere:[46] "There are few writers of modern times who have approached as near to the brilliant originality of Ricardo as Jevons has done," and "There are few thinkers whose claims on our gratitude are as high and as various as those of Jevons."

In truth, Jevons' *Theory of Political Economy* is a brilliant but hasty, inaccurate, and incomplete brochure, as far removed as possible from the painstaking, complete, ultra-conscientious, ultra-unsensational methods of Marshall. It brings out unforgettably the notions of final utility and of the balance between the disutility of labour and the utility of the product. But it lives merely in the tenuous world of bright ideas[47] when we compare it with the great working machine evolved by the patient, persistent toil and scientific genius of Marshall. Jevons saw the kettle boil and cried out with the delighted voice of a child; Marshall too had seen the kettle boil and sat down silently to build an engine.

Meanwhile, Marshall worked on at the generalised diagrammatic scheme disclosed in his papers on the Pure Theory of Foreign Trade and Domestic Values. These must have been substantially complete about 1873 and were communicated to his pupils (particularly to Sir H. H. Cunynghame) about that date. They were drafted as non-consecutive[48] chapters of *The Theory of Foreign Trade, with some Allied Problems relating to the Doctrine of Laisser Faire,* which he nearly completed in 1875-77 after his return from America, embodying the results of his work from 1869 onwards.[49] In 1877 he turned aside to write the *Economics of Industry* with Mrs. Marshall. In 1879 Henry Sidgwick, alarmed at the prospect of Marshall's right of priority being taken from him, printed them for private circulation and copies were sent to leading economists at home and abroad.[50] These chapters, which are now very scarce in their original form, were never published to the world at large,[51] but the most significant parts of them were incorporated in Book V. chaps. xi. and xii. of the *Principles of Economics,* and (fifty years after their origination) in Appendix J of *Money, Credit and Commerce.*

Marshall's mathematical and diagrammatic exercises in Economic Theory were of such a character in their grasp, comprehensiveness, and scientific accuracy, and went so far beyond the "bright ideas" of his predecessors, that we may justly claim him as the founder of modern diagrammatic economics—that elegant apparatus which generally exercises a powerful attraction on clever beginners, which all of us use as an inspirer of, and a check on, our intuitions and as a shorthand record of our results, but which generally falls into the background as we penetrate further into the recesses of the subject. The fact that Marshall's results percolated to the outer world a drop at a time, and reached in their complete form only a limited circle, lost him much international fame which would otherwise have been his, and even, perhaps, retarded the progress of the subject. Nevertheless, we can, I think, on reflection understand Marshall's reluctance to open his career with publishing his diagrammatic apparatus by itself.

For, whilst it was a necessary appurtenance of his intellectual approach to the subject, an appearance of emphasising or exalting such methods pointed right away from what he regarded, quite early in his life, as the proper attitude to economic inquiry. Moreover, Marshall, as one who had been Second Wrangler and had nourished ambitions to explore molecular physics, always felt a slight contempt from the intellectual or aesthetic point of view for the rather "potty" scraps of elementary algebra, geometry, and differential calculus which make up mathematical economics.[52] Unlike physics, for example, such parts of the bare bones of economic theory as are expressible in mathematical form are extremely easy compared with the economic interpretation of the complex and incompletely known facts of experience,[53] and lead one but a very little way towards establishing useful results.

Marshall felt all this with a vehemence which not all his pupils have shared. The preliminary mathematics was for him child's play. He wanted to enter the vast laboratory of the world, to hear its roar and distinguish the several notes, to speak with the tongues of business men, and yet to observe all with the eyes of a highly intelligent angel. So "he set himself," as is recorded in his own words above (p. 329), "to get into closer contact with practical business and with the life of the working classes."

Thus Marshall, having begun by founding modern diagrammatic methods, ended by using much self-obliteration to keep them in their proper place. When the *Principles* appeared, the diagrams were imprisoned in footnotes, or, at their freest, could but exercise themselves as in a yard within the confines of a brief Appendix. As early as 1872, in reviewing Jevons' *Political Economy*, he wrote:

We owe several valuable suggestions to the many investigations in which skilled mathematicians, English and continental, have applied their favourite method to the treatment of economical problems. But all that has been important in their reasonings and results has, with scarcely an exception, been capable of being described in ordinary language. . . . The book before us would be improved if the mathematics were omitted, but the diagrams retained.

In 1881, reviewing Edgeworth's *Mathematical Psychics*, after beginning "This book shows clear signs of genius, and is a promise of great things to come," he adds, "It will be interesting, in particular, to see how far he succeeds in preventing his mathematics from running away with him, and carrying him out of sight of the actual facts of economics." And finally, in 1890, in the Preface to the *Principles*, he first emphasises his preference for diagrams over algebra, then allows the former a limited usefulness[54] and reduces the latter to the position of a convenience for private use.[55]

In his reaction against excessive addiction to these methods, and also (a less satisfactory motive) from fear of frightening "business men" away from reading his book, Marshall may have gone too far. After all, if "there are many problems of pure theory, which no one who has once learnt to use diagrams will willingly handle in any other way," such diagrams must surely form a part of every advanced course in economics[56] and they should be available for students in the fullest and clearest form possible.[57]

Whilst, however, Marshall's reluctance to print the results of his earliest investigations is mainly explained by the profundity of his insight into the true character of his subject in its highest and most useful developments, and by his unwillingness to fall short of his own ideals in what he gave to the world, it was a great pity that *The Theory of Foreign Trade, with some Allied Problems relating to the Doctrine of Laisser Faire,* did not see the light in 1877, even in an imperfect form.[58] After all, he had originally embarked on this particular inquiry because, in this case, "the chief facts relating to it can be obtained from printed documents"; and these facts, supplemented by those which he had obtained first-hand during his visit to the United States about the actual operation of Protection in a new country, might have been deemed sufficient for a monograph. The explanation is partly to be found in the fact that, when his health broke down, he believed that he had only a few years to live and that these must be given to the working out of his fundamental ideas on Value and Distribution.

We must regret still more Marshall's postponement of the publication of his *Theory of Money* until extreme old age, when time had deprived his ideas of freshness and his exposition of sting and strength. There is no part of Economics where Marshall's originality and priority of thought are more marked than here, or where his superiority of insight and knowledge over his contemporaries was greater.

Here too was a semi-independent section of the subject ideally suited to separate treatment in a monograph. Yet apart from what is embedded in his evidence before Royal Commissions and occasional articles, not one single scrap was given to the world in his own words and his own atmosphere at the right time. Since *Money* was from the early seventies onwards one of his favourite topics for lectures, his main ideas became known to pupils in a general way,[59] with the result that there grew up at Cambridge an oral tradition, first from Marshall's own lectures and after his retirement from those of Professor Pigou, different from, and (I think it may be claimed) superior to, anything that could be found in printed books until recently.[60] It may be convenient at this point to attempt a brief summary of Marshall's main contributions to Monetary Theory.

Marshall printed nothing whatever on the subject of Money[61] previously to the Bimetallic controversy, and even then he waited a considerable time before he intervened. His first serious contribution to the subject was contained in his answers to a questionnaire printed by the Royal Commission on the Depression of Trade and Industry in 1886. This was followed by his article on "Remedies for Fluctuations of General Prices" in the *Contemporary Review* for March 1887, and a little later by his voluminous evidence before the Gold and Silver Commission in 1887 and 1888. In 1899 came his evidence before the Indian Currency Committee. But his theories were not expounded in a systematic form until the appearance of *Money, Credit and Commerce* in 1923. By this date nearly all his main ideas had found expression in the works of others. He had passed his eightieth year; his strength was no longer equal to much more than piecing together earlier fragments; and its jejune treatment, carefully avoiding difficulties and complications, yields the mere shadow of what he had had it in him to bring forth twenty[62] or (better) thirty years earlier. It happens, however, that the earliest extant manuscript of Marshall's, written about 1871, deals with his treatment of the Quantity Theory. It is a remarkable example of the continuity of his thought from its first beginnings between 1867 and 1877, that the whole of the substance of Book I. chap. iv. of his *Money, Credit and Commerce* is to be found here, worked out with fair completeness and with much greater strength of exposition and illustration than he could manage fifty years later. I have no evidence at what date he had arrived at the leading

ideas underlying his *Contemporary Review* article or his evidence before the Gold and Silver Commission.[63] But the passages
about Commercial Crises in the *Economics of Industry,* from
which he quoted freely in his reply to the Trade Depression
Commissioners, show that he was on the same lines of thought
in 1879. The following are the most important and characteristic of Marshall's original contributions to this part of Economics.

(1) *The exposition of the Quantity Theory of Money as a part
of the General Theory of Value.* He always taught that the
value of money is a function of its supply on the one hand,
and the demand for it, on the other, as measured by "the average stock of command over commodities which each person
cares to keep in a ready form." He went on to explain how
each individual decides how much to keep in a ready form as
the result of a *balance* of advantage between this and alternative forms of wealth.

The exchange value of the whole amount of coin in the Kingdom [he wrote in the manuscript of 1871 mentioned above] is
just equal to that of the whole amount of the commodities over
which the members of the community have decided to keep a
command in this ready form. Thus with a silver currency if we
know the number of ounces of silver in circulation we can determine what the value of one ounce of silver will be in terms
of other commodities by dividing the value of above given
amount of commodities by the number of ounces. Suppose that
on the average each individual in a community chose to keep
command over commodities in a ready form to the extent of
one-tenth of his year's income. The money, suppose in this case
exclusively silver, in the Kingdom will be equal in value to one-
tenth of the annual income of the kingdom. Let their habits
alter, each person being willing, for the sake of gain in other
ways, to be to a greater extent without the power of having each
want satisfied as soon as it arises. Let on the average each person choose to keep command over commodities in a ready form
only to the extent of a twentieth part of his income. So much
silver as before not being wanted at the old value, it will fall in
value. It would accordingly be more used in manufactures,
while its production from the mines would be checked. . . .[64]

He points out that the great advantage of this method of approach is that it avoids the awkward conception of "rapidity of

circulation" (though he is able to show the exact logical relation between the two conceptions): "When, however, we try to establish a connection between 'the rapidity of circulation' and the value of money, it introduces grave complications. Mr. Mill is aware of the evil (*Political Economy*, Book III. chap. viii. §3, latter part), but he has not pointed the remedy." [65] Marshall also expounded long ago the way in which distrust of a currency raises prices by diminishing the willingness of the public to hold stocks of it—a phenomenon to which recent events have now called everyone's attention; and he was aware that the fluctuation in the price level, which is an accompaniment of the trade cycle, corresponds to a fluctuation in the volume of "ready command" [66] which the public desire to hold.

(2) *The distinction between the "real" rate of interest and the "money" rate of interest, and the relevance of this to the credit cycle, when the value of money is fluctuating.* The first clear exposition of this is, I think, that given in the *Principles* (1890), Book VI. chap. vi. (concluding note).[67]

(3) *The causal train by which, in modern credit systems, an additional supply of money influences prices, and the part played by the rate of discount.* The *locus classicus* for an account of this, and the only detailed account for many years to which students could be referred, is Marshall's Evidence before the Gold and Silver Commission, 1887 (particularly the earlier part of his evidence), supplemented by his Evidence before the Indian Currency Committee, 1899. It was an odd state of affairs that one of the most fundamental parts of Monetary Theory should, for about a quarter of century, have been available to students nowhere except embedded in the form of question-and-answer before a Government Commission interested in a transitory practical problem.

(4) *The enunciation of the "Purchasing Power Parity" Theory as determining the rate of exchange between countries with mutual inconvertible currencies.* In substance this theory is due to Ricardo, but Professor Cassel's restatement of it in a form applicable to modern conditions was anticipated by Marshall in the memorandum[68] appended to his Evidence

before the Gold and Silver Commission (1888). It also had an important place in the conclusions which he laid before the Indian Currency Committee in 1899. The following from an abstract of his opinions handed in by Marshall to the Gold and Silver Commission gives his theory in a nutshell: "Let B have an inconvertible paper-currency (say roubles). In each country prices will be governed by the relation between the volume of the currency and the work it has to do. The gold price of the rouble will be fixed by the course of trade just at the ratio which gold prices in A bear to rouble prices in B (allowing for cost of carriage)."

(5) *The "chain" method of compiling index-numbers.* The first mention of this method is in a footnote to the last section (entitled *How to Estimate a Unit of Purchasing Power*) of his "Remedies for Fluctuations of General Prices" (1887).

(6) *The proposal of paper currency for circulation (on the lines of Ricardo's "Proposals for an Economical and Secure Currency") based on gold-and-silver symmetallism as the standard.* This suggestion is first found in his reply to the Commissioners on Trade Depression in 1886. He argued that ordinary bimetallism would always tend to work out as alternative-metallism.

I submit [he went on] that, if we are to have a great disturbance of our currency for the sake of bi-metallism, we ought to be sure that we get it. . . . My alternative scheme is got from his (Ricardo's) simply by wedding a bar of silver of, say, 2000 grammes to a bar of gold of, say, 100 grammes; the government undertaking to be always ready to buy or sell a wedded pair of bars for a fixed amount of currency. . . . This plan could be started by any nation without waiting for the concurrence of others.

He did not urge the immediate adoption of this system, but put it forward as being at least preferable to bimetallism. The same proposal was repeated in 1887 in his article on "Remedies for Fluctuations of General Prices," and in 1888 in his Evidence before the Gold and Silver Commission.[69]

(7) *The proposal of an official Tabular Standard for optional use in the case of long contracts.* This proposal first ap-

pears in an appendix to a paper on remedies for the discontinuity of employment, which Marshall read at the "Industrial Remuneration Conference" in 1885.[70] He repeated, and added to, what he had said there, in his Reply to the Commissioners on Trade Depression in 1886.

A great cause of the discontinuity of industry [he wrote] is the want of certain knowledge as to what a pound is going to be worth a short time hence. . . . This serious evil can be much diminished by a plan which economists have long advocated. In proposing this remedy I want government to help business, though not to do business. It should publish tables showing as closely as may be changes in the purchasing power of gold, and should facilitate contracts for payments to be made in terms of units of fixed purchasing power. . . . The unit of constant general purchasing power would be applicable, at the free choice of both parties concerned, for nearly all contracts for the payment of interest, and for the repayment of loans; and for many contracts for rent, and for wages and salaries. . . . I wish to emphasise the fact that this proposal is independent of the form of our currency, and does not ask for any change in it. I admit that the plan would seldom be available for the purposes of international trade. But its importance as a steadying influence to our home trade could be so great, and its introduction would be so easy and so free from the evils which generally surround the interference of Government in business, that I venture to urge strongly its claims on your immediate attention.

This important proposal was further developed in Marshall's remarkable essay on "Remedies for Fluctuations of General Prices," which has been mentioned above. The first three sections of this essay are entitled: I. *The Evils of a Fluctuating Standard of Value;* II. *The Precious Metals cannot afford a good Standard of Value;* III. *A Standard of Value independent of Gold and Silver.* Marshall had a characteristic habit in all his writings of reserving for footnotes what was most novel or important in what he had to say,[71] and the following is an extract from a footnote to this essay:

Every plan for regulating the supply of the currency, so that its value shall be constant, must, I think, be national and not international. I will indicate briefly two such plans, though I do not advocate either of them. On the first plan the currency would be inconvertible. An automatic Government Department would buy Consols for currency whenever £1 was worth more than a unit, and would sell Consols for currency whenever it was worth less. . . . The other plan is that of a convertible currency, each £1 note giving the right to demand at a Government Office as much gold as at that time had the value of half a unit together with as much silver as had the value of half a unit.[72]

The *Economist* mocked at Symmetallism and the optional Tabular Standard; and Marshall, always a little over-afraid of being thought unpractical or above the head of the "business man" (that legendary monster), did not persevere.[73]

v

I promised, above, that I would endeavour to set forth the reasons or the excuses for the delay in the publication of Marshall's methods and theories concerning Diagrammatic Methods, the Theory of Foreign Trade, and the Principles of Money and Credit. I think that the reasons, some of which apply to all periods of his life, were partly good and partly bad. Let us take the good ones first.

Marshall, as already pointed out above, arrived very early at the point of view that the bare bones of economic theory are not worth much in themselves and do not carry one far in the direction of useful, practical conclusions. The whole point lies in applying them to the interpretation of current economic life. This requires a profound knowledge of the actual facts of industry and trade. But these, and the relation of individual men to them, are constantly and rapidly changing. Some extracts from his Inaugural Lecture at Cambridge[74] will indicate his position:

The change that has been made in the point of view of Economics by the present generation is due to the discovery that man himself is in a great measure a creature of circumstances and changes with them. The chief fault in English economists at the beginning of the century was not that they ignored history and statistics, but that they regarded man as so to speak a constant quantity, and gave themselves little trouble to study his variations. They therefore attributed to the forces of supply and demand a much more mechanical and regular action than they actually have. Their most vital fault was that they did not see how liable to change are the habits and institutions of industry. But the Socialists were men who had felt intensely and who knew something about the hidden springs of human action of which the economists took no account. Buried among their wild rhapsodies there were shrewd observations and pregnant suggestions from which philosophers and economists had much to learn. Among the bad results of the narrowness of the work of English economists early in the century, perhaps the most unfortunate was the opportunity which it gave to sciolists to quote and misapply economic dogmas. Ricardo and his chief followers did not make clear to others, it was not even quite clear to themselves, that what they were building up was not universal truth, but machinery of universal application in the discovery of a certain class of truths. While attributing high and transcendent universality to the central scheme of economic reasoning, I do not assign any universality to economic dogmas. It is not a body of concrete truth, but an engine for the discovery of concrete truth.[75]

Holding these views and living at a time of reaction against economists when the faults of his predecessors, to which he draws attention above, were doing their maximum amount of harm, he was naturally reluctant to publish the isolated apparatus of economics, divorced from its appropriate applications. Diagrams and pure theory by themselves might do more harm than good, by increasing the confusion between the objects and methods of the mathematical sciences and those of the social sciences, and would give what he regarded as just the wrong emphasis. In publishing his intellectual exercises without facing the grind of discovering their points of contact with the real world he would be following and giving bad example. On the other hand, the relevant facts were extremely hard to come by—much harder than now. The progress of events in the seventies and eighties, particularly in America, was extraordinarily rapid, and organised sources of information, of which there are now so many, scarcely existed. In the twenty years from 1875 to 1895 he was, in fact, greatly increasing his command over real facts and his power of economic judgement, and the work which he could have published between 1875 and 1885 would have been much inferior to what he was capable of between 1885 and 1895.

The other valid reason was a personal one. At the critical moment of his life his health was impaired. After health was restored, the preparation of lectures and the time he devoted to his pupils made big interruptions in the writing of books. He was too meticulous in his search for accuracy, and also for conciseness of expression, to be a ready writer. He was particularly unready in the business of fitting pieces into a big whole and of continually rewriting them in the light of their reactions on and from the other pieces. He was always trying to write big books, yet lacked the power of rapid execution and continuous concentration (such as J. S. Mill had) and that of continuous artistic sensibility to the whole (such as Adam Smith had) which are necessary for the complete success of a Treatise.

We are now approaching in our explanations what we must admit as bad reasons. Given his views as to the impossibility of any sort of finality in Economics and as to the rapidity with which events change, given the limitations of his own literary aptitudes and of his leisure for book-making, was it not a fatal decision to abandon his first intention of separate independent monographs in favour of a great Treatise? I think that it was, and that certain weaknesses contributed to it.

Marshall was conscious of the great superiority of his powers over those of his surviving contemporaries. In his Inaugural lecture of 1885 he said: "Twelve years ago England possessed perhaps the ablest set of economists that there have ever been in a country at one time. But one after another there have been taken from us Mill, Cairnes, Bagehot, Cliffe Leslie, Jevons, Newmarch, and Fawcett." There was no one left who could claim at that date to approach Marshall in stature. To his own pupils, who were to carry on the Economics of the future, Marshall was ready to devote time and strength. But he was too little willing to cast his half-baked bread on the waters, to trust in the efficacy of the co-operation of many minds, and to let the big world draw from him what sustenance it could. Was he not attempting, contrary to his own principles, to achieve an impossible finality? An Economic Treatise may have great educational value. Perhaps we require one treatise, as a *pièce de résistance,* for each generation. But in view of the transitory character of economic facts, and the bareness of economic principles in isolation, does not the progress and the daily usefulness of economic science require that pioneers and innovators should eschew the Treatise and prefer the pamphlet or the monograph? I depreciated Jevons' *Political Economy* above on the ground that it was no more than a brilliant brochure. Yet it was Jevons' willingness to spill his ideas, to flick them at the world, that won him his great personal position and his unrivalled power of stimulating other minds. Every one of Jevons' contributions to Economics was in the nature of a pamphlet. Malthus spoilt the *Essay on Population* when, after the first edition, he converted it into a Treatise. Ricardo's greatest works were written as ephemeral pamphlets. Did not Mill, in achieving by his peculiar gifts a successful Treatise, do more for pedagogics than for science, and end by sitting like an Old Man of the Sea on the voyaging Sinbads of the next generation? [76] Economists must leave to Adam Smith alone the glory of the Quarto, must pluck the day, fling pamphlets into the wind, write always *sub specie temporis,* and achieve immortality by accident, if at all.

Moreover, did not Marshall, by keeping his wisdom at home until he could produce it fully clothed, mistake, perhaps, the true nature of his own special gift? "Economics," he said in the passage quoted above, "is not a body of concrete truth, but an engine for the discovery of concrete truth." This engine, as we employ it to-day, is largely Marshall's creation. He put it in the hands of his pupils long before he offered it to the world. The building of this engine was the essential achievement of Marshall's peculiar genius. Yet he hankered greatly after the "concrete truth" which he had disclaimed and for the discovery of which he was not specially qualified. I have very early memories, almost before I knew what Economics meant, of the sad complaints of my father, who had been able to observe as pupil and as colleague the progress of Marshall's thought almost from the beginning, of Marshall's obstinate refusal to understand where his special strength and weakness really lay, and of how his unrealisable ambitions stood in the way of his giving to the world the true treasures of his mind and genius. Economics all over the world might have progressed much faster, and Marshall's authority and influence would have been far greater, if his temperament had been a little different.

Two other characteristics must be mentioned. First, Marshall was too much afraid of being wrong, too thin-skinned towards criticisms, too easily upset by controversy even on matters of minor importance. An extreme sensitiveness deprived him of magnanimity towards the critic or the adversary. This fear of being open to correction by speaking too soon aggravated other tendencies. Yet, after all, there is no harm in being sometimes wrong—especially if one is promptly found out. Nevertheless, this quality was but the defect of the high standard he never relaxed—which touched his pupils with awe—of scientific accuracy and truth.

Second, Marshall was too anxious to do good. He had an inclination to undervalue those intellectual parts of the subject which were not *directly* connected with human well-being or the condition of the working classes or the like, although *indirectly* they might be of the utmost importance, and to feel that when he was pursuing them he was not occupying himself with the Highest. It came out of the conflict, already remarked, between an intellect, which was hard, dry, critical, as unsentimental as you could find, with emotions and, generally unspoken, aspirations of quite a different type. When his intellect chased diagrams and Foreign Trade and Money there was an evangelical moraliser of an imp somewhere inside him that was so ill-advised as to disapprove. Near the end of his life, when the intellect grew dimmer and the preaching imp could rise nearer to the surface to protest against its lifelong servitude, he once said: "If I had to live my life over again I should have devoted it to psychology. Economics has too little to do with ideals. If I said much about them I should not be read by business men." But these notions had always been with him. He used to tell the following story of his early life: "About the time that I first resolved to make as thorough a study as I could of Political Economy (the word Economics was not then invented) I saw in a shop-window a small oil painting [of a man's face with a strikingly gaunt and wistful expression, as of one 'down and out'] and bought it for a few shillings. I set it up above the chimney-piece in my room in college and thenceforward called it my patron saint, and devoted myself to trying how to fit men like that for heaven. Meanwhile, I got a good deal interested in the semi-mathematical side of pure Economics, and was afraid of becoming a mere thinker. But a glance at my patron saint seemed to call me back to the right path. That was particularly useful after I had been diverted from the study of ultimate aims to the questions about Bimetallism, etc., which at one time were dominant. I despised them, but the 'instinct of the chase' tempted me towards them." This was the defect of that other great quality of his which always touched his pupils—his immense disinterestedness and public spirit.

VI

At any rate, in 1877 Marshall turned aside to help his wife with the *Economics of Industry* (published in 1879), designed as a manual for Cambridge University Extension lecturers, which, as it progressed, became more and more his work. In later years Marshall grew very unfriendly to the little book. After the publication of the *Principles* he suppressed it and replaced it in 1892 with an almost wholly different book under the same title, which was mainly an abridgement of the *Principles* and "an attempt to adapt it to the needs of junior students." Marshall's feelings were due, I think, to the fact that his theory of value, which was here first published to the world, was necessarily treated in a brief and imperfect manner, yet remained for eleven years all that the outside world had to judge from. His controversies in the *Quarterly Journal of Economics* in 1887 and 1888 with American economists who had read the little book accentuated this feeling. He also revolted later on from the conception of Economics as a subject capable of being treated in a light and simple manner for elementary students by half-instructed Extension lecturers[77] aided by half-serious books. "This volume," he wrote in 1910 to a Japanese translator of the 1879 book, "was begun in the hope that it might be possible to combine simplicity with scientific accuracy. But though a simple book can be written on selected topics, the central doctrines of Economics are not simple and cannot be made so."

Yet these sentiments do a real injustice to the book. It won high praise from competent judges and was, during the whole of its life, much the best little text-book available.[78] If we are to have an elementary text-book at all, this one was probably, in relation to its contemporaries and predecessors, the best thing of the kind ever done—much better than the primers of Mrs. Fawcett or Jevons or any of its many successors. Moreover, the later part of Book III. on Trade Combinations, Trade Unions, Trade Disputes, and Co-operation was the first satisfactory treatment on modern lines of these important topics.

After this volume[79] was out of the way, Marshall's health was at its worst. When in 1881 he went abroad to recuperate, his mind did not return to Money or to Foreign Trade, but was concentrated on the central theories which eventually appeared in the *Principles*.[80] Subject to the successive interruptions of his Oxford appointment, his removal to Cambridge, the preparation of his lectures there, his incursion into the Bimetallic controversy and his Evidence before the Gold and Silver Commission, the next nine years were spent on the preparation of this book.

Marshall intended at first to cover the whole field of Economics in a single volume. His theory of Distribution was taking shape in 1883 and 1884.[81] In the summer of 1885 (in the Lakes), the first of his Cambridge Long Vacations, the volume began to assume its final form:

The work done during this year [he wrote] [82] was not very satisfactory, partly because I was gradually outgrowing the older and narrower conception of my book, in which the abstract reasoning which forms the backbone of the science was to be made prominent, and had not yet mustered courage to commit myself straight off to a two-volume book which should be the chief product (as gradually improved) of my life's work.[83]

In 1886:

My chief work was recasting the plan of my book. This came to a head during my stay at Sheringham near Cromer in the summer. I then put the contents of my book into something like their final form, at least so far as the first volume is concerned. And thenceforward for the first time I began to try to put individual chapters into a form in which I expected them to be printed.

In 1887 (at Guernsey):

I did a great deal of writing at my book; and having arranged with Macmillan for its publication, I began just at the end of this academic year to send proofs to the printers: all of it except about half of Book VI. being typewritten in a form not ready for publication, but ready to be put into a form for publication—I mean the matter was nearly all there and the arrangement practically settled.

In 1888:

By the end of the Long Vacation I had got Book V. at the printer's, Book IV. being almost out of my hands. Later on I decided to bring before the Book on Normal Value or Distribution and Exchange a new Book on Cost of Production further considered,[84] putting into it (somewhat amplified) discussions which I had intended to keep for the later part of the Book on Normal Value. That Book now became Book VII. This decision was slowly reached, and not much further progress was made during this Calendar year.

In 1889:

During the first four months of 1889 I worked at Book VI., finishing the first draft of the first four chapters of it, and working off Book V. Meanwhile I had paid a good deal of attention to the Mathematical Appendix and got a good part of that into print. The Long Vacation, of which eight weeks were spent at Bordeaux Harbour, was occupied chiefly with Book VI. chaps. v. and vi., and Book VII. chaps. i.-v.

The work was now pushed rapidly to a conclusion and was published in July 1890.

By 1890 Marshall's fame stood high,[85] and the *Principles of Economics,*[86] Vol. I.,[87] was delivered into an expectant world. Its success was immediate and complete. The book was the subject of leading articles and full-dress reviews throughout the Press. The journalists could not distinguish the precise contributions and innovations which it contributed to science; but they discerned with remarkable quickness that it ushered in a new age of economic thought. "It is a great thing," said the *Pall Mall Gazette,* "to have a Professor at one of our old Universities devoting the work of his life to recasting the science of Political Economy as the Science of Social Perfectibility." The New Political Economy had arrived, and the Old Political Economy, the dismal science, "which treated the individual man as a purely selfish and acquisitive animal, and the State as a mere conglomeration of such animals," had passed away,[88] "It will serve," said the *Daily Chronicle,* "to restore the shaken credit of political economy, and will probably become for the present generation what Mill's *Principles* was for the last." "It has made almost all other accounts of the science antiquated or obsolete," said the *Manchester Guardian.* "It is not premature to predict that Professor Marshall's treatise will form a landmark in the development of political economy, and that its influence on the direction and temper of economic inquiries will be wholly good." These are samples from a general chorus.

It is difficult for those of us who have been brought up entirely under the influences of Marshall and his book to appreciate the position of the science in the long interregnum between Mill's *Principles of Political Economy* and Marshall's *Principles of Economics,* or to define just what difference was made by the publication of the latter. The following is an attempt, with help from notes supplied by Professor Edgeworth, to indicate some of its more striking contributions to knowledge.[89]

(1) The unnecessary controversy, caused by the obscurity of Ricardo and the rebound of Jevons, about the respective parts played by Demand and by Cost of Production in the determination of Value was finally cleared up. After Marshall's analysis there was nothing more to be said.

The new light thrown on Cost of Production [Prof. Edge-worth writes] enabled one more clearly to discern the great part which it plays in the determination of value; that the classical authors had been rightly guided by their intuitions, as Marshall has somewhere said, when they emphasised the forces of Supply above those of Demand. The rehabilitation of the older writers—much depreciated by Jevons, Böhm-Bawerk and others in the seventies and eighties of last century—produced on the reviewer of the first edition an impression which is thus expressed: "The mists of ephemeral criticism are dispelled. The eternal mountains reappear in their natural sublimity, contemplated from a kindred height."

(2) The general idea, underlying the proposition that Value is determined at the equilibrium point of Demand and Supply, was extended so as to discover a whole Copernican system, by which all the elements of the economic universe are kept in their places by mutual counterpoise and interaction.[90] The general theory of economic equlibrium was strengthened and made effective as an organon of thought by two powerful subsidiary conceptions—*the Margin* and *Substitution*. The notion of the Margin was extended beyond Utility to describe the equilibrium point in given conditions of any economic factor which can be regarded as capable of small variations about a given value, or in its functional relation to a given value. The notion of Substitution was introduced to describe the process by which Equilibrium is restored or brought about. In particular the idea of *Substitution at the Margin,* not only between alternative objects of consumption, but also between the factors of production, was extraordinarily fruitful in results. Further, there is

the double relation in which the various agents of production stand to one another. On the one hand, they are often rivals for employment; any one that is more efficient than another in proportion to its cost tending to be substituted for it, and thus limiting the demand price for the other. And on the other hand, they all constitute the field of employment for each other; there is no field of employment for any one, except in so far as it is provided by the others: the national dividend which is the joint product of all, and which increases with the supply of each of them, is also the sole source of demand for each of them.[91]

This method allowed the subsumption of wages and profits under the general laws of value, supply and demand—just as previously the theory of money had been so subsumed. At the same time the peculiarities in the action of demand and supply which determine the wages of the labourer or the profits of the employer were fully analysed.

(3) The explicit introduction of the element of Time as a factor in economic analysis is mainly due to Marshall. The conceptions of the "long" and "short" period are his, and one of his objects was to trace "a continuous thread running through and connecting the applications of the general theory of equilibrium of demand and supply to different periods of time." [92] Connected with these there are further distinctions, which we now reckon essential to clear thinking, which are first explicit in Marshall—particularly those between "external" and "internal" economies[93] and between "prime" and "supplementary" cost. Of these pairs the first was, I think, a complete novelty when the *Principles* appeared; the latter, however, already existed in the vocabulary of manufacture if not in that of economic analysis.

By means of the distinction between the long and the short period, the meaning of "normal" value was made precise; and with the aid of two further characteristically Marshallian conceptions—Quasi-Rent and the Representative Firm—the doctrine of Normal Profit was evolved.

All these are path-breaking ideas which no one who wants to think clearly can do without. Nevertheless, this is the quarter in which, in my opinion, the Marshall analysis is least complete and satisfactory, and where there remains most to do. As he says himself in the Preface to the first edition of the *Principles,* the element of time "is the centre of the chief difficulty of almost every economic problem."

(4) The special conception of Consumers' Rent or Surplus, which was a natural development of Jevonian ideas, has perhaps proved less fruitful of practical results than seemed likely at first. [94] But one could not do without it as part of the apparatus of thought, and it is particularly important in the *Principles* because of the use of it (in Professor Edgeworth's words)

"To show that *laissez-faire*, the maximum of advantage attained by unrestricted competition, is not necessarily the greatest possible advantage attainable." Marshall's proof that *laissez-faire* breaks down in certain conditions *theoretically*, and not merely practically, regarded as a principle of maximum social advantage, was of great philosophical importance. But Marshall does not carry this particular argument very far,[95] and the further exploration of that field has been left to Marshall's favourite pupil and successor, Professor Pigou, who has shown in it what a powerful engine for cutting a way in tangled and difficult country the Marshall analysis affords in the hands of one who has been brought up to understand it well.

(5) Marshall's analysis of Monopoly should also be mentioned in this place; and perhaps his analysis of increasing return, especially where external economies exist, belongs better here than where I have mentioned it above.

Marshall's theoretical conclusions in this field and his strong sympathy with socialistic ideas were compatible, however, with an old-fashioned belief in the strength of the forces of competition. Professor Edgeworth writes:

I may record the strong impression produced on me the first time I met Marshall—far back in the eighties, I think—by his strong expression of the conviction that Competition would for many a long day rule the roost as a main determinant of value. Those were not his words, but they were of a piece with the dictum in his article on "The Old Generation of Economists and the New":[96] "When one person is willing to sell a thing at a price which another is willing to pay for it, the two manage to come together in spite of prohibitions of King or Parliament or of the officials of a Trust or Trade-Union."

(6) In the provision of terminology and apparatus to aid thought I do not think that Marshall did economists any greater service than by the explicit introduction of the idea of "elasticity." Book III. chap. iii. of the first edition of the *Principles*, which introduces the definition of "Elasticity of Demand," [97] is virtually the earliest treatment [98] of a conception without the aid of which the advanced theory of Value and Distribution can scarcely make progress. The notion that

demand may respond to a change of price to an extent that may be either more or less than in proportion had been, of course, familiar since the discussions at the beginning of the nineteenth century about the relation between the supply and the price of wheat.[99] Indeed, it is rather remarkable that the notion was not more clearly disentangled either by Mill or by Jevons.[100] But it was so. And the concept $e = \dfrac{dx}{x} \div -\dfrac{dy}{y}$ is wholly Marshall's.

The way in which Marshall introduces Elasticity, without any suggestion that the idea is novel, is remarkable and characteristic. The field of investigation opened up by this instrument of thought is again one where the full fruits have been reaped by Professor Pigou rather than by Marshall himself.

(7) The historical introduction to the *Principles* deserves some comment. In the first edition, Book I. includes two chapters entitled "The Growth of Free Industry and Enterprise." In the latest editions most of what has been retained out of these chapters has been relegated to an Appendix. Marshall was always in two minds about this. On the one hand, his views as to the perpetually changing character of the subject-matter of Economics led him to attach great importance to the historical background as a corrective to the idea that the axioms of to-day are permanent. He was also dissatisfied with the learned but half-muddled work of the German historical school. On the other hand, he was afraid of spending too much time on these matters (at one period he had embarked on historical inquiries on a scale which, he said, would have occupied six volumes), and of overloading with them the essential matter of his book. At the time when he was occupied with economic history there was very little ready-made material to go upon, and he probably wasted much strength straying unnecessarily along historical by-ways and vacillating as to the importance to be given in his own book to the historical background. The resulting compromise, as realised in the *Principles,* was not very satisfactory. Everything is boiled down into wide generalisations, the evidence for which he has not space to display.[101] Marshall's best historical work is to be found, perhaps, in *Industry and Trade,*

published in 1919, many years after most of the work had been
done. The historical passages of the *Principles* were brusquely
assailed by Dr. William Cunningham in an address before the
Royal Historical Society, printed in the *Economic Journal,* vol.
ii. (1892); and Marshall, breaking his general rule of not replying to criticism, came successfully out of the controversy in a
reply printed in the same issue of the *Journal.*[102]

The way in which Marshall's *Principles of Economics* is
written is more unusual than the casual reader will notice. It
is elaborately unsensational and under-emphatic. Its rhetoric
is of the simplest, most unadorned order. It flows in a steady,
lucid stream, with few passages which stop or perplex the
intelligent reader, even though he know but little economics.
Claims to novelty or to originality on the part of the author
himself are altogether absent.[103] Passages imputing error to
others are rare, and it is explained that earlier writers of repute
must be held to have *meant* what is right and reasonable,
whatever they may have said.[104]

The connexity and continuity of the economic elements, as
signified in Marshall's two mottoes, "Natura non facit saltum"
and "The many in the one, the one in the many," are the
chief grounds of difficulty. But, subject to this, the chief impression which the book makes on the minds of uninitiated readers
—particularly on those who do not get beyond Book IV.—is
apt to be that they are perusing a clear, apt, and humane
exposition of fairly obvious matters.

By this stylistic achievement Marshall attained some of his
objects. The book reached the general public. It increased the
public esteem of Economics. The minimum of controversy was
provoked. The average reviewer liked the author's attitude to
his subject-matter, to his predecessors, and to his readers, and
delighted Marshall by calling attention to the proper stress laid
by him on the ethical element and to the much required
humanising which the dismal science received at his hands;[105]
and, at the same time, could remain happily insensible to the
book's intellectual stature. As time has gone on, moreover, the
intellectual qualities of the book have permeated English eco-

nomic thought, without noise or disturbance, in a degree which can easily be overlooked.

The method has, on the other hand, serious disadvantages. The lack of emphasis and of strong light and shade, the sedulous rubbing away of rough edges and salients and projections, until what is most novel can appear as trite, allows the reader to pass too easily through. Like a duck leaving water, he can escape from this douche of ideas with scarce a wetting. The difficulties are concealed; the most ticklish problems are solved in footnotes; a pregnant and original judgement is dressed up as a platitude. The author furnishes his ideas with no labels of salesmanship and few hooks for them to hang by in the wardrobe of the mind. A student can read the *Principles,* be fascinated by its pervading charm, think that he comprehends it, and yet, a week later, know but little about it. How often has it not happened even to those who have been brought up on the *Principles,* lighting upon what seems a new problem or a new solution, to go back to it and to find, after all, that the problem and a better solution have been always there, yet quite escaping notice! It needs much study and independent thought on the reader's own part before he can know the half of what is contained in the concealed crevices of that rounded globe of knowledge which is Marshall's *Principles of Economics.*

VII

The Marshalls returned in 1885 to the Cambridge of the early years after the reforms which finally removed restrictions upon the marriage of Fellows. They built for themselves a small house, called Balliol Croft, on St. John's College land in the Madingley Road, close to the Backs, yet just on the outskirts of the town, so that on one side open country stretched towards Madingley Hill. Here Alfred Marshall lived for nearly forty years. The house, built in a sufficient garden, on an unconventional plan so as to get as much light as possible, just accommodated the two of them and a faithful maid. His study, lined with books, and filled transversally with shelves, had space by the fire for two chairs. Here were held his innumerable *tête-à-têtes* with pupils, who would be furnished as the afternoon wore on with a cup of tea and a slice of cake on an adjacent stool or shelf. Larger gatherings took place downstairs, where the dining-room and Mrs. Marshall's sitting-room could be thrown into one on the occasion of entertainments. The unvarying character of the surroundings—upstairs the books and nests of drawers containing manuscript, downstairs the Michelangelo figures from the Sistine Chapel let into the furniture, and at the door the face of Sarah the maid [106] —had a charm and fascination for those who paid visits to their Master year after year, like the Cell or Oratory of a Sage.

In that first age of married society in Cambridge, when the narrow circle of the spouses-regnant of the Heads of Colleges and of a few wives of Professors was first extended, several of the most notable Dons, particularly in the School of Moral Science, married students of Newnham. The double link between husbands and between wives bound together a small cultured society of great simplicity and distinction. This circle was at its full strength in my boyhood, and, when I was first old enough to be asked out to luncheon or to dinner, it was to these houses that I went. I remember a homely, intellectual atmosphere which it is harder to find in the swollen, heterogeneous Cambridge of to-day. The entertainments at the Marshalls' were generally occasioned, in later days, by the visit of some fellow-economist, often an eminent foreigner, and the small luncheon party would usually include a couple of undergraduates and a student or young lecturer from Newnham. I particularly remember meeting in this way Adolf Wagner and N. G. Pierson, representatives of a generation of economists which is now almost past. Marshall did not much care about going to other people's houses, and was at his best fitting his guests comfortably into a narrow space, calling out staff directions to his wife, in unembarrassed, half-embarrassed mood, with laughing, high-pitched voice and habitual jokes and phrases. He had great conversational powers on all manner of matters; his cheerfulness and gaiety were unbroken; and, in the presence of his bright eyes and smiling talk and unaffected absurdity, no one could feel dull.

In earlier days, particularly between 1885 and 1900, he was fond of asking working-men leaders to spend a week-end with him—for example, Thomas Burt, Ben Tillett, Tom Mann, and many others. Sometimes these visits would be fitted in with meetings of the Social Discussion Society, which the visitor would address. In this way he came to know most of the leading co-operators and Trade Unionists of the past generation. In truth, he sympathised with the Labour Movement and with Socialism (just as J. S. Mill had) in every way except intellectually.[107]

Marshall was now settled in an environment and in habits which were not to be changed, and we must record in rapid survey the outward events of his life from 1885 to the resignation of his professorship in 1908.

From 1885 to 1890 he was mainly occupied, as we have seen, with the *Principles*. But his other activities included, particularly, his paper before the Industrial Remuneration Conference in 1885, his evidence before the Gold and Silver Commission in 1887-88, and his Presidential Address before the Co-operative Congress in 1889. In the summer of 1890 he delivered his interesting Presidential Address on "Some Aspects of Competition" to the Economic Section of the British Association at Leeds. He was also much occupied with his lectures, and these five years were the most active and productive of his life.

He gave two lectures a week in a general course, and one lecture a week on special theoretical difficulties; but he lectured, as a rule, in only two terms out of three, making about forty-five lectures in the year. Two afternoons a week, from four to seven, Professor Marshall, it was announced, "will be at home to give advice and assistance to any members of the University who may call on him, whether they are attending his lectures or not." In the late eighties the attendance at his general courses would vary between forty and seventy and at his special courses half that number. But his methods choked off—more or less deliberately—the less serious students, and as the academic year progressed the attendance would fall to the lower figure.

It was not Marshall's practice to write out his lectures.

He rarely used notes [Mrs. Marshall writes] except for lectures on Economic History. He sometimes made a few notes before he went to lecture, and thought over them on his way to the class. He said that the reason why he had so many pupils who thought for themselves was that he never cared to present the subject in an orderly and systematic form or to give information. What he cared to do in lectures was to make the students *think with him*. He gave questions once a week on a part of the subject which he had not lectured over, and then answered the questions in class. He took immense pains in looking over the answers, and used red ink on them freely.[108]

I think that the informality of his lectures may have increased as time went on. Certainly in 1906, when I attended them, it was impossible to bring away coherent notes. But the above was always his general method. His lectures were not, like Sidgwick's, books in the making. This practice may have contributed, incidentally, to the retardation of his published work. But the sharp distinction which he favoured between instruction by book and oral instruction by lecture was, as he developed it, extraordinarily stimulating for the better men and where the class was not too large. It is a difficult method to employ where the class exceeds forty at the most (my memory of the size of his class when I attended it is of nearer twenty than forty), and it is not suited to students who have no real aptitude or inclination for economics (in whose interest the curricula of the vast Economic Schools of to-day are mainly designed). The following titles of successive courses, soon after he arrived in Cambridge, indicate the ground which he purported to cover:

1885-86.	October Term :	Foreign Trade and Money.
	Easter ,, :	Speculation, Taxation, etc. (Mill, IV. and V.).
1886-87.	October ,, :	Production and Value.
	Lent ,, :	Distribution.

After the publication of the *Principles* in 1890, his first task was to prepare the abridgement, entitled *Economics of Industry*,[109] which appeared early in 1892.[110] He also spent much time on the successive revisions of the *Principles,* the most important changes being introduced in the third edition, published in 1895, and the fifth edition in 1907. It is doubtful whether the degree of improvement effected corresponded to the labour involved. These revisions were a great obstacle to his getting on with what was originally intended to be volume II. of the *Principles*.

The main interruption, however, came from his membership of the Royal Commission on Labour, 1891-94. He welcomed greatly this opportunity of getting into close touch with the raw material of his subject, and he played a big part in the drafting of the Final Report. The parts dealing with Trade Unions, Minimum Wage, and Irregularity of Employment were especially his work.

Meanwhile he was at work on the continuation of the *Principles*.

But he wasted a great deal of time [Mrs. Marshall writes] because he changed his method of treatment so often. In 1894 he began a historical treatment, which he called later on a White Elephant, because it was on such a large scale that it would have taken many volumes to complete. Later on he used fragments of the White Elephant in the descriptive parts of *Industry and Trade*.

Marshall's work on the Labour Commission was only one of a series of services to Government inquiries. In 1893 he gave evidence before the Royal Commission on the Aged Poor, in which he proposed to associate Charity Organisation Committees with the administration of the Poor Law. Early in 1899 he gave carefully prepared evidence before the Indian Currency Committee. His evidence on monetary theory was in part a repetition of what he had said to the Gold and Silver Commission eleven years earlier, but he himself considered that the new version was an improvement and constituted his best account of the theory of money. The parts dealing with specifically Indian problems were supported by many statistical diagrams. His interest in the economic and currency problems of India had been first aroused during the time at Oxford when it was his duty to lecture to Indian Civil Service Probationers. He was pleased with his detailed realistic inquiries into Indian problems,[111] and the great rolls of Indian charts, not all of which were published, were always at hand as part of the furniture of his study.

Later in the same year, 1899, he prepared Memoranda on the Classification and Incidence of Imperial and Local Taxes for the Royal Commission on Local Taxation. In 1903, at the height of the Tariff Reform controversy, he wrote, at the request of the Treasury, his admirable Memorandum on "The Fiscal Policy of International Trade." This was printed in 1908 as a Parliamentary paper at the instance of Mr. Lloyd George, then Chancellor of the Exchequer, "substantially as it was written originally." The delay of a critical five years in the date of publication was characteristically explained by Marshall as follows:

Some large corrections of, and additions to, this Memorandum were lost in the post abroad[112] in August 1903; and when I re-read the uncorrected proofs of it in the autumn, I was so dissatisfied with it that I did not avail myself of the permission kindly given to me to publish it independently. The haste with which it was written and its brevity are partly responsible for its lack of arrangement, and for its frequent expression almost dogmatically of private opinion, where careful argument would be more in place. It offends against my rule to avoid controversial matters; and, instead of endeavouring to probe to the cause of causes, as a student's work should, it is concerned mainly with proximate causes and their effects. I elected, therefore, to remain silent on the fiscal issue until I could incorporate what I had to say about it in a more careful and fuller discussion; and I am now engaged on that task. But it proceeds slowly; and time flies.

Marshall's growing inhibitions are exposed in these sentences. The difficulties of bringing him to the point of delivering up his mind's possessions were getting almost insuperable. In 1908 he resigned his professorship, in the hope that release from the heavy duties of lecturing and teaching might expedite matters.

VIII

During his twenty-three years as Professor he took part in three important movements, which deserve separate mention— the foundation of the British Economic Association (now the

Royal Economic Society), the Women's Degrees Controversy at Cambridge, and the establishment of the Cambridge Economics Tripos.

1. The circular entitled "Proposal to Form an English Economic Association," which was the first public step towards the establishment of the Royal Economic Society, was issued on October 24, 1890, over the sole signature of Alfred Marshall, though, of course, with the co-operation of others.[113] It invited all lecturers on Economics in any University or public College in the United Kingdom, the members of the Councils of the London, Dublin, and Manchester Statistical Societies, and the members of the London Political Economy Club, together with a few other persons, including members of the Committee of Section F of the British Association, to attend a private meeting at University College, London, on November 20, 1890, under the Chairmanship of Lord Goschen, the Chancellor of the Exchequer, "to discuss proposals for the foundation of an Economic Society or Association, and, in conjunction therewith, of an Economic Journal." This initial circular letter lays down the general lines which the Society has actually pursued during the subsequent years of its existence.[114] The only vocal dissentient was Mr. G. Bernard Shaw,[115] who, whilst approving everything else, suggested, "with all respect to Mr. Goschen, that the head of the Association should not be a gentleman who was identified with any political party in the State."

2. The controversy about admitting women to degrees, which tore Cambridge in two in 1896, found Marshall in the camp which was opposed to the women's claims. He had been in closest touch with Newnham since its foundation, through his wife and through the Sidgwicks. When he went to Bristol he had been, in his own words, "attracted thither chiefly by the fact that it was the first College in England to open its doors freely to women." A considerable proportion of his pupils had been women. In his first printed essay (on "The Future of the Working Classes," in 1873) the opening passage is an eloquent claim, in sympathy with Mill, for the emancipation of women. All Mill's instances "tend to show," he says in that paper, "how our progress could be accelerated if we would unwrap the

swaddling-clothes in which artificial customs have enfolded woman's mind and would give her free scope womanfully to discharge her duties to the world." Marshall's attitude, therefore, was a sad blow to his own little circle, and, being exploited by the other side, it played some part in the overwhelming defeat which the reformers eventually suffered. In his taking this course Marshall's intellect could find excellent reasons. Indeed, the lengthy fly-sheet, which he circulated to members of the Senate, presents, in temperate and courteous terms, a brilliant and perhaps convincing case against the complete assimilation of women's education to that of men. Nevertheless, a congenital bias, which by a man's fifty-fourth year of life has gathered secret strength, may have played a bigger part in the conclusion than the obedient intellect.

3. Lastly, there are Marshall's services in the foundation of the Cambridge School of Economics.

When Marshall came back to Cambridge in 1885, papers on Political Economy were included both in the Moral Sciences Tripos and in the History Tripos.[116] The separate foundation of these two schools some twenty years earlier had worked a great revolution in liberalising the studies of the University.[117] But, almost as soon as he was Professor, Marshall felt strongly that the time had come for a further step forward; and he particularly disliked the implication of the existing curriculum, that Economics was the sort of subject which could be satisfactorily undertaken as a subsidiary study. Immediately that he was back in Cambridge in 1885 he was in rebellion against the idea that his lectures must be adapted to the requirements of an examination of which Economics formed but a part.[118] His Inaugural Lecture constituted, in effect, a demand that Economics should have a new status; and it was so interpreted by Sidgwick. The following declaration from that Lecture is of some historical importance as almost the first blow in the struggle for the independent status which Economics has now won almost everywhere:

There is wanted wider and more scientific knowledge of facts: an organon stronger and more complete, more able to analyse and help in the solution of the economic problems of the age. To develop and apply the organon rightly is our most urgent need; and this requires all the faculties of a trained scientific mind. Eloquence and erudition have been lavishly spent in the service of Economics. They are good in their way; but what is most wanted now is the power of keeping the head cool and clear in tracing and analysing the combined action of many combined causes. Exceptional genius being left out of account, this power is rarely found save amongst those who have gone through a severe course of work in the more advanced sciences. Cambridge has more such men than any other University in the world. But, alas! few of them turn to the task. Partly this is because the only curriculum in which Economics has a very important part to play is that of the Moral Sciences Tripos. And many of those who are fitted for the highest and hardest economic work are not attracted by the metaphysical studies that lie at the threshold of that Tripos.

This claim of Marshall's corresponded to the conception of the subject which dominated his own work. Marshall was the first great economist *pur sang* that there ever was; the first who devoted his life to building up the subject as a separate science, standing on its own foundations, with as high standards of scientific accuracy as the physical or the biological sciences. It was Marshall who finally saw to it that "never again will a Mrs. Trimmer, a Mrs. Marcet, or a Miss Martineau earn a goodly reputation by throwing economic principles into the form of a catechism or of simple tales, by aid of which any intelligent governess might make clear to the children nestling around her where lies economic truth." [119] But—much more than this—after his time Economics could never be again one of a number of subjects which a Moral Philosopher would take in his stride, one Moral Science out of several, as Mill, Jevons, and Sidgwick took it. He was the first to take up this professional scientific attitude to the subject, as something above and outside current controversy, as far from politics as physiology from the general practitioner.

As time went on Political Economy came to occupy, in Part II. of the Moral Sciences Tripos, a position nearer to Marshall's ideal. But he was not satisfied until, in 1903, his victory was complete by the establishment of a separate School and Tripos in Economics and associated branches of Political Science.[120]

Thus in a formal sense Marshall was Founder of the Cambridge School of Economics. Far more so was he its Founder in those informal relations with many generations of pupils, which played so great a part in his life's work and in determining the course of their lives' work.

To his colleagues Marshall might sometimes seem tiresome and obstinate; to the outside world he might appear pontifical or unpractical; but to his pupils he was, and remained, a true sage and master, outside criticism, one who was their father in the spirit and who gave them such inspiration and comfort as they drew from no other source. Those eccentricities and individual ways, which might stand between him and the world, became, for them, part of what they loved. They built up sagas round him (of which Mr. Fay is, perhaps, the chief repository), and were not content unless he were, without concession, his own unique self. The youth are not satisfied unless their Socrates is a little odd.

It is difficult to describe on paper the effect he produced or his way of doing it. The pupil would come away with an extraordinary feeling that he was embarked on the most interesting and important voyage in the world. He would walk back along the Madingley Road, labouring under more books, which had been taken from the shelves for him as the interview went on, than he could well carry, convinced that here was a subject worthy of his life's study. Marshall's double nature, coming out informally and spontaneously, filled the pupil seated by him with a double illumination. The young man was presented with a standard of intellectual integrity, and with it a disinterestedness of purpose which satisfied him intellectually and morally at the same time. The subject itself had seemed to grow under the hands of master and pupil as they had talked. There were endless possibilities, not out of reach. "Everything was friendly and informal," Mr. Sanger has written of these occasions (*Nation*, July 19, 1924):

There was no pretence that economic science was a settled affair—like grammar or algebra—which had to be learnt, not criticised; it was treated as a subject in the course of development. When once Alfred Marshall gave a copy of his famous book to a pupil, inscribed "To——, in the hope that in due course he will render this treatise obsolete," this was not a piece of mock modesty, but an insistence on his belief that economics was a growing science, that as yet nothing was to be considered as final.

It must not be supposed that Marshall was undiscriminating towards his pupils. He was highly critical and even sharp-tongued. He managed to be encouraging, whilst at the same time very much the reverse of flattering. Pupils, in after life, would send him their books with much trepidation as to what he would say or think. The following anecdote of his insight and quick observation when lecturing is told by Dr. Clapham: "You have two very interesting men from your College at my lecture," he said to a College Tutor. "When I come to a very stiff bit, A. B. says to himself, 'This is too hard for me: I won't try to grasp it.' C. D. tries to grasp it but fails"—Marshall's voice running off on to a high note and his face breaking up into his smile. It was an exact estimate of the two men's intelligences and tempers.

It is through his pupils, even more than his writings, that Marshall is the father of Economic Science as it exists in England to-day. So long ago as 1888, Professor Foxwell was able to write: "Half the economic chairs in the United Kingdom are occupied by his pupils, and the share taken by them in general economic instruction in England is even larger than this." [121] To-day, through pupils and the pupils of pupils, his dominion is almost complete. More than most men he could, when the time came for him to go away, repeat his *Nunc Dimittis,* on a comparison of his achievement with the aim he had set himself in the concluding sentence of his Inaugural Lecture in 1885:

It will be my most cherished ambition, my highest endeavour, to do what with my poor ability and my limited strength I may, to increase the numbers of those whom Cambridge, the great mother of strong men,[122] sends out into the world with cool heads but warm hearts, willing to give some at least of their best powers to grappling with the social suffering around them; resolved not to rest content till they have done what in them lies to discover how far it is possible to open up to all the material means of a refined and noble life.

IX

Marshall retired from the Chair of Political Economy at Cambridge in 1908, aged sixty-six. He belonged to the period of small salaries and no pensions. Nevertheless, he had managed out of his professional stipend (of £700, including his fellowship), which he never augmented either by examining or by journalism,[123] to maintain at his own expense a small lending library for undergraduates, to found a triennial Essay Prize of the value of £60[124] for the encouragement of original research, and privately to pay stipends of £100 a year to one, or sometimes two, young lecturers for whom the University made no provision and who could not have remained otherwise on the teaching staff of the School of Economics. At the same time, with the aid of receipts from the sales of his books,[125] he had saved just sufficient to make retirement financially possible. As it turned out, the receipts from his books became, after the publication of *Industry and Trade*, so considerable that, at the end of his life, he was better off than he had ever been; and he used to say, when Macmillan's annual cheque arrived, that he hardly knew what to do with the money. He left his Economic library to the University of Cambridge, and most of his estate and any future receipts from his copyrights are also to fall ultimately to the University for the encouragement of the study of Economics.

Freed from the labour of lecturing and from the responsibility for pupils,[126] he was now able to spend what time and strength were left him in a final effort to gather in the harvest of his prime. Eighteen years had passed since the publication of the *Principles*, and masses of material had accumulated for consolidation and compression into books. He had frequently changed his plans about the scope and content of his later volumes, and the amount of material to be handled exceeded his powers of co-ordination. In the preface to the fifth edition of the *Principles* (1907) he explains that in 1895 he had decided to arrange his material in three volumes: I. *Modern Conditions of Industry and Trade;* II. *Credit and Employment;* III. *The Economic Functions of Government.* By 1907 four volumes were becoming necessary. So he decided to concentrate upon two of them, namely: I. *National Industry and Trade;* and II. *Money, Credit and Employment.* This was the final plan, except that, as time went on, *Employment* was squeezed out of the second of these volumes in favour of International Trade or *Commerce.* Even so, twelve more years passed by before, in his seventy-seventh year, *Industry and Trade* was published.

During this period the interruptions to the main matter in hand were inconsiderable. He wrote occasional letters to *The Times*—on Mr. Lloyd George's Budget (1909), in controversy with Professor Karl Pearson on "Alcoholism and Efficiency" (1910), on "A Fight to a Finish" and "Civilians in Warfare" on the outbreak of war (1914), and on Premium Bonds (1919). He wrote to the *Economist* in 1916 urging increased taxation to defray the expenses of the war; and in 1917 he contributed a chapter on "National Taxation after the War" to *After-War Problems,* a volume edited by Mr. W. H. Dawson.

Marshall's letters to *The Times* on the outbreak of war are of some interest. When he was asked, before war was actually declared, to sign a statement that we ought not to go to war because we had no interest in the coming struggle, he replied: "I think the question of peace or war must turn on national duty as much as on our interest. I hold that we ought to mobilise instantly, and announce that we shall declare war if the Germans invade Belgium; and everybody knows they will." For many years he had taken seriously Pan-Germanic ambitions, and he headed his letter "A Fight to a Finish." Thus he took up a definitely anti-pacifist attitude, and did not fluctuate from this as time went on. But he was much opposed to the inflaming of national passions. He remembered that he had "known and loved Germany," and that they were "a people exceptionally conscientious and upright." [127] He held, therefore, that "it is our interest as well as our duty to respect them and make clear that we desire their friendship, but yet to fight them with all our might." And he expressed "an anxiety lest popular lectures should inflame passions which will do little or nothing towards securing victory, but may very greatly increase the slaughter on both sides, which must be paid as the price of resisting Germany's aggressive tendencies." These sentiments brought down on him the wrath of the more savage patriots.

At last, in 1919, *Industry and Trade* appeared, a great effort of will and determination on the part of one who had long passed the age when most men rest from their labours.

It is altogether a different sort of book from the *Principles*. The most part of it is descriptive. A full third is historical and summarises the results of his long labours in that field. The co-ordination of the parts into a single volume is rather artificial. The difficulties of such co-ordination, which had beset him for so many years, are not really overdone. The book is not so much a structural unity as an opportunity for bringing together a number of partly related matters about which Marshall had something of value to say to the world. This is particularly the case with its sixteen Appendices, which are his device for bringing to birth a number of individual monographs or articles. Several of these had been written a great number of years before the book was issued. They were quite well suited to separate publication, and it must be judged a fault in him that they were hoarded as they were.

The three books into which the volume is divided would, like the Appendices, have suffered very little if they had been published separately. Book I., entitled *Some Origins of Present Problems of Industry and Trade,* is a history of the claims to industrial leadership of England, France, Germany, and the United States, mainly during the second half of the nineteenth century. Book II., on *Dominant Tendencies of Business Organisation,* whilst not definitely historical, is also in the main an account of the evolution of the forms of Business Organisation during the second half of the nineteenth century. Book I. is an account of the economic evolution of that period considered nationally; Book II. is an account of it considered technically.

Book III., on *Monopolistic Tendencies: their Relations to Public Well-being,* deals in more detail with the special problems which arose in regard to Transport and to Trusts, Cartels, and Combinations during the same period.

Thus such unity as the book possesses derives from its being an account of the forms of individualistic capitalism as this had established itself in Western Europe at about the year 1900, of how they came to pass, and of how far they served the public interest. The volume as a whole also serves to illustrate what Marshall was always concerned to emphasise, namely, the transitory and changing character of the forms of business organisation and of the shapes in which economic activities embody themselves. He calls particular attention to the precarious and impermanent nature of the foundations on which England's industrial leadership had been built up.

The chief value of the book lies, however, in something less definite and more diffused than its central themes. It represents the fruits of Marshall's learning and ripe wisdom on a host of different matters. The book is a mine rather than a railway—like the *Principles,* a thing to quarry in and search for buried treasure. Like the *Principles,* again, it appears to be an easy book; yet it is more likely, I believe, to be useful to one who knows something already than to a beginner. It contains the suggestions, the starting points for many investigations. There is no better book for suggesting lines of original inquiry to a reader so disposed. But for the ignorant the broad generalisations of the book are too quiet, smooth, urbane, undogmatic, to catch him.

Industry and Trade was a remarkable success with the public. A second edition was called for immediately, and by the end of 1932, 16,000 copies had been printed. The fact that it was reaching wide circles of readers and met with no damaging criticisms was a cause of great encouragement and consolation to the aged author, who could feel that, after all, he had not been prevented by time, the enemy, from delivering his words to the world.

But, all the same, time's wingèd chariot was hurrying near. "Old age," as he wrote in the preface of *Industry and Trade,* "indicates that my time for thought and speech is nearly ended." The composition of great Treatises is not, like that of great pictures, a work which can be continued into extreme old age. Much of his complete scheme of ordered knowledge would never be delivered. Yet his determination and his courage proved just equal to the publication of one more volume.

His powers of concentration and of memory were now beginning to fail somewhat rapidly. More and more he had to live for the book alone and to save for that every scrap of his strength. Talk with visitors tired him too much and interfered too seriously with his power of work. More and more Mrs. Marshall had to keep them away from him, and he lived alone with her, struggling with time. He would rest much, listening to his favourite melodies on the auto-piano, which was a great solace to him during the last ten years of his life, or hearing Mrs. Marshall read over again a familiar novel. Each night he walked alone in the dark along the Madingley Road. On his seventy-eighth birthday he said that he did not much want a future life. When Mrs. Marshall asked him whether he would not like to return to this world at intervals of (say) a hundred years, to see what was happening, he replied that he should like it from pure curiosity. "My own thoughts," he went on, "turn more and more on the millions of worlds which may have reached a high state of morality before ours became habitable, and the other millions of worlds that may have a similar development after our sun has become cool and our world uninhabitable." [128] His greatest difficulty, he said, about believing in a future life was that he did not know at what stage of existence it could begin. One could hardly believe that apes had a future life or even the early stages of tree-dwelling human beings. Then at what stage could such an immense change as a future life begin?

Weaknesses of digestion, which had troubled him all his life, increased in later years. In September 1921, in his eightieth year, he made the following notes:

Tendency of work to bring on feeling of pressure in the head, accompanied by weariness, is increasing; and it troubles me. I must work on, so far as strength permits, for about two full years (or say four years of half-time) if that is allowed to me: after that, I can say "Nunc dimittis." I care little for length of life for its own sake. I want only so to arrange my work as to increase my chance of saying those things which I think of chief importance.

In August 1922, soon after his eightieth birthday, *Money, Credit and Commerce* was finished, and it was published in the following year, 1923.[129] The scope of the volume differed from his design, in that it did not include "a study of the influences on the conditions of man's life and work which are exerted by the resources available for employment." But he managed to bring within the covers of a book his chief contributions to the theories of Money and of Foreign Trade. The book is mainly pieced together from earlier fragments, some of them written fifty years before, as has been recorded above, where also the nature of his main contributions to these subjects have been summarised. It shows the marks of old age in a way which *Industry and Trade* did not. But it contains a quantity of materials and ideas, and collects together passages which are otherwise inaccessible to the student or difficult of access. "If much of it might have been written in the eighties of last century," Professor Edgeworth wrote of it in the *Economic Journal,* "much of it will be read in the eighties of this century."

"Although old age presses on me," he wrote in the preface to *Money, Credit and Commerce,* "I am not without hopes that some of the notions which I have formed as to the possibilities of social advance may yet be published." Up to his last illness, in spite of loss of memory and great feebleness of body, he struggled to piece together one more volume. It was to have been called *Progress: its Economic Conditions*. But the task was too great. In a way his faculties were still strong. In writing a short letter he was still himself. One day in his eighty-second year he said that he was going to look at Plato's *Republic,* for he would like to try and write about the kind of Republic that Plato would wish for had he lived now. But though, as of old, he would sit and write, no advance was possible.

In these last days, with deep-set and shining eyes, wisps of white hair, and black cap on his head, he bore, more than ever, the aspect of a Sage or Prophet. At length his strength ebbed from him. But he would wake each morning, forgetful of his condition and thinking to begin his day's work as usual. On July 13, 1924, a fortnight before his eighty-second birthday, he passed away into rest.

FRANCIS YSIDRO EDGEWORTH

1845-1926

Francis Ysidro Edgeworth was almost the last in the male line of a famous family—illustrating his own favourite Law of Averages; for his great-great-grandfather, Francis Edgeworth, married three wives,[1] and his grandfather, the eccentric and celebrated Richard Lovell Edgeworth, married four wives[2] and had twenty-two children, of whom seven sons and eight daughters survived him. F. Y. Edgeworth himself was the fifth son of a sixth son. Yet, in 1911, after the other heirs had died without leaving male issue,[3] he succeeded to the family estate of Edgeworthstown, Co. Longford, where the Edgeworths, whose name was taken from Edgeware, formerly Edgeworth, in Middlesex, had established themselves in the reign of Queen Elizabeth. After his succession he had taken interest in gathering up family records and in seeking to restore Edgeworthstown House to something of its former tradition under the care of a married niece, Mrs. Montagu. Whilst visiting Ireland every summer, he did not live at Edgeworthstown, but declared that he looked forward to a happy "old age"—though when, if ever, he would have deemed this period to have arrived I do not know[4]—in the home of his forefathers.

Edgeworth was a notable link with celebrities of almost a

century ago—a nephew of the novelist Maria Edgeworth,[5] who was born in 1767 and was already famous in the eighteenth century, and a first cousin of the poet Thomas Lovell Beddoes, who died in 1847. Sir Walter Scott sent a copy of *Waverley* to Edgeworth's aunt on its first publication, and wrote in the last chapter of it (and afterwards in the preface to the novels) that it was her descriptions of Irish character which first encouraged him to make a similar experiment in Scotland; and Jane Austen sent her a copy of *Emma* on its first publication; and Macaulay sent her his *History,* which contains a reference to her. And in her later days she had visited Ricardo at Gatcomb Park.

F. Y. Edgeworth's father, Francis Beaufort Edgeworth, born in 1809, who had been educated at Charterhouse[6] and Cambridge, where he was a prominent member of Sterling's set, has been immortalised in none too flattering terms by Thomas Carlyle, who devoted some three pages to him in his *Life of John Sterling* (Part II. chap. iv.). "Frank was a short neat man," Carlyle wrote, "of sleek, square, colourless face (resembling the portraits of his Father), with small blue eyes in which twinkled curiously a joyless smile; his voice was croaky and shrill, with a tone of shrewish obstinacy in it, and perhaps of sarcasm withal. A composed, dogmatic, speculative, exact, and not melodious man. He was learned in Plato and likewise in Kant; well-read in philosophies and literature; entertained not creeds, but the Platonic or Kantian *ghosts* of creeds; coldly sneering away from him, in the joyless twinkle of those eyes, in the inexorable jingle of that shrill voice, all manner of Toryisms, superstitions: for the rest, a man of perfect veracity, of great diligence and other worth."

The Reverend Thomas Mozley, who devotes a chapter to Frank Edgeworth in his *Reminiscences,* does not confirm this account of "the good little Frank," as Carlyle calls him: "My ear still testifies that there was sweetness in Edgeworth's voice, and gentleness in his manner and tone. . . . Frank Edgeworth was torn by conflicting systems, and I may add conflicting sensibilities, from childhood. He was a most sympathetic, self-sacrificing being." [7] In Sterling's own description one can gain a further glimpse of the inherited temperament of the son. "Edgeworth seems to me not to have yet gone beyond a mere notional life. It is manifest that he has no knowledge of the necessity of a progress from *Wissen* to *Wesen* (say, *Knowing to Being*). . . . I regard it as a very happy thing for Edgeworth that he has to come to England. In Italy he probably would never have gained any intuition into the reality of Being as different from a mere power of Speculating and Perceiving; and, of course, without this he can never reach to more than the merest Gnosis; which taken alone is a poor inheritance, a box of title-deeds to an estate which is covered with lava, or sunk under the sea." [8]

But Sterling's friend was only one of the ingredients which went to the making of Francis Ysidro Edgeworth. For Francis Beaufort Edgeworth "had married a young Spanish wife, whom by a romantic accident he came upon in London." [9] Edgeworth's mother was a Spanish lady, Rosa Florentina Eroles. Frank Edgeworth, on his way to Germany to study philosophy in the company of his nephew, T. L. Beddoes, stopped in London to read in the British Museum, and accidentally made the acquaintance of Senorita Eroles, aged sixteen, daughter of a political refugee from Catalonia, married her within three weeks, and carried her off to Florence, where the couple lived for a few years. F. Y. Edgeworth was a good linguist, reading French, German, Spanish, and Italian, and his mixed Irish-Spanish-French[10] origin may have contributed to the markedly international sympathies of his mind.

The external landmarks of Edgeworth's life are soon told. He was born at Edgeworthstown House, where, after returning from Florence and an unsuccessful attempt at school-mastering, Frank Edgeworth had settled down to manage the family property, on February 8, 1845. His father died when he was two years old. He was brought up at Edgeworthstown under tutors until he went to Trinity College, Dublin, at the age of seventeen. His memory and agility of mind were already at that time remarkable. He told his Oxford cousins[11] only a few weeks before his death how well he still remembered the poetry he had learnt in his youth, and complete books of Milton, Pope, Virgil, and Homer would readily come to his memory. At the end of his life he was one of the very few survivors of the tradition of free quotation from the Classics on all occasions and in all contexts.[12]

He entered Oxford as a scholar of Magdalen Hall, proceeding from there to Balliol, where he obtained a First Class in *Lit. Hum.* There is a tradition in Oxford concerning his "Viva" in the Final Schools. It is said that, being asked some abstruse question, he inquired "Shall I answer briefly, or at length?" and then spoke for half an hour in a manner which converted what was to have been a Second Class into a First. He was called to the Bar by the Inner Temple in 1877, and spent some years in London with but straitened means, the youngest son of a younger son of an impoverished Irish estate, before he could find, amidst the multiplicity of his intellectual gifts and interests, his final direction. He became a Lecturer in Logic and afterwards Tooke Professor of Political Economy at King's College, London. In 1891 he succeeded Thorold Rogers as Drummond Professor of Political Economy at Oxford, and was elected a Fellow of All Souls, which became his home for the rest of his life. He retired from the Oxford professorship with the title of Emeritus Professor in 1922. He was President of the Economic Section of the British Association in 1889 and again in 1922. He was an ex-President of the Royal Statistical Society, a Vice-President of the Royal Economic Society, and a Fellow of the British Academy. Above all, Edgeworth was the first Editor of the *Economic Journal* and designed and moulded it. He had been continuously responsible for it as Editor, Chairman of the Editorial Board, and Joint Editor from the first issue in March 1891 down to the day of his death, February 13, 1926. As his fellow-editor I received a final letter from him about its business after the news of his death.

At Balliol, Edgeworth had been a favourite of Jowett's, and it may have been from Jowett, who was always much interested in Political Economy and was occasionally teaching the subject at about that time, that he received his first impulse to the subject. The most important influence, however, on his early economic thought was, I think, Jevons, whom he got to know in London, where his Hampstead lodgings were but a short distance from Jevons' house. His contact with Marshall, for whom his respect was unmeasured, came a little later. In *The Academy* for 1881, Marshall reviewed Edgeworth's *Mathematical Psychics*—one of the only two reviews which Marshall ever wrote, the other being of Jevons' *Theory of Political Economy*. This review led to an acquaintanceship which ripened into a lifelong personal and intellectual friendship. Mrs. Marshall has many pleasant memories of Edgeworth's visits to Cambridge—though there can seldom have been a couple whose conversational methods were less suited to one another than Francis Edgeworth and Alfred Marshall.

To judge from his published works, Edgeworth reached Economics, as Marshall had before him, through Mathematics and Ethics. But here the resemblance ceases. Marshall's interest was intellectual and moral, Edgeworth's intellectual and aesthetic. Edgeworth wished to establish *theorems* of intellectual and aesthetic interest, Marshall to establish *maxims* of practical and moral importance. In respect of technical training and of lightness and security of touch, Marshall was much his superior in the mathematical field—Marshall had been Second Wrangler, Edgeworth had graduated in *Litteris Humanioribus*. Yet Edgeworth, clumsy and awkward though he often was in his handling of the mathematical instrument, was in originality, in accomplishment, and in the bias of his natural interest considerably the greater mathematician. I do not think it can be disputed that for forty years Edgeworth was the most distinguished and the most prolific exponent in the world of what he himself dubbed *Mathematical Psychics*—the niceties and the broadnesses of the application of quasi-mathematical method of the Social Sciences.

It would be a formidable task to draw up a complete list of Edgeworth's writings,[13] almost entirely in the shape of contributions to learned journals. The earliest with which I am acquainted is his *New and Old Methods of Ethics,* published by Parker and Co. of Oxford in 1877, when he was thirty-two years of age—a paper-covered volume of 92 pages. It mainly consists of a discussion of the quantitative problems which arise in an examination of Utilitarianism, in the form of a commentary on Sidgwick's *Methods of Ethics* and Barratt's criticisms of Sidgwick in *Mind* for 1877. Edgeworth's peculiarities of style, his brilliance of phrasing, his obscurity of connection, his inconclusiveness of aim, his restlessness of direction, his courtesy, his caution, his shrewdness, his wit, his subtlety, his learning, his reserve—all are there full-grown. Quotations from the Greek tread on the heels of the differential calculus, and the philistine reader can scarcely tell whether it is a line of Homer or a mathematical abstraction which is in course of integration. The concluding words of Edgeworth's first flight would have come as well at the end of his long travelling:

Where the great body of moral science is already gone before, from all sides ascending, under a master's guidance, towards one serene commanding height, thither aspires this argument, a straggler coming up, *non passibus aequis,* and by a devious route. A devious route, and verging to the untrodden method which was fancifully delineated in the previous section; so far at least as the mathematical handling of pleasures is divined to be conducive to a genuinely physical ethic, προοίμια αὐτοῦ τοῦ νόμου.

Another slim volume (150 pages), *Mathematical Psychics: An Essay on the Application of Mathematics to the Moral Sciences,* appeared in 1881. This was Edgeworth's first contribution to Economics and contains some of the best work he ever did.[14] During the last months of his life he nursed the intention of reprinting a portion of it.[15]

The volume on Ethics had attempted to apply mathematical method to Utilitarianism. In *Mathematical Psychics* Edgeworth carried his treatment of "the calculus of *Feeling,* of Pleasure and Pain" a stage further. The Essay consists of two parts "concerned respectively with principle and practice, root and fruit, the applicability and the application of Mathematics to Sociology." In the First Part, which is very short, "it is attempted to illustrate the possibility of Mathematical reasoning without *numerical* data"—a thesis which at the time it was written was of much originality and importance. "We cannot *count* the golden sands of life; we cannot *number* the 'innumerable' smiles of seas of love; but we seem to be capable of observing that there is here a *greater,* there a *less,* multitude of pleasure-units, mass of happiness; and that is enough."

The Second Part contains the roots of much of Edgeworth's work on mathematical economics, in particular the treatment of Contract in a free market and its possible indeterminateness; and it is here that his famous *Contract-Curves* first appear.

I have dwelt on these two early works at disproportionate length, because in them, and particularly in *Mathematical Psychics,* the full flavour and peculiarity of Edgeworth's mind and art are exhibited without reserve. The latter is a very eccentric book and open to mockery. In later works, it seems to me, Edgeworth did not ever give quite a full rein to his natural self. He feared a little the philistine comment on the strange but charming amalgam of poetry and pedantry, science and art, wit and learning, of which he had the secret; and he would endeavour, however unsuccessfully, to draw a veil of partial concealment over his native style, which only served, however, to enhance the obscurity and allusiveness and half-apologetic air with which he served up his intellectual dishes. The problem of the inequality of men's and women's wages interested him all his life and was the subject of his Presidential address to Section F of the British Association in 1922; but who in space and time but Edgeworth in the eighties, whose sly chuckles one can almost hear as one reads, would treat it thus?

The aristocracy of sex is similarly grounded upon the supposed superior capacity of the man for happiness, for the ἐνεργεῖαι of action and contemplation; upon the sentiment:

Woman is the lesser man, and her passions unto mine
Are as moonlight unto sunlight and as water unto wine.

Her supposed generally inferior capacity is supposed to be compensated by a special capacity for particular emotions, certain kinds of beauty and refinement. Agreeably to such finer sense of beauty, the modern lady has received a larger share of certain *means,* certain luxuries and attentions (Def. 2; *a sub finem*). But gallantry, that "mixed sentiment which took its rise in the ancient chivalry," has many other elements. It is explained by the polite Hume as attention to the weak, and by the passionate Rousseau φυσικωτέρως .... Altogether, account being taken of existing, whether true or false, opinions about the nature of woman, there appears a nice consilience between the deductions from the utilitarian principle and the disabilities and privileges which hedge round modern womanhood.[16]

Edgeworth next proceeded to the second great application of mathematics to the Moral Sciences, namely, its application "to *Belief*, the Calculus of Probabilities," which became perhaps his favourite study of all. In 1883 and 1884 he contributed seven papers on Probability and the Law of Error to the *Philosophical Magazine*, to *Mind*, and to *Hermathena*. These were the first of a very long series of which the last, one more elaborate discussion of the Generalised Law of Error, still remained at the date of his death to appear in the *Statistical Journal*.

As regards Probability proper, Edgeworth's most important writings are his article on "The Philosophy of Chance" in *Mind*, 1884, and on "Probability" in the *Encyclopaedia Britannica* (revived up to 1911). Edgeworth began as an adherent of the Frequency Theory of Probability, with a strong bias in favour of a physical rather than a logical basis for the conception, just as he was an adherent of the Utilitarian Ethics with a bias in favour of a physical rather than a metaphysical basis. But in both cases his mind was alive to the objections, and in both cases the weight of the objections increased in his mind, as time went on, rather than diminished. Nevertheless, he did not in either case replace these initial presumptions by any others, with the result that he took up increasingly a sceptical attitude towards philosophical foundations combined with a pragmatic attitude towards practical applications which had been successfully erected upon them, however insecure these foundations might really be. The consequence was that the centre of his interest gradually passed from Probability to the Theory of Statistics, and from Utilitarianism to the Marginal Theory of Economics. I have often pressed him to give an opinion as to how far the modern theory of Statistics and Correlation can stand if the Frequency Theory falls as a logical doctrine. He would always reply to the effect that the collapse of the Frequency Theory would affect the *universality* of application of Statistical Theory, but that large masses of statistical data did, nevertheless, in his opinion, satisfy the conditions required for the validity of Statistical Theory, whatever these might be. I expect that this is true. It is a reasonable attitude for one who is mainly interested in statistics to take up. But it implied in Edgeworth an unwillingness to revise or take up again the more speculative studies of his youth. The same thing was true of his work in Economics. He was disinclined, in company with most other economists of the Classical School, to reconsider how far the initial assumptions of the Marginal Theory stand or fall with the Utilitarian Ethics and the Utilitarian Psychology, out of which they sprang and which were sincerely accepted, in a way no one accepts them now, by the founders of the subject. Mill, Jevons, the Marshall of the seventies, and the Edgeworth [17] of the late seventies and the early eighties *believed* the Utilitarian Psychology and laid the foundations of the subject in this belief. The later Marshall and the later Edgeworth and many of the younger generation have not fully believed; but we still trust the superstructure without exploring too thoroughly the soundness of the original foundations.

Thus, as time went on, Edgeworth's technical statistical work became more important than his contributions to the theory of probability. From 1885 onwards his more general articles, especially his "Methods of Statistics" in the Jubilee Volume of the *Statistical Journal,* 1885, and his "Application of the Calculus of Probabilities to Statistics" in the *Bulletin of the International Statistical Institute,* 1910, were of great value in keeping English students in touch with the work of the German school founded by Lexis and in sponsoring, criticising, and applauding from their first beginnings the work of the English statisticians on Correlation. His constructive work, particularly in his later years, centred in highly elaborate and difficult discussions of his own "Generalised Law of Error." Edgeworth's particular affection for the mode of treatment which he here adopted was partly due, I think, to its requiring the minimum of assumption, so that he was able to obtain his results on more generalised hypotheses than will yield results in the case of other statistical formulae. In this way he could compensate, as it were, his bad conscience about the logical, as distinct from the pragmatic, grounds of current statistical theory.

At about the same time as his first papers on Probability and the Law of Error, namely, in 1883, in his thirty-eighth year, Edgeworth embarked on the fifth topic, which was to complete the range of the main work of his life, that is to say, Index Numbers, or the application of mathematical method to the measurement of economic value.[18] These five applications of Mathematical Psychics—to the measurement of Utility or ethical value, to the algebraic or diagrammatic determination of economic equilibriums, to the measurement of Belief or Probability, to the measurement of Evidence or Statistics, and to the measurement of economic value or Index Numbers—constitute, with their extensions and ramifications and illustrations, Edgeworth's life work. If he had been of the kind that produce Treatises, he would doubtless have published, some time between 1900 and 1914, a large volume in five books entitled *Mathematical Psychics*. But this was not to be. He followed up his two monographs of 1877 and 1881 with a third entitled *Metretike, or the Method of Measuring Probability and Utility,* in 1887. It is a disappointing volume and not much worth reading (a judgement with which I know that Edgeworth himself concurred). After this, so far from rising from the Monograph to the Treatise, moving to the opposite extreme from Marshall's, he sank from the Monograph to the paper, essay, article, or transaction. For forty years a long stream of splinters split off from his bright mind to illumine (and to obscure) the pages of the *Statistical* and *Economic Journals*.

Once when I asked him why he had never ventured on a Treatise he answered, with his characteristic smile and chuckle, that large-scale enterprise, such as Treatises and marriage, had never appealed to him. It may be that he deemed them industries subject to diminishing return, or that they lay outside his powers or the limits he set to his local universe. Such explanations are more than enough and Occam's razor should forbid me to mention another. But there may have been a contributory motive.

Mathematical Psychics has not, as a science or study, fulfilled its early promise. In the seventies and eighties of the last century it was reasonable, I think, to suppose that it held great prospects. When the young Edgeworth chose it, he may have looked to find secrets as wonderful as those which the physicists have found since those days. But, as I remarked in writing about Alfred Marshall's gradual change of attitude towards mathematico-economics (p. 158 above), this has not happened, but quite the opposite. The atomic hypothesis which has worked so splendidly in Physics breaks down in Psychics. We are faced at every turn with the problems of Organic Unity, of Discreteness, of Discontinuity—the whole is not equal to the sum of the parts, comparisons of quantity fail us, small changes produce large effects, the assumptions of a uniform and homogeneous continuum are not satisfied. Thus the results of Mathematical Psychics turn out to be derivative, not fundamental, indexes, not measurements, first approximations at the best; and fallible indexes, dubious approximations at that, with much doubt added as to what, if anything, they are indexes or approximations of. No one was more conscious of all this than Edgeworth. All his intellectual life through he felt his foundations slipping away from under him. What wonder that with these hesitations added to his cautious, critical, sceptical, diffident nature the erection of a large and heavy superstructure did not appeal to him. Edgeworth knew that he was skating on thin ice; and as life went on his love of skating and his distrust of the ice increased, by a malicious fate, *pari passu*. He is like one who seeks to avert the evil eye by looking sideways, to escape the censure of fate by euphemism, calling the treacherous sea Euxine and the unfriendly guardians of Truth the kindly ones. Edgeworth seldom looked the reader or interlocutor straight in the face; he is allusive, obscure, and devious as one who would slip by unnoticed, hurrying on if stopped by another traveller.

After the appearance of *Metretike* in 1887, Edgeworth ventured on no separate publication, apart from four lectures delivered during the war, which were printed in pamphlet form,[19] until in 1925 the Royal Economic Society published under his own editorship his *Collected Economic Papers* in three substantial volumes. These volumes preserve in accessible form the whole of Edgeworth's contribution to the subject of Economics, which he himself wished to see preserved, apart from some portions of *Mathematical Psychics* alluded to above.

The publication of his Economic Papers was a great satisfaction to Edgeworth. His modest and self-effacing ways would always have prevented him from undertaking such an enterprise on his own initiative. But as soon as others were prepared to take the responsibility, the business of selection and preparation for the press was a congenial task. Moreover, the publication proved a great success in every way, and was reviewed in learned journals throughout the world with expressions of esteem such as the author's previous modes of publication had cut him off from hearing. I think that Edgeworth was genuinely surprised at the extent of his international reputation, and it gave him as much pleasure as surprise.

In spite of his constant flow of learned papers, a great part of Edgeworth's time for the last thirty-five years of his life was occupied with the editorship of the Economic Journal. His practical gifts as an editor were quite other than might have been expected from his reputation as an unpractical, unbusinesslike person, remote from affairs, living on abstractions in the clouds, illuminating the obscure by the more obscure. As one who was associated with him in the conduct of the *Journal* for fifteen years, I can report that this picture was the opposite of the truth. He was punctual, businesslike, and dependable in the conduct of all routine matters. He was quite incapable of detecting misprints in what he wrote himself,[20] but had an exceptionally sharp eye for other people's. He had an unfailing instinct for good "copy" (except, again, in what he wrote himself), exercised his editorial powers with great strictness to secure brevity from the contributors,[21] and invariably cast his influence in favour of matter having topical interest and against tedious expositions of methodology and the like (which often, in his opinion, rendered German journals unuseful). I have often found myself in the position of defending the heavier articles against his strictures. He established and was always anxious to maintain the international sympathies and affiliations of the *Journal*. I am sure that there was no economist in England better read than he in foreign literature. He added to this what must have been the widest personal acquaintance in the world with economists of all nations. Edgeworth was the most hospitable of men, and there can have been very few foreign economists, whether of established reputation or not, who visited London in his time and were not entertained by Edgeworth. He had a strong feeling for the solidarity of economic science throughout the world and sought to encourage talent wherever he found it, and to extend courtesies in the most exquisite traditions of Ireland and Spain. His tolerance was all-embracing, and he combined a respect for established reputation which might have been thought excessive if there had not been a flavour of mockery in it, with a natural inclination to encourage the youthful and the unknown. All his eccentricity and artistic strangeness found its outlet in his own writings. All his practical good sense and daily shrewdness was devoted to the *Economic Journal*.

On anyone who knew Edgeworth he must have made a strong individual impression as a person. But it is scarcely possible to portray him to those who did not. He was kind, affectionate, modest, self-depreciatory, humorous, with a sharp and candid eye for human nature; he was also reserved, angular, complicated, proud, and touchy, elaborately polite, courteous to the point of artificiality, absolutely unbending and unyielding in himself to the pressure of the outside world. Marshall, remembering his mixed parentage, used to say: "Francis is a charming fellow, but you must be careful with Ysidro."

His health and vigour of body were exceptional. He was still a climber in the mountains, bather in the cold waters of the morning at Parson's Pleasure, unwearying pedestrian in the meadows of Oxfordshire, after he had passed his seventieth year. He was always at work, reading, correcting proofs, "verifying references" (a vain pursuit upon which his ostensible reverence for authority and disinclination to say anything defi-

nite on his own responsibility led him to waste an abundance
of time), working out on odd bits of paper long arithmetical
examples of abstruse theorems which he loved to do (just as
Maria Edgeworth has recorded of his grandfather), writing letters, building up his lofty constructions with beautiful bricks
but too little mortar and no clear architectural design. Towards the end of his life it was not easy to carry through with
him a consecutive argument *viva voce*—he had a certain dissatisfied restlessness of body and attention which increased
with age and was not good to see. But on paper his intellectual
powers even after his eightieth year were entirely unabated;
and he died, as he would have wished, in harness.

Edgeworth was never married; but it was not for want of
susceptibility. His difficult nature, not his conception of life,
cut him off from a full intimacy in any direction. He did not
have as much happiness as he might have had. But in many
ways a bachelor life suited his character. He liked to have the
fewest possible material cares; he did not want to be loaded
with any sort of domestic responsibility; and he was content
without private comfort. No one lived more continuously than
he in Common Rooms, Libraries, and Clubs, or depended more
completely upon such adjuncts for every amenity. He had but
few possessions—scarcely any furniture or crockery, not even
books (he preferred a public library near at hand), no proper
notepaper of his own or stationery or stamps. Red tape and
gum are the only material objects with the private ownership
of which I associate him. But he was particular about his appearance and was well dressed in his own style. There was
more of Spain than of Edgeworth in his looks. With broad
forehead, long nose, olive colouring, trimly pointed beard, and
strong hands, his aspect was distinguished but a little belied by
his air of dwelling *uncomfortably* in his clothes or in his body.
He lived at Oxford in spartanic rooms at All Souls; in London
lodgings at 5 Mount Vernon, two small bare rooms, pitched
high on the cliff of Hampstead with a wide view over the
metropolitan plain, which he had taken on a weekly tenancy
more than fifty years before and had occupied ever since; in
Ireland, where he would spend some weeks of the summer, at

the St. George Club, Kingstown. For meals the Buttery and Hall of All Souls, the Athenaeum, the Savile, or the Albemarle; for books the libraries of these places, of the British Museum, of Trinity College, Dublin, of the Royal Statistical Society.

It is narrated that in his boyhood at Edgeworthstown he would read Homer seated aloft in a heron's nest. So, as it were, he dwelt always, not too much concerned with the earth.

F. P. RAMSEY

1903-1930

I. RAMSEY AS AN ECONOMIST

The death at the age of twenty-six of Frank Ramsey, Fellow of King's College, Cambridge, sometime scholar of Winchester and of Trinity, son of the President of Magdalene, was a heavy loss—though his primary interests were in Philosophy and Mathematical Logic—to the pure theory of Economics. From a very early age, about sixteen I think, his precocious mind was intensely interested in economic problems. Economists living in Cambridge have been accustomed from his under-graduate days to try their theories on the keen edge of his critical and logical faculties. If he had followed the easier path of mere inclination, I am not sure that he would not have exchanged the tormenting exercises of the foundations of thought and of psychology, where the mind tries to catch its own tail, for the delightful paths of our own most agreeable branch of the moral sciences, in which theory and fact, intuitive imagination and practical judgement, are blended in a manner comfortable to the human intellect.

When he did descend from his accustomed stony heights, he still lived without effort in a rarer atmosphere than most economists care to breathe, and handled the technical apparatus of our science with the easy grace of one accustomed to something far more difficult. But he has left behind him in print (apart from his philosophical papers) only two witnesses to his powers—his papers published in the *Economic Journal* on "A Contribution to the Theory of Taxation" in March 1927, and on "A Mathematical Theory of Saving" in December 1928. The latter of these is, I think, one of the most remarkable contributions to mathematical economics ever made, both in respect of the intrinsic importance and difficulty of its subject, the power and elegance of the technical methods employed, and the clear purity of illumination with which the writer's mind is felt by the reader to play about its subject. The article is terribly difficult reading for an economist, but it is not difficult to appreciate how scientific and aesthetic qualities are combined in it together.

The loss of Ramsey is, therefore, to his friends, for whom his personal qualities joined most harmoniously with his intellectual powers, one which it will take them long to forget. His bulky Johnsonian frame, his spontaneous gurgling laugh, the simplicity of his feelings and reactions, half-alarming sometimes and occasionally almost cruel in their directness and literalness, his honesty of mind and heart, his modesty, and the amazing, easy efficiency of the intellectual machine which ground away behind his wide temples and broad, smiling face, have been taken from us at the height of their excellence and before their harvest of work and life could be gathered in.

March 1930.

II. RAMSEY AS A PHILOSOPHER

Logic, like lyrical poetry, is no employment for the middle-aged, and it may be that we have in this volume[1] some of the best illumination which one of the brightest minds of our generation could give, though he died at twenty-six. I do not think that there is any book of equal importance for those who would think about fundamental matters in a modern way, and the circumstance that much of it is tentative and inconclusive and not finally corrected is no impediment in subject where an author's vanity in giving his finished work a rounded surface is pure deception.

Seeing all of Frank Ramsey's logical essays published together, we can perceive quite clearly the direction which his mind was taking. It is a remarkable example of how the young can take up the story at the point to which the previous generation had brought it a little out of breath, and then proceed forward without taking more than about a week thoroughly to digest everything which had been done up to date, and to understand with apparent ease stuff which to anyone even ten years older seemed hopelessly difficult. One almost has to believe that Ramsey in his nursery near Magdalene was unconsciously absorbing from 1903 to 1914 everything which anyone may have been saying or writing in Trinity. In the year 1903, in which Frank Ramsey was born, Bertrand Russell's *Principles of Mathematics* was published, giving a new life to formal logic and seeming to bring new kingdoms within its scope. This book raised certain fundamental problems without solving all of them satisfactorily, but for the next seven years Russell and Whitehead were more concentrated on the technical problem of exhibiting in their *Principia Mathematica* the actual links between mathematics and formal logic than on strengthening the foundations on which they were building. But meanwhile Ludwig Wittgenstein had been attracted to Cambridge by the desire to talk with Russell, and Wittgenstein was wholly occupied with the fundamental matters of logical analysis. His *Tractatus Logico-Philosophicus* was mainly worked out before the war, but it was not published until 1922, by which time Frank Ramsey was on the scene, aged nineteen, to assist in the preparation of an English version and to expound its obscure contents to the world. Today Russell is recognising that each period of life has its appropriate avocation, and that the fundamental exercises of logic are not for those who have reached their sixtieth year. Wittgenstein is wondering if his next book will be finished before time's chariots are too near, and Ramsey, alas! who entered into their harvest as easily as a young lord into his estates, is dead.

The first part of this book, comprising papers which have

been previously published, consists in tackling fundamental problems at the point at which the work of Russell and Wittgenstein had left them. They are handled with great power, and at the same time elegance of treatment and lucidity, and probably with success. The second part, which has not previously been published, deals with Probability and associated subjects, starting from a criticism of my *Treatise on Probability*, which was published in 1921. This latter part had not been published because it was fragmentary and not completely satisfactory. But it is of the greatest interest both in itself and as showing in some detail how far his mind was departing, in pursuance of certain hints thrown out in the first part, from the formal and objective treatment of his immediate predecessors. The first impression conveyed by the work of Russell was that the field of formal logic was enormously extended. The gradual perfection of the formal treatment at the hands of himself, of Wittgenstein and of Ramsey had been, however, gradually to empty it of content and to reduce it more and more to mere dry bones, until finally it seemed to exclude not only all experience, but most of the principles, usually reckoned logical, of reasonable thought. Wittgenstein's solution was to regard everything else as a sort of inspired nonsense, having great value indeed for the individual, but incapable of being exactly discussed. Ramsey's reaction was towards what he himself described as a sort of pragmatism, not unsympathetic to Russell but repugnant to Wittgenstein. "The essence of pragmatism," he says, "I take to be this, that the meaning of a sentence is to be defined by reference to the actions to which asserting it would lead, or, more vaguely still, by its possible causes and effects. Of this I feel certain, but of nothing more definite."

Thus he was led to consider "human logic" as distinguished from "formal logic." Formal logic is concerned with nothing but the rules of *consistent* thought. But in addition to this we have certain "useful mental habits" for handling the material with which we are supplied by our perceptions and by our memory and perhaps in other ways, and so arriving at or towards truth; and the analysis of such habits is also a sort of logic. The application of these ideas to the logic of probability is very fruitful. Ramsey argues, as against the view which I had put forward, that probability is concerned not with objective relations between propositions but (in some sense) with degrees of belief, and he succeeds in showing that the calculus of probabilities simply amounts to a set of rules for ensuring that the system of degrees of belief which we hold shall be a *consistent* system. Thus the calculus of probabilities belongs to formal logic. But the basis of our degrees of belief—or the *a priori* probabilities, as they used to be called—is part of our human outfit, perhaps given us merely by natural selection, analogous to our perceptions and our memories rather than to formal logic. So far I yield to Ramsey—I think he is right. But in attempting to distinguish "rational" degrees of belief from belief in general he was not yet, I think, quite successful. It is not getting to the bottom of the principle of induction merely to say that it is a useful mental habit. Yet in attempting to distinguish a "human" logic from formal logic on the one hand and descriptive psychology on the other, Ramsey may have been pointing the way to the next field of study when formal logic has been put into good order and its highly limited scope properly defined.

Ramsey reminds one of Hume more than of anyone else, particularly, in his common sense and a sort of hard-headed practicality towards the whole business. The reader will find many passages which convey the peculiar flavour of his mind, the expression of which—though not included by him amongst the purposes of philosophy!—was a delightful thing.

October 1931.

III. A SHORT ANTHOLOGY

Most of Ramsey's writings, as published in the posthumous collection *The Foundations of Mathematics,* in the *Economic Journal,* and in the *Encyclopaedia Britannica,* are very technical. But amongst his notes, not published in his lifetime and none of them polished for the press, which have been brought together at the end of *The Foundations of Mathematics*[2] are some aphorisms and fragmentary essays from which I give below a few selections, because they may convey a little of what I have called above "the peculiar flavour of his mind"; though nothing will ever fully convey to those, who never came into direct acquaintance with the workings of his intellect and personality as given to one in a single joint impression, why Mr. Braithwaite could write with justice that his death deprived Cambridge of one of its chief intellectual glories. Let me also quote what Goldsworthy Lowes Dickinson wrote of Frank Ramsey and of C. P. Sanger, another scholar of Winchester and Trinity, who died, though in his maturity, nearly at the same time:

It does not become a Cambridge man to claim too much for his university, nor am I much tempted to do so. But there is, I think, a certain type, rare, like all good things, which seems to be associated in some peculiar way with my alma mater. I am thinking of men like Leslie Stephen (the original of Meredith's Vernon Whitford), like Henry Sidgwick, like Maitland, like one who died but the other day with all his promise unfulfilled. It is a type unworldly without being saintly, unambitious without being inactive, warmhearted without being sentimental. Through good report and ill such men work on, following the light of truth as they see it; able to be sceptical without being paralyzed; content to know what is knowable and to reserve judgment on what is not. The world could never be driven by such men, for the springs of action lie deep in ignorance and madness. But it is they who are the beacon in the tempest, and they are more, not less, needed now than ever before. May their succession never fail!

1. *Philosophy*

Philosophy must be of some use and we must take it seriously; it must clear our thoughts and so our actions. Or else it is a disposition we have to check, and an inquiry to see that this is so; *i.e.* the chief proposition of philosophy is that philosophy is nonsense. And again we must then take seriously that it is nonsense, and not pretend, as Wittgenstein does, that it is important nonsense!

In philosophy we take the propositions we make in science and everyday life and try to exhibit them in a logical system with primitive terms and definitions, etc. Essentially a philosophy is a system of definitions or, only too often, a system of descriptions of how definitions might be given.

I do not think it is necessary to say with Moore that the definitions explain what we have hitherto meant by our propositions, but rather that they show how we intend to use them in future. Moore would say they were the same, that philosophy does not change what anyone meant by "This is a table." It seems to me that it might; for meaning is mainly potential, and a change might therefore only be manifested on rare and critical occasions. Also, sometimes philosophy should clarify and distinguish notions previously vague and confused, and clearly this is meant to fix our future meaning only. But this is clear, that the definitions are to give at least our future meaning, and not merely to give any pretty way of obtaining a certain structure.

I used to worry myself about the nature of philosophy through excessive scholasticism. I could not see how we could understand a word and not be able to recognise whether a proposed definition of it was or was not correct. I did not realise the vagueness of the whole idea of understanding, the reference it involves to a multitude of performances any of which may fail and require to be restored. Logic issues in tautologies, mathematics in identities, philosophy in definitions; all trivial, but all part of the vital work of clarifying and organising our thought.[3]

2. Philosophical Thinking

It seems to me that in the process of clarifying our thought we come to terms and sentences which we cannot elucidate in the obvious manner by defining their meaning. For instance, theoretical terms we cannot define, but we can explain the way in which they are used, and in this explanation we are forced to look not only at the objects which we are talking about, but at our own mental states.

Now this means that we cannot get clear about these terms and sentences without getting clear about meaning, and we seem to get into the situation that we cannot understand, *e.g.* what we say about time and the external world, without first understanding meaning, and yet we cannot understand meaning without first understanding certainly time and probably the external world which are involved in it. So we cannot make our philosophy into an ordered progress to a goal, but have to take our problems as a whole and jump to a simultaneous solution; which will have something of the nature of a hypothesis, for we shall accept it not as the consequence of direct argument, but as the only one we can think of which satisfies our several requirements.

Of course, we should not strictly speak of argument, but there is in philosophy a process analogous to "linear inference" in which things become successively clear; and since, for the above reason, we cannot carry this through to the end, we are in the ordinary position of scientists of having to be content with piecemeal improvements; we can make several things clearer, but we cannot make anything clear.

I find this self-consciousness inevitable in philosophy except in a very limited field. We are driven to philosophise because we do not know clearly what we mean; the question is always "What do I mean by *x*?" And only very occasionally can we settle this without reflecting on meaning. But it is not only an obstacle, this necessity of dealing with meaning; it is doubtless an essential clue to the truth. If we neglect it I feel we may get into the absurd position of the child in the following dialogue: "Say breakfast." "Can't." "What can't you say?" "Can't say breakfast."

The chief danger to our philosophy, apart from laziness and woolliness, is scholasticism, the essence of which is treating what is vague as if it were precise and trying to fit it into an exact logical category. A typical piece of scholasticism is Wittgenstein's view that all our everyday propositions are completely in order and that it is impossible to think illogically. (This last is like saying it is impossible to break the rules of bridge, because if you break them you are not playing bridge but, as Mrs. C. says, not-bridge.) [4]

3. *Is There Anything to Discuss?*

Science, history, and politics are not suited for discussion except by experts. Others are simply in the position of requiring more information, and, till they have acquired all available information, cannot do anything but accept on authority the opinions of those better qualified. Then there is philosophy; this, too, has become too technical for the layman. Besides this disadvantage, the conclusion of the greatest modern philosopher is that there is no such subject as philosophy; that it is an activity, not a doctrine; and that, instead of answering questions, it aims merely at curing headaches. It might be thought that, apart from this technical philosophy whose centre is logic, there was a sort of popular philosophy which dealt with such subjects as the relation of man to nature, and the meaning of morality. But any attempt to treat such topics seriously reduces them to questions either of science or of technical philosophy, or results more immediately in perceiving them to be nonsensical. . . .

I think we rarely, if ever, discuss fundamental psychological questions, but far more often simply compare our several experiences, which is not a form of discussing. I think we realise too little how often our arguments are of the form:—A: "I went to Grantchester this afternoon." B: "No I didn't." Another thing we often do is to discuss what sort of people or behaviour we feel admiration for or ashamed of. *E.g.* when we discuss constancy of affection it consists in A saying he would feel guilty if he weren't constant, B saying *he* wouldn't feel guilty in the least. But that, although a pleasant way of passing the time, is not discussing anything whatever, but simply comparing notes.

Genuine psychology, on the other hand, is a science of which we most of us know far too little for it to become us to venture an opinion.

Lastly, there is aesthetics, including literature. This always excites us far more than anything else; but we don't really discuss it much. Our arguments are so feeble; we are still at the stage of "Who drives fat oxen must himself be fat," and have very little to say about the psychological problems of which aesthetics really consists, *e.g.* why certain combinations of colours give us such peculiar feelings. What we really like doing is again to compare our experience; a practice which in this case is peculiarly profitable because the critic can point out things to other people to which, if they attend, they will obtain feelings which they value which they failed to obtain otherwise. We do not and cannot discuss whether one work of art is better than another; we merely compare the feelings it gives.

I conclude that there really is nothing to discuss; and this conclusion corresponds to a feeling I have about ordinary conversation also. It is a relatively new phenomenon which has arisen from two causes which have operated gradually through the nineteenth century. One is the advance of science, the other the decay of religion, which have resulted in all the old general questions becoming either technical or ridiculous. This process in the development of civilisation we each of us have to repeat in ourselves. I, for instance, came up as a freshman enjoying conversation and argument more than anything else in the world; but I have gradually come to regard it as of less and less importance, because there never seems to be anything to talk about except shop and people's private lives, neither of which is suited for general conversation. . . .

If I was to write a *Weltanschauung* I should call it not "What I believe" but "What I feel." This is connected with Wittgenstein's view that philosophy does not give us beliefs, but merely relieves feelings of intellectual discomfort. Also, if I were to quarrel with Russell's lecture,[5] it would not be with what he believed but with the indications it gave as to what he felt. Not that one can really quarrel with a man's feelings; one can only have different feelings oneself, and perhaps also regard one's own as more admirable or more conducive to a happy life. From this point of view, that it is a matter not of fact but of feeling, I shall conclude by some remarks on things in general, or as I would rather say, not things but *life* in general.

Where I seem to differ from some of my friends is in attaching little importance to physical size. I don't feel the least hum-ble before the vastness of the heavens. The stars may be large, but they cannot think or love; and these are qualities which impress me far more than size does. I take no credit for weighing nearly seventeen stone.

My picture of the world is drawn in perspective and not like a model to scale. The foreground is occupied by human beings and the stars are all as small as three-penny bits. I don't really believe in astronomy, except as a complicated description of part of the course of human and possibly animal sensation. I apply my perspective not merely to space but also to time. In time the world will cool and everything will die; but that is a long time off still and its present value at compound discount is almost nothing. Nor is the present less valuable because the future will be blank. Humanity, which fills the foreground of my picture, I find interesting and on the whole admirable. I find, just now at least, the world a pleasant and exciting place. You may find it depressing; I am sorry for you, and you despise me. But I have reason and you have none; you would only have a reason for despising me if your feeling corresponded to the fact in a way mine didn't. But neither can correspond to the fact. The fact is not in itself good or bad; it is just that it thrills me but depresses you. On the other hand, I pity you with reason, because it is pleasanter to be thrilled than to be depressed, and not merely pleasanter but better for all one's activities.

February 28, 1925.

WILLIAM STANLEY JEVONS

1835-1882

A CENTENARY ALLOCUTION ON HIS LIFE AND WORK
AS ECONOMIST AND STATISTICIAN [1]
Read before the Royal Statistical Society, 21 April 1936

I

Stanley Jevons was born in the year after Malthus's death. But he was only seven years senior to Marshall and ten years senior to Edgeworth. Professor Foxwell lectured in his stead at University College *before* Jevons took up his professorship there. He examined my father in the Moral Sciences Tripos of 1875, his name being known to me from my early years as, in my father's mind, the pattern of what an economist and logician should be. Thus, though we celebrate to-day (a little late) the centenary of his birth, though it is sixty years ago that Professor Foxwell lectured in his stead and more than fifty years since his death, nevertheless, Jevons belongs to the group of economists whose school of thought dominated the subject for the half-century after the death of Mill in 1873, who are the immediate teachers and predecessors of ourselves here assembled to pay our duty to his memory.

His family belonged to the class of educated nonconformists, who, without academic connections, made up, in the first half of the nineteenth century, the intelligentsia of Liverpool, Man-

chester, Leeds and Birmingham, and became the backbone of
Bentham's foundation (in 1826) at University College, London, and of Owens College, Manchester (founded in 1846).
The family, and many of their connections, were Unitarians;
and in substance Stanley Jevons remained of that faith to the
end of his life. His father was an iron merchant, a friend of
Stephenson, much interested in the engineering innovations of
the age, said to have constructed (in 1815) the first iron boat
that sailed on seawater, a supporter of the construction of the
Thames Tunnel to his own financial loss, author of a small
book on law and of an economic pamphlet. His mother, whose
ninth child he was, herself a poetess, was the eldest of the
gifted family of William Roscoe, the solicitor and banker of
Liverpool, collector and dilettante, but also a learned historian,
author of the *Life of Lorenzo de Medici* and the *Life and
Pontificate of Leo X* amongst much else (including the children's classic *The Butterfly's Ball and the Grasshopper's
Feast*²). Stanley Jevons himself married a daughter of J. E.
Taylor, the founder of the *Manchester Guardian,* and was a
connection by marriage of R. H. Hutton of the *Spectator.*

His father and his grandfather Roscoe, though both unusually gifted and of unquestioned probity, were both of them
bankrupted, the former in the financial crisis of 1848 and the
latter through a run on his bank in 1816; so that he had
good hereditary cause not to overlook the phenomenon of business fluctuations, Stanley Jevons took much interest in his own
investments and financial position, which he managed, if certain hints in his correspondence are to be trusted, with close
regard to his theories concerning the Trade Cycle and the gradual exhaustion of our reserves of coal. His own capital was
small, but his wife had some means of her own, and Jevons, I
am told, augmented their income by good investment of their
savings. He was an example of a man who at every critical
stage of his affairs sacrificed his income relentlessly in order to
secure his major purposes in life, but was far, nevertheless,
from despising money, and suffered severe pangs each time that
a sacrifice was called for. In many, perhaps in most, respects he
was a good Victorian, averse both intellectually and morally to

the outlook of the extreme Left, appreciative alike of a Conservative Party "desirous at all costs"—I quote his own words —"to secure the continued and exclusive prosperity of this country as a main bulwark of the general good," and, on the other hand, of a Liberal Party "less cautious, more trustful in abstract principles and the unfettered tendencies of nature." [3]

The circle in which Stanley Jevons grew up was interested in social and economic problems. His grandfather, William Roscoe, was an ardent social reformer, active over the abolition of the slave trade. His father wrote a pamphlet entitled *The Prosperity of the Landlords not Dependent on the Corn Laws*. It is recorded that his mother read with him Archbishop Whateley's *Easy Lessons on Money Matters*. His headmaster, Dr. Hodgson, at the Mechanics' Institute High School in Liverpool, where he first went to school, was afterwards Professor of Political Economy at Edinburgh. Nevertheless, Jevons was educated, not in the moral sciences, but in mathematics and in biology, chemistry and metallurgy.[4] In 1852, seven years before the publication of Darwin's *Origin of Species*, when he was seventeen years old he wrote in his journal:

I have had several rather learned discussions with Harry about moral philosophy, from which it appears that I am decidedly a "dependent moralist," not believing that we have any "moral sense" altogether separate and of a different kind from our animal feelings. I have also had a talk about the origin of species, or the manner in which the innumerable races of animals have been produced. I, as far as I can understand at present, firmly believe that all animals have been transformed out of one primitive form by the continued influence, for thousands and perhaps millions of years, of climate, geography, etc. Lyell makes great fun of Lamarck's, that is, of this theory, but appears to me not to give any good reason against it.[5]

When he was eighteen the financial difficulties of his family led to his accepting an appointment as an assayer at the Sydney Mint, lately opened as a result of the Australian gold discoveries. In this post he remained for nearly five years. To his ambitions it was a great disappointment to leave University College half-way through his studies, and his main object in leaving Australia was to return there to complete his course for the M.A. degree. But his long period of solitary thought and slow gestation in Australia, at an age when the powers of pure originality are at their highest, had been abundantly fruitful. For soon after his return, the outlines of his principal contributions to knowledge were firmly fixed in his mind. The last third of Jevons's life after he was thirty was mainly devoted to the elucidation and amplification of what in essence he had already discovered.

The results of his solitary thinking in Australia and afterwards, which were produced in a series of studies covering a little more than the decade following his return to England at the end of 1859, fall into two distinct groups, both foreshadowed by his communications to the Cambridge meeting of the British Association in 1862—the first concerned with his inductive studies of fluctuations, and the second with his deductive contributions to pure theory. But before considering these in detail, it will be convenient to mention *The Coal Question,* his first book and the first occasion of his coming prominently before the public.

II

The Coal Question: An Inquiry concerning the Progress of the Nation and the Probable Exhaustion of our Coal Mines is by no means one of Jevons's best works. It is most brilliantly and engagingly written, with nothing omitted which could add to its attractiveness and the effect of its impact. But its prophecies have not been fulfilled, the arguments on which they were based are unsound, and re-read to-day it appears over-strained and exaggerated.

It was Jevons's thesis in this book that the maintenance of Great Britain's prosperity and industrial leadership required a continuous growth of her heavy industries on a scale which would mean a demand for coal increasing in a geometrical progression. Jevons advanced this principle as an extension of Malthus's law of population, and he designated it the *Natural Law of Social Growth.* In the form in which he enunciated the principle—namely, "that living beings of the same nature and in the same circumstances multiply in the same geometrical ratio"—it is, as he said, "self-evident when the meanings of the words are understood." [6] Yet in spite of his warning that "even if we do not change in inward character, yet our exterior circumstances are usually changing," Jevons's extension of the truism can easily mislead. For he continues:

Now what is true of the mere number of the people is true of other elements of their condition. If our parents made a definite social advance, then, unless we are unworthy of our parents, or in different circumstances, we should make a similar advance. If our parents doubled their income, or doubled the use of iron, or the agricultural produce of the country, then so ought we, unless we are either changed in character or circumstances.[7]

From this it is a short step to put *coal* into the position occupied in Malthus's theory by *corn*:

Our subsistence no longer depends upon our produce of corn. The momentous repeal of the Corn Laws throws us from corn upon coal. It marks, at any rate, the epoch when coal was finally recognized as the staple product of the country; it marks the ascendancy of the manufacturing interest, which is only another name for the development of the use of coal.[8]

It is easy to see what alarming deductions from this could be made convincing to a generation which accepted without question a crude version of Malthus. For, as Jevons pointed out, "the quantity of coal consumed is really a quantity of two dimensions, the number of people, and the average quantity used by each. In round numbers, the population has about doubled since the beginning of the century, but the consumption of coal has increased eightfold and more. Again, the quantity consumed by each individual is a composite quantity, increased either by multiplying the scale of former applications of coal, or finding wholly new applications. We cannot, indeed, always be doubling the length of our railways, the magnitude of our ships, and bridges, and factories. But the new applications of coal are of an unlimited character." [9]

By this time the reader has been carried away from the carefully qualified truisms with which he began, and Jevons concludes in splendid and exciting terms:

We are growing rich and numerous upon a source of wealth of which the fertility does not yet apparently decrease with our demands upon it. Hence the uniform and extraordinary rate of growth which this country presents. We are like settlers spreading in a new country of which the boundaries are yet unknown and unfelt.

But then I must point out the painful fact that such a rate of growth will before long render our consumption of coal comparable with the total supply. In the increasing depth and difficulty of coal mining we shall meet that vague, but inevitable boundary that will stop our progress. We shall begin as it were to see the further shore of our Black Indies. The wave of population will break upon that shore, and roll back upon itself. And as settlers, unable to choose in the fair inland new and virgin soil of unexceeded fertility, will fall back upon that which is next best, and will advance their tillage up the mountain side, so we, unable to discover new coal-fields as shallow as before, must deepen our mines with pain and cost.

There is, too, this most serious difference to be noted. A farm, however far pushed, will under proper cultivation continue to yield for ever a constant crop. But in a mine there is no reproduction and the produce once pushed to the utmost will soon begin to fail and sink to zero.

So far, then, as our wealth and progress depend upon the superior command of coal, we must not only stop—we must go back.[10]

Jevons, it must be confessed, meant the book to be *épatant*. For it is not, I think, unfair to attribute the striking manner in which it is written to his extreme anxiety that his ideas should not be overlooked. His highly original communications to the British Association (in 1862) had fallen flat. His diagrams for business forecasting (also in 1862), the precursor, sixty years too soon, of so many half-baked loaves, had been published at his own expense and, barely mentioned in *The Times* and the *Economist*, lost him money. His pamphlet on Gold [11] (in 1863), though it attracted attention a little later on,[12] had sold 74 copies.[13] Yet he had a passionate sense of vocation and of having something valuable to give the world. On April 25, 1863, he wrote in his Journal:

Now, I suppose I am low because my essay on "Gold" is out, and as yet no one has said a word in its favour except my sister, who of course does it as a sister. What if all I do or can do were to be received so? In the first place, one might be led to doubt whether all one's convictions concerning oneself were not mere delusions. Secondly, one might at last learn that even the best productions may never be caught by the breath of popular approval and praise. It would take infinite time and space to write all I have thought about my position lately. As I have even thought myself in many ways a fool, I am in no way surprised to find that many notions which I have had are ridiculous. At last I fairly allow that the one great way of getting on in this world is to get friends, and impress them with a notion of your cleverness. Send them about to advertise your cleverness, get their testimonials like so many levers to force yourself where you wish to go. How well did Shakespeare see through all these things when he wrote his sixty-sixth sonnet.

It is quite obvious to me that it is useless to go on printing works which cost great labour, much money, and are scarcely noticed by any soul. I must begin life again, and by another way, ingratiating myself where and when I can: only after long years of slow progress can one's notions be brought out with any chance of being even examined by those capable of judging of them.

Faulty as I am in so many ways, I yet feel that my inmost motives are hardly selfish. I believe they grow by degrees less so. Sometimes I even feel that I should not care for reputation, wealth, comfort, or even life itself, if I could feel that all my efforts were not without their use. Could I do all anonymously I perhaps might consent to it. And yet the condemnation of friends and all you meet is hard to be borne, and their praise or admiration must be sweet. . . . I must go upon a different tack.[14]

This time, therefore, he was determined that the public should listen to him. All the arts of showmanship are exercised to recall Political Economy from Saturn. It took Mr. Alexander Macmillan but a few days to perceive that he had been sent a best-seller.[15] Within a year success was complete. He wrote in his Journal:

Sunday Evening, 3rd December, 1865.—The work of the thinker and inventor may indeed prove for ever futile and mistaken; but even if it be in the true and successful path, it is not, and perhaps can hardly be, recognized at once. At least it is not. One of my chief reasons for the little love of society, is that in most company my hopes and feelings seem snuffed out.

14th December, 1865.—Yesterday I had a letter from Sir John Herschel, approving in the most complete manner of my *Coal*

Question, which I lately had sent to him. Long periods of labour and depression have to be repaid in brief moments of such satisfaction as that letter gave me—perhaps I may say amply repaid. If the book, which was to me a work of intense interest and feeling, is read by few and understood by fewer, it has at least the endorsement of one scientific man whom I should perhaps of all in the world select as the most competent judge of the subject as a whole.[16]

The shrewd publisher sent a copy to Mr. Gladstone, who replied, "I think it is a masterly review of a vast, indeed a boundless subject," [17] and invited the author to call upon him. "My visit to Gladstone, however, was the striking event, which I shall not easily forget—as an author to meet a great minister in the height of his power." [18] Mill drew attention to the book in Parliament in a speech "in which he urged, for the sake of posterity, the present duty of making greater efforts for the reduction of the National Debt." [19] Indeed, the book came opportunely as political ammunition in the controversy over the Sinking Fund. Jevons had written:

A multiplying population, with a constant void for it to fill; a growing revenue, with lessened taxation; accumulating capital, with rising profits and interest. *This is a union of happy conditions which hardly any country has before enjoyed, and which no country can long expect to enjoy.*[20]

Thus it was easy to invoke the proposition that we were living on our natural capital, as a reason why the times were suitable for the rapid reduction of the dead-weight debt. Yet a little reflection might have shown that, if our demand for coal was going to increase indefinitely in a geometrical ratio, our future national income would be so much greater than our present income that the dead-weight debt would become of little account. Indeed, there is not much in Jevons's scare which can survive cool criticism. His conclusions were influenced, I suspect, by a psychological trait, unusually strong in him, which many other people share, a certain hoarding instinct, a readiness to be alarmed and excited by the idea of the exhaustion of resources. Mr. H. S. Jevons has communicated to me an amusing illustration of this. Jevons held similar ideas as to the approaching scarcity of paper as a result of the vastness of the demand in relation to the supplies of suitable material (and here again he omitted to make adequate allowance for the progress of technical methods). Moreover, he acted on his fears and laid in such large stores not only of writingpaper, but also of thin brown packing paper, that even to-day, more than fifty years after his death, his children have not used up the stock he left behind him of the latter; though his purchases seem to have been more in the nature of a speculation than for his personal use, since his own notes were mostly written on the backs of old envelopes and odd scraps of paper, of which the proper place was the waste-paper basket.[21]

III

We must now turn back to Jevons's long series of inductive studies of commercial fluctuations and of prices which began with his paper "On the Study of Periodic Commercial Fluctuations, with Five Diagrams" read before the British Association in 1862.[22] This brief paper of less than a dozen pages marks the beginning of a new stage in economic science. Others before Jevons had noticed seasonal changes and the alternations of good and bad business. He was not the first to plot economic statistics in diagrams; some of his diagrams bear, indeed, a close resemblance to Playfair's, with whose work he seems to have been acquainted.[23] But Jevons compiled and arranged economic statistics for a new purpose and pondered them in a new way. The significance of his method may be expressed by saying that he approached the complex economic facts of the real world, both literally and metaphorically, as meteorologist. Most of his previous papers were in fact concerned with meteorology,[24] and he begins his association with economics by the declaration:

It seems necessary, then, that all commercial fluctuations should be investigated according to the same scientific methods with which we are familiar in other complicated sciences, such especially as meteorology and terrestrial magnetism." [25]

As we shall see subsequently, Jevons was equally at home in the simplified abstractions of pure theory. But this did not blind him to the fact that the material to be handled is shifting and complicated, and will only yield up its answer if it is arranged, compared and analysed for the discovery of uniformities and tendencies. Jevons was the first theoretical economist to survey his material with the prying eyes and fertile, controlled imagination of the natural scientist. He would spend hours arranging his charts, plotting them, sifting them, tinting them neatly with delicate pale colours like the slides of the anatomist, and all the time poring over them and brooding over them to discover their secret. It is remarkable, looking back, how few followers and imitators he had in the black arts of inductive economics in the fifty years after 1862. But to-day he can certainly claim an unnumbered progeny, though the scientific flair which can safely read the shifting sands of economic statistics is no commoner than it was.

In the first instance Jevons was primarily interested in the discovery and elimination of *seasonal* fluctuations. Indeed, the title of his early paper before the British Association is misleading if it suggests that it was concerned with the trade cycle. He points out that, although there had always been an unwritten knowledge of seasonal fluctuations in the minds of business men, he was only aware of two scientific studies of such matters—Gilbart on the bank-note circulation, and Babbage on the Clearing House statistics, published in the *Statistical Journal* for 1854 and 1856 respectively; and he then proceeds to study the seasonal movements of the rate of discount, of bankruptcies, of the price of Consols and of the price of wheat. He is not yet concerned with the larger swings, and his meteorological interests have not yet led him to sunspots. Nevertheless, his study of the monthly prices of many articles since 1844 put an idea into his head. "I was so much struck with the enormous and almost general rise of prices about the year 1853, that I was led to suspect an alteration of the standard of value." [26] As a result, in the next year (1863) his pamphlet on *A Serious Fall in the Value of Gold* leads him, not to cyclical, but to secular movements.

The state of the subject, when this unknown young man spent his savings on printing his notions about it, was extraordinarily backward. The Californian and Australian gold discoveries had led Chevalier (in 1859) to predict a large fall in the value of gold. But the meaning to be attached to the latter phrase and the method of measurement appropriate to the problem were involved in deep obscurity. Newmarch (in 1857) and McCulloch (in 1858) doubted the existence of any depreciation in the purchasing power of gold, and subsequently in the pages of the *Statistical Journal* (1859, 1860 and 1861) Newmarch had suspended judgement. Jevons had to solve the problem of price index-numbers practically from the beginning,[27] and it is scarcely an exaggeration to say that he made as much progress in this brief pamphlet as has been made by all succeeding authors put together. He examines the logical and dialectical problem, the question of weighting, the choice between an arithmetic and a geometric mean, whether articles which have moved abnormally should be excluded, and, generally speaking, what classes of commodities can best be taken as representative. He then compiles a series of index numbers based on the average monthly prices of thirty-nine commodities for each of the years 1845 to 1862; and supplements and checks the results by considering a further seventy-nine minor articles. His final conclusion he expressed as follows:

While I must assert the fact of a depreciation of gold with the utmost confidence, I assign the numerical amount of it with equal diffidence. The lowest estimate of the fall that I arrive at is 9 per cent., and I shall be satisfied if my readers accept this. At the same time, in my own opinion the fall is nearer 15 per cent. It may even be more than this. Many years, however, must pass before numerical estimates can be properly stated to possess more than a slight degree of probability.[28]

Finally, Jevons examined the social consequences of the change in the value of money, classifying incomes according as they suffer from depreciation, estimating its effect on the Budget and the National Debt, enquiring "Whether a remedy is needful or possible," "Ought gold as a standard of value to be abandoned?" "Have the gold discoveries added to the wealth of the world?" and concluding:

I cannot but agree with Macculloch, that, putting out of sight individual cases of hardship, if such exist, a fall in the value of

gold must have, and, as I should say, has already, a most power-
fully beneficial effect. It loosens the country, as nothing else
could, from its old bonds of debt and habit. It throws increased
rewards before all who are making and acquiring wealth. It
excites the active and skilful classes of the community to new
exertions, and is, to some extent, like a discharge from his debts
is to the bankrupt long struggling against his burdens. All this
is effected without a breach of national good faith, which nothing could compensate.[29]

For unceasing fertility and originality of mind applied, with
a sure touch and unfailing control of the material, to a mass of
statistics, involving immense labours for an unaided individual
ploughing his way through with no precedents and labour-
saving devices to relieve his task, this pamphlet stands unrivalled in the history of our subject. The numerous diagrams
and charts which accompany it are also of high interest in the
history of statistical description.

Just as Jevons's study of seasonal fluctuations had led to his
detection of the secular movement of prices, so his task of analysing the latter brought to the surface the character of the
cyclical movements over the same period. The analysis and
elimination of the latter played, indeed, an important part in
his controversial objective. For the doubt which existed as to
the secular depreciation of gold was due to the movement being overlaid by the price changes of the trade cycle; those who
denied the long-period change in the value of the standard,
ascribing the observed movements to the familiar alternation of
good and bad trade. It was, therefore, necessary for Jevons to
endeavour to eliminate the effect of the latter, which led him,
incidentally, to date and to measure the trade cycle with a new
precision. This was to lead him at a later date to famous conclusions. For the time being his observations on the underlying
causes of the trade cycle, though merely *obiter dicta,* strike
deeper, in my judgement, than those which he popularized
later. He summed them up as follows:

That great commercial fluctuations, completing their course
in some ten years, diversify the progress of trade, is familiar to
all who attend to mercantile matters. The remote cause of these
commercial tides has not been so well ascertained. It seems to

lie in the *varying proportion which the capital devoted to per-manent and remote investment bears to that which is but tem-porarily invested soon to reproduce itself.*[30]

Were a certain definite proportion of the capital of the coun-try set apart every year for such long-dated investments, the returns of capital which they would make would be as regular as the absorption of capital. But this is not the case. It is the peculiarity of these great and permanent works to be multi-plied at particular periods.[31]

Jevons supported this conclusion by a graph showing annually over a period of thirty-seven years the quantity of bricks made in the United Kingdom, the loads of timber imported and the price of iron—a remarkable example (in what is merely a pa-renthesis) of the range of Jevons's inductive curiosity and of his intense industry at this period of his life.[32]

Speaking in this place, it is suitable to mention that at this point Jevons felt himself ripe to apply for membership of our body. In his Journal of June 4, 1864, he wrote:

I am on the point of getting myself proposed and perhaps elected a Fellow of the Statistical Society, as the use of the title F.S.S., the use of the library, and possible acquaintance with other statisticians, will be of high advantage to me.[33]

His next contribution, *On the Variation of Prices and the Value of the Currency since 1782,* in which he further devel-oped this theory of index numbers and carried through the im-mense labour of continuing his series backwards into the eight-eenth century, was read before the Statistical Society in May 1865; and in the following year he read before the Society his extensive study *On the Frequent Autumnal Pressure in the Money Market, and the Action of the Bank of England.* These papers were the beginning of a close association, which in 1877 culminated in his becoming one of the secretaries of the So-ciety and a member of the Council. By this time he was resi-dent in London, and frequently attended our meetings. In 1880 he was appointed a Vice-President on resigning his secre-taryship.

The four years from 1862 to 1866 had been a period of in-tense activity of mind.[34] Jevons was living on the money he had

saved in Australia. He had no post, and had a sense of loneli-
ness and failure. Even in the early part of 1866, when his name
had been established, his Journal shows that he suffered from
anxiety and depression. So is it always. In May 1866 he was
appointed Professor of Logic and Mental and Moral Philosophy
and Cobden Professor of Political Economy in Owens College,
Manchester. "I shall now have about £300 a year from the
college," he wrote in his Journal, "and nearly £108 from my
own money. What can I not do with it?" But he now had
much to do besides think and write; and in 1867 he married.
Nearly ten years were to pass before he again attempted a major statistical enquiry.[35]

It is often forgotten how comparatively late in his career
Jevons developed the theory of solar variation as the explanation of the period of the Trade Cycle, which is immortally associated with his name. It was published in two papers read
before the British Association in 1875 and 1878. The first of
these papers is brief and goes little further than to suggest a
matter for enquiry. In 1801 Sir William Herschel had "endeavoured to discover a connection between the price of corn
and the power of the sun's rays as marked by the decennial
variation of the sun's spots."[36] In 1861 R. C. Carrington, "in
his standard work upon the sun, gave a diagram comparing the
price of corn with the sunspot curve during portions of the
last and present centuries."[37] The results of both these enquir-
ies were negative. But Arthur Schuster, Jevons's colleague at
Owens College, revived the matter by pointing out "that the
years of good vintage in Western Europe have occurred at intervals somewhat approximating to eleven years, the average
length of the principal sunspot cycle."[38] Thorold Rogers' *History of Agriculture and Prices in England,* which began to
appear in 1866, provided Jevons with material for analysing
wheat prices over a long period. The commercial crises in his
own lifetime had occurred at intervals of ten or eleven years:
1825, 1836–39, 1847, 1857, 1866. Might there not be a connection between these things? "I am aware," Jevons concluded,
"that speculations of this kind may seem somewhat far-fetched
and finely-wrought; but financial collapses have recurred with

such approach to regularity in the last fifty years, that either this or some other explanation is needed." [39] Nevertheless, he soon repented of publishing what was no better than a bright idea. "Subsequent enquiry convinced me that my figures would not support the conclusion I derived from them, and I withdrew the paper from publication." [40]

The virus, however, had entered into his system. No one who has once deeply engaged himself in coincidence-fitting of this character will easily disembarrass himself of the enquiry. In 1878 Jevons returned to it in his second paper before the British Association, and in an article contributed to *Nature* in which the argument was recapitulated. Three new discoveries were his excuse. In the first place, he had succeeded in carrying back the history of commercial crises at ten- or eleven-year intervals almost to the beginning of the eighteenth century. In the second place, he was now advised by his astronomical friends that the solar period was not 11.1 years, as he had previously supposed, but 10.45 years, which fitted much better his series of commercial crises. In the third place, he now abandoned European harvests, the price statistics for which yielded negative results, as the intermediary through which sunspots affected business, in favour of Indian harvests, which, he argued, transmitted prosperity to Europe through the greater margin of purchasing power available to the Indian peasant to buy imported goods.[41]

Jevons's argument is by no means so clear as is usual with him. He produced considerable evidence for the view that commercial crises had occurred at intervals of about 10½ years. The astronomers told him that the solar period was about 10½ years. This "beautiful coincidence," as he called it, produced in him an unduly strong conviction of causal nexus. "I beg leave to affirm," he wrote in his article for *Nature*, "that I never was more in earnest, and that after some further careful enquiry, I am perfectly convinced that these decennial crises do depend upon meteorological variations of like period." [42] But he devoted far too little attention to the exact dating of deficient harvests in relation to the dating of commercial crises, which was a necessary first step to tracing the intermediate links. In his paper of 1875, when he believed his evidence to depend on European harvests, he discovered the link in the spirit of optimism produced by good crops:

Mr. John Mills in his very excellent papers upon Credit Cycles in the *Transactions of the Manchester Statistical Society* (1867-68) has shown that these periodic collapses are really mental in their nature, depending upon variations of despondency, hopefulness, excitement, disappointment and panic.[43] . . . Assuming that variations of commercial credit and enterprise are essentially mental in their nature, must there not be external events to excite hopefulness at one time or disappointment and despondency at another? It may be that the commercial classes of the English nation, as at present constituted, form a body suited by mental and other conditions to go through a complete oscillation in a period nearly corresponding to that of the sunspots. In such conditions a comparatively slight variation of the prices of food, repeated in a similar manner, at corresponding points of the oscillation, would suffice to produce violent effects.[44]

But in 1878 he described this theory as a "rather fanciful hypothesis," [45] and made everything to depend on the decennial fluctuations in foreign trade consequent on cyclical crop changes in India and elsewhere. Unfortunately this involved a difficulty in dating which he passes over with surprising levity:

One difficulty which presents itself is that the commercial crises in England occur simultaneously with the high prices in Delhi, or even in anticipation of the latter; now the effect cannot precede its cause, and in commercial matters we should expect an interval of a year or two to elapse before bad seasons in India made their effects felt here. The fact, however, is that the famines in Bengal appear to follow similar events in Madras.[46]

Thus the details of the inductive argument are decidedly flimsy. If, however, it could be established that, generally speaking and on the average of different crops and countries, years when the world draws for current consumption on the stocks carried forward from one harvest to another alternate, in accordance with the solar period, with years when bountiful harvests serve to increase the stocks carried forward, Jevons could have linked his thesis, on the broadest possible grounds, with his forgotten theory of 1863 that the trade cycle depended on fluctuations of investment. For alternating investment and disinvestment in the aggregate stocks of the produce of the soil held in excess of current consumption might be capable of consequences closely analogous to those he had previously ascribed to fluctuations in the rate of new investment in durable goods.

Whether or not Jevons was wrong or rash in the hypotheses he framed on the basis of his inductive studies, it was a revolutionary change, for one who was a logician and a deductive economist, to approach the subject in this way. By using these methods Jevons carried economics a long stride from the *à priori* moral sciences towards the natural sciences built on a firm foundation of experience. But the material of economics is shifting as well as complex. Jevons was pursuing a singularly difficult art, and he has had almost as few successors as predecessors, who have attained to his own level of skill.

The sun-spot papers cannot be ranked on at all the same plane of genius or of achievement as *A Serious Fall in the Value of Gold*. Since his time, unfortunately for his conclusions, the astronomers have reverted to 11.125 as the average of the solar period,[47] whilst the trade cycles have recurred at intervals of 7 or 8, rather than of 10 or 11 years. In 1909 the problem was reconsidered in an ingenious manner by his son Prof. H. S. Jevons,[48] who argued that the harvest statistics could be interpreted in terms of a 3½-year cycle, which was combined in twos or threes to produce either 7- or 10½-year periods. This was followed up after the War by Sir William Beveridge's much more elaborate studies of harvest statistics, which led him to the conclusion of a complex 15.2-years period which he further analysed into sub-periods.[49] It is now generally agreed that, even if a harvest period can be found associated with the solar period or with more complex meteorological phenomena, this cannot afford a complete explanation of the trade cycle. The theory was prejudiced by being stated in too precise and categorical a form. Nevertheless, Jevons's notion, that meteorological phenomena play a part in harvest fluctuations and that harvest fluctuations play a part (though more important formerly than to-day) in the trade cycle, is not to be lightly dismissed.

IV

Meanwhile Jevons was contributing with equal originality to the study of deductive economics based on simplified and abstract assumptions. His thoughts can be traced back to his period of solitary thought in Australia in 1858–9 when he was 22 or 23 years old.[50] By 1860, when he was working at University College, a definite theory was taking shape in his mind. On June 1, 1860, he wrote to his brother Herbert:

During the last session I have worked a good deal at political economy; in the last few months I have fortunately struck out what I have no doubt is *the true Theory of Economy,* so thorough-going and consistent, that I cannot now read other books on the subject without indignation. While the theory is entirely mathematical in principle, I show, at the same time, how the data of calculation are so complicated as to be for the present hopeless. Nevertheless, I obtain from the mathematical principles all the chief laws at which political economists have previously arrived, only arranged in a series of definitions, axioms, and theories almost as rigorous and connected as if they were so many geometrical problems. One of the most important axioms is, that as the quantity of any commodity, for instance, plain food, which a man has to consume, increases, so the utility or benefit derived from the last portion used decreases in degree. The decrease of enjoyment between the beginning and end of a meal may be taken as an example. And I assume that on an average, the *ratio of utility* is some continuous mathematical function of the quantity of commodity. This law of utility has, in fact, always been assumed by political economists under the more complex form and name of the Law of Supply and Demand. But once fairly stated in its simple form, it opens up the whole of the subject. Most of the conclusions are, of course, the old ones stated in a consistent form; but my definition of capital and law of the interest of capital are, as far as I have seen, quite new. I have no idea of letting these things lie by till somebody else has the advantage of them, and shall therefore try to publish them next spring.[51]

More than two years passed by, however, before the outline of his theory was made public. Jevons sent a short paper entitled *Notice of a General Mathematical Theory of Political*

Economy to Section F of the British Association to be read in his absence before the 1862 Meeting held at Cambridge, where Marshall was an undergraduate in his first year. He had no diffidence about its worth and high, though doubtful, hopes about its effect. He wrote to his brother in September 1862:

Although I know pretty well the paper is perhaps worth all the others that will be read there put together, I cannot pretend to say how it will be received—whether it will be read at all, or whether it won't be considered nonsense. . . . I am very curious, indeed, to know what effect my theory will have both upon my friends and the world in general. I shall watch it like an artilleryman watches the flight of a shell or shot, to see whether its effects equal his intentions.[52]

The paper attracted no attention whatever and was not printed, the Secretary of the British Association writing to him that "a further explanation and publication of the above-mentioned theory is deferred until a more suitable period for establishing a matter of such difficulty." Four years later it was published in the *Statistical Journal* (June 1866), where it occupies about five pages.[53] Though to a modern reader Jevons's 27 paragraphs are perfectly lucid, they are little more than an abstract or syllabus of a complete theory. But the substance of all his subsequent ideas is there. A hedonistic calculus allows us to balance the utility of consumption against the disutility of labour. The price of a commodity is determined not by its aggregate utility but by balancing the marginal utility of its consumption, or, as he here expresses it, "the *co-efficient of utility* (which) is the ratio between the last increment or infinitely small supply of the object, and the increment of pleasure which it occasions," against the marginal disutility of its production, "labour (being) exerted both in intensity and duration until a further increment will be more painful than the increment of produce thereby obtained is pleasurable." [54] " (The) amount of capital is estimated by the amount of utility of which the enjoyment is deferred. . . . As labour must be supposed to be aided with some capital, the rate of interest is always determined by the *ratio which a new increment of produce bears to the increment of capital by which it was produced.*" [55] In a concluding sentence the extent of his departure from the classical school is indicated: "The interest of capital has no relation to the absolute returns to labour, but only to the increased return which the last increment of capital allows." [56]

Another five years passed by before this abstract, which had attracted no more attention than at its first reading, was fully clothed, *The Theory of Political Economy* being published in October 1871. Prof. H. S. Jevons records[57] that "according to one of my father's MS. notes,[58] the publication might have been delayed considerably later than 1871 had it not been for the appearance in 1868 and 1870 of articles by Professor Fleeming Jenkin." The book follows very closely both the order and substance of the abstract of nearly ten years before. But it carries out what was only the promise of the latter to "reduce the main problem of this science to a mathematical form," by introducing diagrams and expressing the argument in mathematical form with a frequent use of the notation of the differential calculus.

Jevons's *Theory of Political Economy* and the place it occupies in the history of the subject are so well known that I need not spend time in describing its contents. It was not as uniquely original in 1871 as it would have been in 1862. For, leaving on one side the precursors Cournot, Gossen, Dupuit, Von Thünen and the rest, there were several economists, notably Walras and Marshall, who by 1871, were scribbling equations with x's and y's, big Deltas and little d's. Nevertheless, Jevons's *Theory* is the first treatise to present in a finished form the theory of value based on subjective valuations, the marginal principle and the now familiar technique of the algebra and diagrams of the subject. The first modern book on economics, it has proved singularly attractive to all bright minds newly attacking the subject;—simple, lucid, unfaltering, chiselled in stone where Marshall knits in wool. Let me open it almost at random and quote you a passage to remind you of its quality:

The fact is, that *labour once spent has no influence on the future value of any article:* it is gone and lost for ever. In commerce bygones are for ever bygones; and we are always starting clear at each moment, judging the values of things with a view to future utility. Industry is essentially prospective, not retro-spective; and seldom does the result of any undertaking exactly coincide with the first intentions of its promoters.

But though labour is never the cause of value, it is in a large proportion of cases the determining circumstance, and in the following way: *Value depends solely on the final degree of util-ity. How can we vary this degree of utility?* —*By having more or less of the commodity to consume. And how shall we get more or less of it?*—*By spending more or less labour in obtaining a supply.* According to this view, then, there are two steps between labour and value. Labour affects supply, and sup-ply affects the degree of utility, which governs value, or the ratio of exchange. In order that there may be no possible mis-take about this all-important series of relations, I will re-state it in a tabular form, as follows:

> *Cost of production determines supply;*
> *Supply determines final degree of utility;*
> *Final degree of utility determines value.*[59]

In recent times Jevons has received special praise for his Theory of Capital, inasmuch as he anticipated the Austrian School by emphasizing as two distinct dimensions the quantity of capital and the period for which it has to be employed in order to yield up its product. Nevertheless, his treatment as a whole is somewhat vitiated (as Prof. Robbins has pointed out) by echoes of "wage-fund" ideas. Capital, according to Jevons, "consists merely in the aggregate of those commodities which are required for sustaining labourers of any kind or class en-gaged in work." [60] He prefers to say, "not that a factory, or dock, or railway, or ship *is capital,* but that *it represents so much capital sunk in the enterprise.*" "Accordingly, I would not say that a railway *is fixed capital,* but that *capital is fixed in the railway.* The capital is not the railway, but the food of those who made the railway." On the other hand, there are admir-able passages where he conceives of capital as being measured on the supply side by the amount of the present utility fore-gone and on the demand side by the discounted value of the future utilities expected from it.

It is somewhat surprising that even the book did not win any immediate success.[61] The only reviews of importance were those by Cairnes, representing the older generation, and by Alfred Marshall, representing the younger, in what was the latter's first appearance in print. Cairnes declared that ignorance of mathematics made most of the book unintelligible to him, but this did not prevent him from concluding that it was all wrong. Marshall's review was tepid and grudging. "We may read far into the present book," he wrote, "without finding any important proposition which is new in substance." [62] "The main value of the book does not lie in its more prominent theories, but in its original treatment of a number of minor points, its suggestive remarks and careful analogies." [63] And he characteristically concludes: "The book before us would be improved if the mathematics were omitted, but the diagrams retained." [64] Jevons, writing to a correspondent, commented as follows: "There was indeed a review in the *Academy* of 1st April, 1872, but though more fair than that of the *Saturday Review*, it contained no criticism worthy of your notice." [65] So late as 1874 Jevons wrote:

While I am not aware that my views have been accepted by any well-known English economist, there are a certain number of younger mathematicians and economists who have entered into the subject, and treated it in a very different manner. Among these I may mention Mr. George Darwin, the son of the eminent naturalist; he is a very good mathematician and an acute economist.[66]

The relations between Jevons and Marshall are of some interest. Nearly twenty years later, and eight years after Jevons's death, the references to Jevons in the *Principles* are still somewhat grudging.[67] Marshall was extraordinarily reluctant to admit that he owed anything to Jevons. There is no evidence that Jevons was aware of the authorship of the *Academy* review. He never visited Cambridge before 1874, when he first examined in the Moral Sciences Tripos. "The only time I saw him," Mrs. Marshall writes to me, "was in 1874 when he was one of my examiners and gave rise to Dr. Kennedy's lines:

"Were they at sixes and at sevens?
Oh Pearson Gardiner Foxwell Jevons." [68]

He was, of course, close friends with Professor Foxwell, with whom he frequently corresponded, and whom he again visited at Cambridge towards the end of 1880. In a letter of Jevons's to Professor Foxwell written in 1875 and again in 1879 there are echoes of talk in which Professor Foxwell seems to have been advancing Marshall's claims. In 1875 Jevons writes:

I have been very much interested in your letter concerning my paper. It has told me much, which I had no previous means of knowing, concerning the ideas current in philosophical subjects in Cambridge. I was not aware that Marshall had so long entertained notions of a quantitative theory of political economy, and think it a pity that he has so long delayed publishing something on the subject.

It is, of course, open to you or him or others to object to the special way in which I have applied mathematics, and I should like to see other attempts in different directions, but what I contend is that my notion of utility is the correct one, and the only sound way of laying the foundation for a mathematical theory.[69]

And in 1879:

As regards the analogy of the laws of wages and rents, of course I do not know what Marshall gave in his lectures in 1869, as I neither attended them nor have seen notes, unless, indeed, the answers of some of the candidates. But I do not remember that they said anything on the matter. . . .

As regards Marshall's originality, I never called it in question in the slightest degree, having neither the wish nor the grounds. On the other hand, you seem to forget that the essential points of my theory were fully indicated as far back as 1862, at the Cambridge Meeting of the British Association. I have no reason to suppose that Marshall saw any printed report of my first brief paper; but of course, on the other hand, in my book of 1871 (*Theory of Political Economy*) I could not possibly have borrowed anything from Marshall. But these questions are really of little or no importance now that we have found such earlier books as those of Gossen, Cournot, Dupuit, etc. We are all shelved on the matter of priority, except, of course, as regards details and general method of exposition, etc.[70]

Jevons omits to point out that an abstract of his whole theory had been printed in the *Statistical Journal* in 1866—not a very obscure source. Indeed, it was preposterous to suggest that Jevons could have derived anything from Marshall. But for more than another decade after Jevons wrote the above, "what

Marshall gave in his lectures in 1869" was to be an inhibition and a taboo on the publications of others. In later years Marshall was, perhaps, a little uneasy whether a certain fundamental lack of sympathy had led him to do injustice to Jevons. The following undated [71] fragment was found amongst his papers:

I looked with great excitement for Jevons's *Theory:* but he gave me no help in my difficulties and I was vexed. I have since learnt to estimate him better. His many-sidedness, his power of combining statistical with analytical investigations, his ever fresh honest sparkling individuality and suggestiveness impressed me gradually; and I reverence him now as among the very greatest of economists. But even now I think that the central argument of his *Theory* stands on a lower plane than the work of Cournot and von Thünen. They handled their mathematics gracefully: he seemed like David in Saul's armour. They held a mirror up to the manifold interactions of nature's forces: and, though none could do that better than Jevons when writing on money or statistics or on practical issues, he was so encumbered by his mathematics in his central argument, that he tried to draw nature's actions out into a long queue. This was partly because the one weakness of his otherwise loyal and generous character showed itself here: he was impressed by the mischief which the almost pontifical authority of Mill exercised on young students; and he seemed perversely to twist his own doctrines so as to make them appear more inconsistent with Mill's and Ricardo's than they really were. But the genius which enabled Ricardo—it was not so with Mill—to tread his way safely through the most slippery paths of mathematical reasoning, though he had no aid from mathematical training, had made him one of my heroes; and my youthful loyalty to him boiled over when I read Jevons's *Theory*. The editor of the *Academy* having heard that I had been working on the same lines, asked me to review the book: and, though a quarter of a century has passed, I have a vivid memory of the angry phrases which would force themselves into my draft, only to be cut out and then reappear in another form a little later on, and then to be cut out again. . . . On many aspects of economics I have learnt more from Jevons than from any one else. But the obligations which I had to acknowledge in the Preface to my *Principles* were to Cournot and von Thünen and not to Jevons.[72]

This passage brings to the surface a deeper cause of the lack of sympathy between these two founders of modern economics than a sense of rivalry arising out of the similarity of their approach—namely, out of their *dissimilarity* in standing, each with the deep emotion which the subject commands, on opposite sides in the still unresolved debate whether Ricardo was a true or a false prophet. In 1875 Jevons wrote to Professor Foxwell:

"I am beginning to think very strongly that the true line of economic science descends from Smith through Malthus to Senior, while another branch through Ricardo to Mill has put as much error into the science as they have truth." [73] And the preface to the second edition of his *Theory of Political Economy* (1879) concludes as follows:

When at length a true system of Economics comes to be established, it will be seen that that able but wrong-headed man, David Ricardo, shunted the car of Economic science on to a wrong line, a line, however, on which it was further urged towards confusion by his equally able and wrong-headed admirer John Stuart Mill. There were Economists, such as Malthus and Senior, who had a far better comprehension of the true doctrines (though not free from the Ricardian errors), but they were driven out of the field by the unity and influence of the Ricardo-Mill school. It will be a work of labour to pick up the fragments of a shattered science and to start anew, but it is a work from which they must not shrink who wish to see any advance of Economic Science. [74]

The violence of Jevons's aversion to Mill, pursued almost to the point of morbidity, is well known. All Jevons's nonconformist heredity rose up against the orthodoxy which the prestige of Mill in the 'sixties and 'seventies imposed on the subject and particularly on its educational side. He wrote to a correspondent in 1874:

I fear it is impossible to criticize Mr. Mill's writings without incurring the danger of rousing animosity, but I hope and believe you are right in saying that I have said nothing from petulance or passion. Whatever I have said or shall say of Mr. Mill is due to a very long consideration of his works, and to a growing conviction that, however valuable they are in exciting thought and leading to the study of social subjects, they must not be imposed upon us as a new creed. [75]

Of the younger men with whom he was intimate, he fully converted Professor Foxwell to his point of view, and it was a bond of sympathy. But he could not forgive Edgeworth, with whom he used to walk on Hampstead Heath, by which they both lived in the last years of his life, for being "still deep in the fallacies of Mill." The aversion had some of its roots, I think, in a personal experience. In 1860, shortly after his return from Australia, he was working at University College for the B.A. degree. At this time his own theories were seething in his head.[76] In his heart he believed himself to be in embryo the only economist in the world with a conception of the truth. This was a dangerous state of mind for an examinee, and after the College Examinations in June, 1860, he has to confess:

> In political economy I had a sad reverse, such indeed as I never had before, for in spite of having studied the subject independently and originally, and having read some dozens of the best works in it, almost neglecting other classes for the purpose, I was placed third or fourth when I felt confident of the first prize. This I can only attribute to a difference of opinion, which is perfectly allowable, having prejudiced the professor against my answers. However, I shall fully avenge myself when I bring out my *Theory of Economy,* and reestablish the science on a sensible basis.[77]

It is interesting to record, that the first prize was awarded to H. H. Cozens-Hardy, afterwards Master of the Rolls, who was, however, three years Jevons's junior, and that in the examination for the Ricardo Scholarship in Political Economy, a few months later in the same year, Jevons defeated Cozens-Hardy and was awarded the scholarship.[78] Moreover in the June examination in Philosophy of Mind and Logic Jevons was bracketed first (with Theodore Waterhouse). So he had not, in fact, much to complain of. Nevertheless the effect on his mind was curious. The students whom he had to teach when he became Professor at Owens College were accustomed to sit for the London examinations. As he thought it would be unfair to expose his own pupils to the rebuff he himself had suffered, his conscience did not allow him to teach them his own characteristic doctrine. His courses at Manchester were mainly confined to an exposition of Mill.[79] I had long ago heard this from my father, and how his repression of his own theories had brought his feeling against Mill to boiling point. A book of careful lecture notes taken down by a member of his class, which I lately came across, confirms that this was so.[80]

V

In my memoir of Alfred Marshall I called attention to the many-sidedness which seems to be a necessary equipment for an economist.[81] Jevons was certainly a notable example of this. To his scientific and experimental training which led him to his inductive studies and his logical and analytical bent which led him to his deductive studies there was added an unusually strong historical, and even antiquarian, bias. From his earliest days Jevons had a native inclination to carry his inductive studies backwards in point of time, and to discover the historical origins of any theory in which he was interested. This is first apparent in the quantity of historical material with which he adorned the *Coal Question,* material much of which it would have occurred to few other authors to bring in. He carried back his series of index numbers into the eighteenth century. When he came to study solar variations, he traced back the history of the trade cycle to the beginning of the eighteenth century and examined harvest statistics over many centuries. Thus in the field of economic history he made himself a pioneer in the history of prices and of trade fluctuations.

In the history of economic thought and theory he was even more deeply interested. In every branch of the subject that he touched he sought out the unknown or forgotten precursors of his favourite theories. His most brilliant contribution in this field was his discovery of the work and significance of Cantillon; whilst his most substantial contribution was his pioneer work in economic bibliography summed up in his hand-list of "Mathematico-Economic Books, Memoirs, and other published Writings," printed as an appendix to the second edition of his *Theory of Political Economy* and in his hand-list of writings on monetary problems appended to the *Investigations in Currency and Finance.*

Beyond this, Jevons was a born collector, the first of the distinguished tribe of economic bibliomaniacs who have contrived to set a fashion amongst librarians which has entitled the booksellers to run the obscurest fragments of economic literature up to fancy figures. Jevons invented the collecting of obscure economic books and pamphlets; though it was, of course, Lord Macaulay who first drew attention to their importance as historical sources. Professor Foxwell [82] first caught the affliction from him; though Jevons never paid high prices or proceeded to the extremer stages where condition and collector's "points" are paramount,—his was primarily a far flung working library for which any usable copy would do. Nevertheless, there are entries scattered through his letters tantalizing to the modern collector. On April 8, 1879, he writes to his wife from The Three Swans, Salisbury:

I have done a great stroke in book-buying, having bought a remarkable collection of nearly five hundred economical and political pamphlets at about a half-penny each. Some of them are evidently valuable and rare. One of them contains copper-plate diagrams of prices for some centuries. One or two are by Robert Owen. I also got a carefully-written list of them all, as good as a catalogue.[83]

In 1881 he writes from Paris:

A large part of my time has been taken up in book-hunting on the banks of the Seine. I have secured almost a trunkful of books on economics, of much scientific and historic value, but often at ridiculously low prices.[84]

His wife records:

On a leisure afternoon he thoroughly enjoyed making a round of several old bookshops, and his kindly, courteous manners—as courteous always to his inferiors in position as to those of his own station—were fully appreciated by the owners. At two at least of the shops which he most frequented he was regarded as a friend, and the booksellers took a pleasure in looking out at the sales they attended for the books they thought might suit him, reserving them from their other customers until he had seen them.[85]

By the end of his life he had accumulated several thousand volumes, lining the walls and passages of the house and packed in heaps in the attics, an embarrassment to his wife and family both then and in their subsequent removals. These latter led to the gradual dispersal of the books. In 1907 the Library of Owens College, Manchester, was given the first choice to take what they wanted and some 2,400 volumes are incorporated in that library with a special label. After that the Library of University College, London, was given the opportunity to take some hundreds. Out of the residue his son, Prof. H. S. Jevons, maintained a working collection, mainly of the more modern books, which he added to the notable economics library which he had built up at the University of Allahabad, when he gave up his Professorship there. Jevons also had a collection of old bank-notes which he described as "such a collection as probably hardly anyone else has." [86]

VI

We have now traversed Jevons's outstanding contributions to Economics and Statistics. But we are far from having surveyed the whole of his work. During his lifetime the reputation of Jevons as a logician stood nearly as high as his reputation as an economist. The English school of Logic of the post-Mill period has not held its own in the judgment of modern opinion, and the interest of Jevons's work has declined along with that of his contemporaries. But during the second phase of his work from about 1866 to 1876 logic occupied a large part of his time and thought, and also (so long as he was at Owens College) of his teaching duties. More than half of the books published during his lifetime related to logic. One of them, *The Principles of Science, A Treatise on Logic and Scientific Method,* is his largest work, and was widely used for many years. Nevertheless, the part Jevons played in the development of logic is in no way comparable to his position in the history of Economics and Statistics. It is, however, no part of my present task to review his contributions to knowledge in that field.

In the last decade of his life he discovered in himself a remarkable aptitude for writing in a simple, clear and interesting style the elementary outlines of his favourite subjects. Apart from numerous editions printed in America and in six or seven foreign languages, there have sold up to the present time 130,-000 copies of his *Elementary Lessons in Logic* (published in 1870), 148,000 copies of his *Primer of Logic* (1876), and 98,-000 copies of his *Primer of Political Economy* (1878). Another elementary book, though on a somewhat larger scale, his *Money and the Mechanism of Exchange* (1875), has sold about 20,000 copies in this country, apart from large sales in America, where there was at one time a cheap pirated edition. For a period of half a century practically all elementary students both of Logic and of Political Economy in Great Britain and also in India and the Dominions were brought up on Jevons. His little books involve few perplexities, are never dull, and give the effect of lucidity and certainty of outlook without undue dogmatism,—indeed ideal for the purpose. Simple and definite examination questions can be set upon them;—no blame to them in the eyes of Jevons, who was, rightly, a great believer in the system of examinations which was one of the great contributions of his generation to education and administration. The conclusion of his article on "Cram," published in *Mind* (1877), is worth quoting:

I should not venture to defend University examinations against all the objections which may be brought against them. My purpose is accomplished in attempting to show that examination is the most effective way of enforcing a severe and definite training upon the intellect, and of selecting those for high position who show themselves best able to bear this severe test. It is the popular cry against "Cram" that I have answered, and I will conclude by expressing my belief that any mode of education which enables a candidate to take a leading place in a severe and well-conducted open examination, must be a good system of education. Name it what you like, but it is impossible to deny that it calls forth intellectual, moral, and even physical powers, which are proved by unquestionable experience to fit men for the business of life.

This is what I hold to be Education. We cannot consider it the work of teachers to make philosophers and scholars and geniuses of various sorts: these, like poets, are born, not made. Nor, as I have shown, is it the business of the educator to impress indelibly upon the mind the useful knowledge which is to guide the pupil through life. This would be "Cram" indeed. It is the purpose of education so to exercise the faculties of mind that the infinitely various experience of after-life may be observed and reasoned upon to the best effect. What is popularly condemned as "Cram" is often the best-devised and best-conducted system of training towards this all-important end.[87]

Finally, in the last period of his life Jevons became much interested in the relation of the State to the economic life of the community. On the side of morals and sentiment Jevons was, and always remained, an impassioned individualist. There is a very odd early address of his, delivered to the Manchester Statistical Society in 1869,[88] in which he deplores free hospitals and medical charities of all kinds, which he regarded as undermining the character of the poor (which he seems to have preferred to, and deemed independent of, their health). "I feel bound," he said, "to call in question the policy of the whole of our medical charities, including all free public infirmaries, dispensaries, hospitals, and a large part of the vast amount of private charity. What I mean is that the whole of these charities nourish in the poorest classes a contented sense of dependence on the richer classes for those ordinary requirements of life which they ought to be led to provide for themselves." Perhaps it would brace us and strengthen us if we could feel again those astringent sentiments, and face that vigorous East wind, believing so firmly in the future as to make almost anything tolerable in the present. For the feeling behind this Victorian hardness was grand. "We cannot be supposed," Jevons concludes, "yet to have reached a point at which the public or private charity of one class towards another can be dispensed with, but I do think we ought to look towards such a state of things. True progress will tend to render every class self-reliant and independent."

Nevertheless, considerations of expediency influenced Jevons, as time went on, to move just a little to the Left, though never to nearly the extent that Mill had moved before the end of his life. He had always advocated a large public expenditure on education (for this, unlike medical attention apparently, would improve the "characters" of the poor), and on the right kind of museums.[89] His essay on "Amusements of the People" [90] follows Aristotle in thinking it a public duty to provide good music for universal consumption. The Hallé orchestra, which he attributed to the presence there of "a large resident, well-cultured German middle-class population," was for him the best thing in Manchester. In the London of his day, he writes, "one craves sometimes the stirring clang of the trombones, the roll of the drums, the solemn boom of the diapason, and the exciting crescendo of a great orchestra." It is evident that, whatever Jevons felt about the hospitals, he would have acclaimed the B.B.C. He became, moreover, exceedingly interested in State Trading, as exemplified in the Post Office, and wrote more than once concerning the criteria of policy towards the parcels traffic and telegrams. The last book published in his lifetime, *The State in Relation to Labour* (1882), takes up a cautious, intermediate position. "The all-important point," he explains in the preface, "is to explain if possible why, in general, we uphold the rule of *laisser-faire,* and yet in large classes of cases invoke the interference of local or central authorities. . . . The outcome of the inquiry is that we can lay down no hard-and-fast rules, but must treat every case in detail upon its merits."

It may be interesting to put on record the circulation up to the present time of Jevons's publications,[91] apart from the popular text-books already mentioned:

Pure Logic (1863), 1,000.
The Coal Question (1865), 2,000.
The Theory of Political Economy (1871), 7,000.
The Principles of Science (1874), 9,000.
Studies in Deductive Logic (1880), 6,000.
The State in Relation to Labour (1882), 9,000.
Methods of Social Reform (1883), 2,000.
Investigations in Currency and Finance (1884), 2,000.
Principles of Economics (1905), 1,000.[92]

Of the outward facts of his life there is little more to record. In 1876 he succeeded to the Professorship of Political Economy at University College, London.[93] He took a house high up in Hampstead at the edge of the heath. In 1880 increasing uncertainty of health and a great preference for writing rather than lecturing caused him to resign his professorship. He planned to spend three or four years in Switzerland completing his projected *Principles of Economics,* of which a fragment was published posthumously in 1905. On a Sunday morning, August 13, 1882, he was overcome by faintness while bathing off Galley Hill, between Bexhill and Hastings, and was drowned. He left three children, a son and two daughters. His son, Herbert Stanley Jevons, was, like his father, educated in science—in his case geology and chemistry—but found his way by natural bent to economics, and has successively occupied the chairs of economics at Cardiff, Allahabad and Rangoon. Jevons's wife survived him nearly thirty years until 1910.

Although Jevons died, greatly lamented by his own world, at the early age of forty-six, I think that his work was done. It was in the decade of his youth from 1857 to 1865 that he had genius and divine intuition and a burning sense of vocation. His flame was paler and less steady at the close.

VII

What sort of man was Jevons in himself? There is no strong personal impression of him which has been recorded, and 54 years after his death it is not easy to find a definite imprint on the minds of the few now left who knew him. My belief is that Jevons did not make a strong impression on his companions at any period of his life. He was, in modern language, strongly introverted. He worked best alone with flashes of inner light. He was repelled, as much as he was attracted, by contact with the outside world. He had from his boyhood unbounded belief in his own powers; but he desired greatly to influence others whilst being himself uninfluenced by them. He was deeply affectionate towards the members of his family, but not intimate with them or with anyone. When he was 27, he wrote the following about his own state of mind at the age of 16:

It was during the year 1851, while living almost unhappily among thoughtless, if not bad companions, in Gower Street—a gloomy house on which I now look with dread—it was then, and when I had got a quiet hour in my small bedroom at the top of the house, that I began to think that I could and ought to do more than others. . . . My reserve was so perfect that I suppose no one had the slightest comprehension of my motives or ends. My father probably knew me but little. I never had any confidential conversation with him. At school and college the success in the classes was the only indication of my powers. All else that I intended or did was within or carefully hidden. The reserved character, as I have often thought, is not pleasant or lovely. But is it not necessary to one such as I? [94]

In Australia he lived almost entirely by himself, and was reluctant to join in the social events of colonial life. In 1857, when he was 22, he wrote home to his sister the following analysis of his own powers:

I have scarcely a spark of imagination and no spark of wit. I have but a poor memory, and consequently can retain only a small portion of learning at any one time, which great numbers of other persons possess. But I am not so much a storehouse of goods as I am a machine for making those goods. Give me a few facts or materials, and I can work them up into a smoothly-arranged and finished fabric of theory, or can turn them out in a shape which is something new. My mind is of the most regular structure, and I have such a strong disposition to classify things as is sometimes almost painful. I also think that if in anything I have a chance of acquiring the power, it is that I have some *originality,* and can strike out new things. This consists not so much in quickness of forming new thoughts or opinions but in seizing upon one or two of them and developing them into something symmetrical. It is like a kaleidoscope; just put a bent pin in, or any little bit of rubbish, and a perfectly new and symmetrical pattern will be produced. [95]

In 1865, not long before he married, he wrote in his Journal:

At intervals success rewards me deliciously, but at other times it seems but to oppress me with a burden of duty. More and more I feel a lifelong work defined beforehand for me, and its avoidance impossible. Come what will, I cannot but feel that I have faculties which are to be cultivated, and developed at any risk. To misuse or neglect them would be treason of the deepest kind. And yet the troubles are not slight which such a high and difficult work brings upon me. One duty, too, seems to clash with others. My idea seems to involve contradictories. I would be loved and loving. But the very studies I have to cultivate absorb my thoughts so that I hardly feel able to be what I would in other ways. And, above all, poverty is sure to be my lot. I cannot aid others as I would wish. Nor in a money-making and loving world is it easy to endure the sense of meanness and want which poverty brings. And if I could endure all this myself, I could not expect nor hardly wish for a wife nor any relative to endure it. Half my feelings and affections, then, must be stifled and disappointed.[96]

After his marriage (his wife had private means) his disposition was not radically changed. He went out very little. He had only a few intimates. Music, which was almost a necessity of life to him,[97] bathing and solitary walks were his favourite relaxations at all times. He was not an easy man to live with, a little irritable towards the interruptions of family life, excessively sensitive to noise, liable to depression and valetudinarianism, without much conversation. But it is recorded that "his hearty laugh was something unique in itself and made everyone the happier who heard it." [98] From an early age he was liable to attacks of liverishness and dyspepsia and constipation, which latterly became so acute as to overshadow everything and interrupt his work, suggesting perhaps some deeper cause.

He was a reluctant and unsuccessful lecturer. "Sometimes I have enjoyed lecturing," he wrote on his retirement from University College, "especially on logic, but for years past I have never entered the lecture room without a feeling probably like that of going to the pillory." [99] The value of his lectures was impaired by his resolution seldom to introduce any of his own ideas but to retail mainly the purest milk of Mill, which he believed to be poison. He never, so far as I know, bred up a worthy pupil; though he was in close touch, at the end of his life, with his two younger contemporaries, Foxwell and Edgeworth.[100] Almost every Sunday when he was in London, Foxwell would call on him in Hampstead for a long walk on the Heath; and Edgeworth, who lived close by, was his frequent companion. When I talked of Jevons the other day to Professor Foxwell, recalling these days, "he did not talk much," he said, "there never was a worse lecturer, the men would not go to his classes, he worked in flashes and could not finish anything thoroughly," and then after a pause with a different sort of expression, "the only point about Jevons was that he was a genius."

A photograph of him in later life, which is prefixed to the *Letters and Journal*, is familiar. With crinkly beard, curling hair, a broad brow and square face, full nostrils and a full, somewhat protruding lower lip his countenance was almost, one might say, of a Jewish cast, as Professor Foxwell confirms, explicable, doubtless, by his partly Welsh descent, *Jevons* being a variant of *Evans*. His complexion was florid, his hair a darkish brown, and his eyes bluish-grey. It is a powerful, but not a brilliant face. He would pass for a Victorian banker of high standing. There is also a photograph of him when he was 22 or 23 years old.[101] This is much more interesting, exceedingly strong, keener, clearer, clean-shaven, with a straight lean nose, fine eyes and look, and a tangle of dark unbrushed hair standing back from a high, wide forehead,—a genius then and not at all a banker. These two photographs confirm one's impression that the greatness of Jevons was in his youth.

I have frequently quoted from his Journal, which he kept from 1852, when he was 17, up to the time of his marriage at the end of 1867.[102] This Journal is of the highest interest both in itself and for the light which it casts on his nature. I wish I could have had access to the complete text and had not been limited to the extracts published by his wife in her selection of *Letters and Journal*. The volumes are believed to be extant in the possession of his children, but their present whereabouts is uncertain and they are not accessible. This Journal received all his confidences and the fruits of his introspection, of his excessive introspection. The Journal often, as we have seen, records depression but also the delight of a creative mind in moments of illumination. In March 1866, for example, he writes: "As I awoke in the morning, the sun was shining brightly into my room. There was a consciousness on my mind that I was the discoverer of the true logic of the future. For a few minutes I felt a delight such as one can seldom hope to feel." But he quickly adds: "I remembered only too soon how unworthy and weak an instrument I was for accomplishing so great a work, and how hardly could I expect to do it." [103]

Part II: Sketches of Politicians

WINSTON CHURCHILL

MR. CHURCHILL ON THE WAR

This brilliant book[1] is not a history. It is a series of episodes, a
succession of bird's-eye views, designed to illuminate certain
facets of the great contest and to confirm the author's thesis
about the conduct, in its broadest strategic aspects, of modern
warfare. There are great advantages in this procedure. Mr.
Churchill tells us many details of extraordinary interest, which
most of us did not know before, but he does not lose himself
in detail. He deals in the big with the essential problems of the
higher thought of the conduct of the war. The book is written,
like most books of any value, with a purpose. It does not pretend to the empty impartiality of those dull writers before
whose minds the greatest and most stirring events of history
can pass without producing any distinct impression one way
or the other. Mr. Churchill's was, perhaps, the most acute and
concentrated intelligence which saw the war at close quarters
from beginning to end with knowledge of the inside facts
and of the inner thoughts of the prime movers of events. He
formed clear conclusions as to where lay truth and error—not
only in the light of afterevents. And he here tells them to us
in rhetorical, but not too rhetorical, language. This naturally
means telling us most where he was nearest, and criticising

chiefly where he deemed himself the wisest. But he contrives to do this without undue egotism. He pursues no vendettas, discloses no malice. Even the admirals and generals, who are the victims of his analysis, are not pursued too far. Mr. Asquith, Mr. Lloyd George, Mr. Balfour, Mr. Bonar Law, Sir Edward Carson—he speaks them all fair and friendly in recognition of their several qualities, not striking down those who did service because they have joints in their armour. Mr. Churchill writes better than any politician since Disraeli. The book, whether its bias is right or wrong, will increase his reputation.

Mr. Churchill's principal thesis amounts to the contention that, broadly speaking, in each country the professional soldiers, the "brass-hats," were, on the great questions of military policy, generally wrong—wrong on the weight of the argument beforehand and wrong on the weight of the evidence afterwards—whilst the professional politicians, the "frocks," as Sir Henry Wilson called them (a bit of a "frock" himself), were generally right. This is a question upon which at the time it was impossible for an outside observer to form a judgement, since, whilst it appeared to be the case that both sides committed cardinal errors at each turning-point of the war, no one could divide the responsibility between the Cabinets and the General Staffs. In England, popular opinion rallied on the whole to the generals—more picturesque, much more glorious figures than our old knock-about friends the "frocks," and enjoying the enormous advantage of never having to explain themselves in public. Mr. Churchill sets himself to redress this balance, to convince us, in the light of the full disclosures now available from every side, that wisdom lay on the whole with Asquith, Lloyd George, and himself, with Briand, Painlevé, and Clemenceau, with Bethmann-Hollweg and even the Crown Prince, and that it was Haig and Robertson, Joffre and Nivelle, Falkenhayn and Ludendorff who jeopardised or lost the war.

Let me try to summarise Mr. Churchill's indictment of the General Staffs. Each side signally lacked a Cunctator Maximus. No Fabius arose to wait, to withdraw, to entice. The "brass-hats" were always in a hurry, hurrying to disclose their possession of new weapons of offence—the German poison-gas, the German U-boats, the British tanks—before they had accumulated enough of them to produce a decisive effect; hurrying to the useless slaughter of their dreadful "pushes." The strategic surrender, the deliberate withdrawal, the attempt to lure the enemy into a pocket where he could be taken in flank, all such expedients of the higher imagination of warfare, were scarcely attempted. Mangin's counter-stroke under the direction of Foch in July 1918, which both the French and British Staffs were inclined to deprecate and distrust, was one of the few such efforts. The ideas of the Staffs were from beginning to end elementary in the extreme—in attack, to find out the enemy in his strongest place and hurl yourself on him; in defence, to die heroically in the first ditch. There were only two important exceptions to this rule—the withdrawal of the Germans to the Hindenburg line in 1917, and the unchanging demeanour of Sir John Jellicoe. Mr. Churchill's fascinating analysis of the Battle of Jutland seems to the layman to show that Jellicoe missed his chances—chances which he ought to have taken. But Jellicoe, carrying a greater burden of risk and responsibility than any other single individual, the only man on either side, as Mr. Churchill admits, who could have lost the war in an afternoon, does stand out as the one triumphant Cunctator who, though he may have missed chances, carried through from start to finish without a single disastrous mistake. I do not think, even in the light of some incisive criticisms which Mr. Churchill is able to make, that one would have wished to see any other personality, which the war threw up in any country, in charge of the North Sea.

Mr. Churchill's next point concerns the narrow geographical vision of the General Staffs, their inability on both sides to throw out wide-ranging glances of strategic and political imagination over the whole potential field of hostilities. The armies were drawn to one another like magnets. The soldiers were always busy discerning where the enemy was strongest and then demanding equal or greater forces to counter him, never testing where he was weakest and thrusting there. This

is an old controversy upon which we have long known where
Mr. Churchill stood, and Mr. Lloyd George also. I do not
know that this book adds much directly to their case, but Mr.
Churchill's third point, which I come to later, does confirm, I
think, the potential value of the restless visions of the politicians as hints towards victory, as against the dogged dullness
of the Staffs. Mr. Churchill holds that the Germans, especially
Falkenhayn, were at least as much at fault in this respect as
we were. The Generals on both sides were equally confirmed
"Westerners," and supported one another, by their disposi-
tions, against their respective Governments at home.

Akin to this narrow geographical and political outlook was
the narrow scientific vision of the professional soldiers, their
extraordinary slowness to take up with new mechanical ideas,
as illustrated by the history of the tanks, which our Staff dep-
recated in their inception and never demanded from the Ministry of Munitions in adequate quantity, even after they had
become enthusiastic of their results, and which Ludendorff
never imitated on a serious scale, even after their existence had
been prematurely discovered to him. The overdoing of the
artillery and the maintenance of cavalry, which even in 1918
occupied nearly the same numbers of British personnel as
the machine guns and nearly twice those of the tanks, are
further examples of inelasticity of mind, as compared with the
alternative policy, never adopted, except by Mr. Churchill himself in 1918 with a view to the unfought campaign of 1919, of
an immense concentration of man-power on aeroplanes, machine guns, tanks, and gas.

The third point, which probably constitutes the most novel
and interesting part of Mr. Churchill's book, concerns the
actual value, as judged by the results now fully known from
the records of both sides, of the great offensive on the Western
Front. It is here that there was the sharpest and most continuing divergence of opinion between the professional politicians
and the professional soldiers. Apart from a temporary conversion of Mr. Lloyd George to the Staff view in 1917, the former
were ever of the opinion that the soldiers were underestimat-
ing the opportunities of defence and overestimating the poten-

tial gains of an offensive, and that no decision would ever be reached by assaulting the enemy in his fortified positions on the Western Front. The influence of the War Cabinet was almost invariably cast against the "pushes" of 1915, 1916, and 1917. Since the successive Cabinets expected little from these appalling offensives, there was nothing to mitigate the effect on their minds of the cruel and useless losses. By the end of 1917 a situation was actually reached in which Mr. Lloyd George was preventing available troops from being sent across the Channel which were certainly required in reserve there, because he could not trust his power to prevent Sir Douglas Haig from sending them to the massacre once they were in France. "But for the horror which Passchendaele inspired in the minds of the Prime Minister and the War Cabinet," Mr. Churchill writes, "Haig would no doubt have been supplied with very much larger reinforcements." Beginning with Mr. Asquith's prolonged and tenacious opposition to conscription down to this episode in the winter of 1917, Mr. Churchill's evidence goes to show that it was the politicians who had the soft hearts, but also that it was they on the whole who, on military grounds, were right.

The General Staffs were ready to admit after each offensive that the results were disappointing, but they were apt to console themselves with the consideration of the great losses inflicted on the enemy and on some satisfactory progress towards the objective of attrition. Mr. Churchill claims that he distrusted these conclusions at the time, and that the figures of casualties now available from both sides show that the result of almost every offensive was to leave the attacking side relatively weaker in man-power than it was before. Sir Frederick Maurice, in a letter to *The Times,* has disputed this interpretation of the statistics. But even if Mr. Churchill has pushed his case too far, he seems on the whole to have established it. In particular it was Ludendorff's apparently successful offensive of 1918 which really prepared the way for, and indeed rendered inevitable, the final German collapse.

Nothing is more interesting in Mr. Churchill's book than his impressions of the prevailing types of the High Command on each side. "There was altogether lacking," he says, "that supreme combination of the King-Warrior-Statesman which is apparent in the persons of the great conquerors of history." Most of the great Commanders with the possible exception of Joffre, were undoubtedly men of outstanding ability in their profession, but they were prevailingly of the heavy blockhead type, men whose nerves were much stronger than their imaginations. Hindenburg was not the only wooden image. Joffre, Kitchener, Haig, Robertson, Ludendorff—they also might be commemorated in the same medium. They slept well, they ate well—*nothing* could upset them. As they could seldom explain themselves and preferred to depend on their "instincts," they could never be refuted. Mr. Churchill, quoting from a letter from Robertson to Haig in which the former proposes to stick to offensives in the West "more because my instinct prompts me to stick to it, than because of any good argument by which I can support it," comments: "These are terrible words when used to sustain the sacrifice of nearly four hundred thousand men." The type reached its furthest limit in Mr. Churchill's semi-comic portrait of Père Joffre. No doubt more highly strung men could not stand the wear and tear of High Command in modern warfare. They were necessarily eliminated in favour of those who, in Mr. Churchill's words, could preserve their sang-froid amid disastrous surprises "to an extent almost indistinguishable from insensibility." Moreover, the Commander-in-Chief may be almost the last person even to hear the truth. "The whole habit of mind of a military staff is based upon subordination of opinion." This meant that the lighter mind of the politician, surrounded by candid friends and watchful opponents, was indispensable to the right conclusions. The final defeat of Germany was in fact due to the supreme strength of her Great General Staff. If Germany's politicians had had the same influence as ours or France's or America's she could never have suffered a similar defeat. Her three cardinal errors, according to Mr. Churchill—the invasion of Belgium, the unrestricted use of U-boats, the offensive of March 1918—were all the peculiar and exclusive responsibility of the General Staff. Ludendorff was the final embodiment both of the influence of the General Staff and of its highest qualities—of that General Staff whose members

were bound together by the closest ties of professional comradeship and common doctrine. They were to the rest of the Army what the Jesuits in their greatest period had been to the Church of Rome. Their representatives at the side of every Commander and at Headquarters spoke a language and preserved confidences of their own. The German Generals of Corps and Armies, Army-Group Commanders, nay, Hindenburg himself, were treated by this confraternity, to an extent almost incredible, as figureheads, and frequently as nothing more.

It was this extraordinary confraternity which raised the German military might to monstrous dimensions, provoked and organised inhuman exertions, and yet, by the inevitable workings of its own essence, brought down upon itself the great defeat.

Mr. Churchill does not dissemble his own delight in the intense experiences of conducting warfare on the grand scale which those can enjoy who make the decisions. Nor, on the other hand, does he conceal its awfulness for those who provide the raw material of those delights. The bias of emphasis is on the grand decisions and high arguments. But, not the less for this reason, is his book, in its final impression on the reader, a tractate against war—more effective than the work of a pacifist could be, a demonstration from one who loves the game, not only of the imbecility of its aims and of its methods, but, more than this, that the imbecility is not an accidental quality of the particular players, but is inherent in its spirit and its rules.

March 1927.

MR. CHURCHILL ON THE PEACE

Mr. Churchill has finished his task—by far and away the greatest contribution to the history of the war, the only one which combines the gifts of the historian and born writer with the profound experiences and direct knowledge of one of the prime movers of events. This last volume[2] is not so good, I think, as the two which preceded it—a falling away which is probably one more of the disappointing consequences of the author's latest bout of office. For authorship is a whole-time job; and so is the Chancellorship of the Exchequer. But it is much better than those who have read the rather flat, rhetorical extracts published by *The Times* will have surmised. For these lose, as extracts do, the sweep and impression of the whole.

Mr. Churchill records in his preface what a number of important events in which he was personally concerned had utterly passed from his mind. This, he adds, is probably an experience common to most of the principal actors—"one impression effaced another." So with anyone who lived in the administrative flux. For me the quality of the Midland Railway breakfast marmalade served up in the Hotel Majestic has stuck faster than anything else; I know *exactly* what that experience was like. It is only for those who lived for months in the trenches or suffered some repetitive military routine, where one impression reinforced another, that the war can in memory be lived over again. Yet Mr. Churchill has contrived to convey a contemporary impression of motives and atmosphere—though, curiously, least of all by the contemporary documents he quotes, which the reader will instinctively skip—such as posterity would never be able to reconstruct for itself. The book contains, too, some singularly moving passages, where the emotions of the moment had left behind them a permanent furrow, of which I would particularly instance the accounts of the British Demobilisation and of the Irish Treaty. Moreover, it serves to bring back to us with overwhelming effect what of everything we are most disposed to forget—the violence, bloodshed, and tumult of the *post*-war years, the "Aftermath" of Mr. Churchill's title.

The book is mainly made up of four distinct topics, of which the successive chapters are, rather distractingly, intermixed—the Peace Conference, the Russian Revolution, the Irish Rebellion, and the Greco-Turkish Imbroglio. Of these the account of the Russian business is—as one might expect—the least satisfactory. Mr. Churchill does not seek to defend unduly his own part in the fiascos of the Russian Civil Wars. But he fails to see—or at least to set—in perspective the bigness of the events in their due relations, or to disentangle the essential from casual episodes. He half admits the inevitable futility of the proceedings which he supported; he lets one see the wretched character and effete incompetence of the Russian Whites whom he would have so much liked to idealise ("It was not the want of material means, but of comradeship, will-power, and rugged steadfastness that lost the struggle"); and he quotes Foch, who firmly refused to have anything to do with the affair, as remarking "with much discernment" that "these armies of Koltchak and Denikin cannot last long be-cause they have no civil Governments behind them." But the Bolsheviks remain for him, in spite of his tribute to the great-ness of Lenin, nothing more than an imbecile atrocity. His imagination cannot see them as the Great Scavengers, and the officers of the Whites as better employed on the films. Yet can he believe that his fine peroration—"Russia, self-outcast, sharpens her bayonets in her Arctic night, and mechanically proclaims through self-starved lips her philosophy of hatred and death"—is really the whole of the truth?

Apart from Russia, Mr. Churchill appears, in a degree to which public opinion has done much less than justice, as an ardent and persistent advocate of the policy of appeasement—appeasement in Germany, in Ireland, in Turkey. As he wrote to Mr. Lloyd George in March 1920—"Since the Armistice my policy would have been, 'Peace with the German people, war on the Bolshevik tyranny.'" Throughout the Peace Conference such influence as he had was cast on the side of moderation.

His account of the Peace Conference itself is less personal in character than any other part of the book, for he was, indeed, but little directly concerned with it. He visited Paris once or twice, but was mainly in London preoccupied with other matters. It is, therefore, a general view which he presents, as it appeared to a member of the British Cabinet who was out-side the main stream of the negotiations. His attitude is to deplore—but to shrug his shoulders. There has been too much shrugging of the shoulders both at the time and since. He justifies his shrug on two grounds: firstly, because politicians are not only pusillanimous, but rightly so, their pusillanimity being merely a realisation of their actual impotence; and, secondly, because financial and economic mistakes work themselves out in due course, whereas frontiers, which were not so badly handled by the Conference, are the only long-period realities. One could say the same thing about the miseries of the war itself—they are all over now—and indeed about most things, for the consequences, even if they persist, are generally lost in the river of time; and the doctrine that statesmen must always act contrary to their convictions, when to do otherwise would lose them office, implies that they are less easily replaceable than is really the case. I believed then, and I believe now, that it was a situation where an investment in political courage would have been marvellously repaid in the end.

Mr. Churchill's account of the Conference lacks the intensity of feeling which would be natural to one who had been tormented on the spot. But it is, all the same, the best short handbook yet written to the general character of what really happened. There are one or two points in it worth picking out. Mr. Churchill does well to emphasise the prolongation of the blockade of Germany through the first half of 1919 as a question of first-rate importance. The remarkable history of the successive negotiations for the renewal of the Armistice and the provisioning of Germany has never yet been printed.[3] He recognises their importance, but his account of them (pages 66, 67) is by no means accurate, and indicates that he was not conversant with, or has forgotten, the details. It was not the "officials" who were to blame. If any individual is to be picked out as chiefly responsible for prolonging the dreadful privations of Central Europe, it must certainly be the celebrated Monsieur Klotz. I think he is right in saying that Mr. Lloyd George was quite genuine about hanging the Kaiser and continued to harbour such sentiments long after others had cooled off; but that he never, at any time, entertained an illusion about Reparations or made any statement which did not, if read carefully, include a saving clause.

It is well, too, that he gives the world a fuller account than has been published before of the meeting of the British Empire Delegation convened by Mr. Lloyd George in Paris on June 1, 1919, to consider the German reply to the draft Treaty of Peace. The Prime Minister had called this meeting "to strengthen himself in his efforts to obtain a mitigation of the peace terms." Mr. Churchill himself circulated a memorandum, endorsed by the Chief of the Imperial General Staff, urging that we should, at least, meet the Germans half-way. These views were accepted by practically the whole of the Delegation and of the Cabinet, including Mr. Austen Chamberlain, who was then Chancellor of the Exchequer, Lord Birkenhead, Lord Milner, and Mr. Balfour. The meeting resolved that many important concessions should be made, and added a rider authorising the Prime Minister "to use the full weight of the entire British Empire even to the point of refusing the services of the British Army to advance into Germany, or the services of the British Navy to enforce the blockade of Germany." This was the second time that Mr. Lloyd George had made a genuine, but abortive, effort for a "good" Peace. But it was not to be. The plebiscite for Upper Silesia was obtained as an almost solitary concession. For the rest, it was President Wilson—as I have described in *The Economic Consequences of the Peace*—who at this stage was "not taking any."

Mr. Churchill has a good deal to say about President Wilson. He has had the advantage not only of his own memories, but of Colonel House's latest volumes, which have cast on the scene so bright a side-light. As the evidence accumulates, the impression is confirmed of a blind man, unbelievably out of touch with the realities of things, filled with all the wrong suspicions. But peace to his spirit. Mr. Churchill's summing up is just:

The influence of mighty, detached, and well-meaning America upon the European settlement was a precious agency of hope. It was largely squandered in sterile conflicts and half-instructed and half-pursued interferences. If President Wilson had set himself from the beginning to make common cause with Lloyd George and Clemenceau, the whole force of these three great men, the heads of the dominant nations, might have played with plenary and beneficent power over the wide scene of European tragedy. He consumed his own strength and theirs in conflict in which he was always worsted. He gained as an antagonist and corrector results which were pitifully poor compared to those which would have rewarded comradeship. He might have made everything swift and easy. He made everything slower and more difficult. He might have carried a settlement at the time when leadership was strong. He acquiesced in second-rate solutions when the phase of exhaustion and dispersion had supervened.

However, as Captain he went down with his ship.

The chronicle is finished. With what feelings does one lay down Mr. Churchill's two-thousandth page? Gratitude to one who can write with so much eloquence and feeling of things which are part of the lives of all of us of the war generation, but which he saw and knew much closer and clearer. Admiration for his energies of mind and his intense absorption of intellectual interest and elemental emotion in what is for the moment the matter in hand—which is his best quality. A little envy, perhaps, for his undoubting conviction that frontiers, races, patriotisms, even wars if need be, are ultimate verities for mankind, which lends for him a kind of dignity and even nobility to events, which for others are only a nightmare interlude, something to be permanently avoided.

March 1929.

MR. LLOYD GEORGE

A FRAGMENT

I wrote the preceding description of the Council of Four in the summer of 1919 immediately after my resignation as Treasury representative at the Peace Conference. Friends, to whom I showed it for criticism, pressed me to add a further passage concerning Mr. Lloyd George, and in an attempt to satisfy them I wrote what here follows. But I was not content with it, and I did not print it in *The Economic Consequences of the Peace,* where the chapter on "The Conference" appeared as it was originally written with no addendum. I was also influenced by a certain compunction. I had been very close to Mr. Lloyd George at certain phases of the Conference, and I felt at bottom that this, like almost everything else that one could say about him, was only partial. I did not like to print in the heat of the moment what seemed to me, even in the heat of the moment, to be incomplete.

I feel some compunction still. But nearly fourteen years have passed by. These matters belong now to history. It is easier to explain than it was then, that this is an aspect, a thing seen but not the whole picture and to offer it as a record of how one, who saw the process at close quarters, sincerely felt at the time.

I should prefer to end this chapter here. But the reader may ask, What part in the result did the British Prime Minister play? What share had England in the final responsibility? The answer to the second question is not clear-cut. And as to the first, who shall paint the chameleon, who can tether a broomstick? The character of Lloyd George is not yet rendered, and I do not aspire to the task.

The selfish, or, if you like, the legitimate interests of England did not, as it happened, conflict with the Fourteen Points as vitally as did those of France. The destruction of the fleet, the expropriation of the marine, the surrender of the colonies, the suzerainty of Mesopotamia—there was not much here for the President to strain at, even in the light of his professions, especially as England, whose diplomatic moderation as always was not hampered by the logical intransigency of the French mind, was ready to concede in point of form whatever might be asked. England did not desire the German fleet for herself, and its destruction was a phase of Disarmament. The expropriation of the marine was a legitimate compensation, specifically provided for in the Pre-Armistice conditions, for the lawless campaign of submarines which had been the express occasion of America's entering the war. Over the colonies and Mesopotamia England demanded no exclusive sovereignty, and they were covered by the Doctrine of Mandates under the League of Nations.

Thus when the British Delegation left for Paris there seemed no insuperable obstacles to an almost complete understanding between the British and the American negotiators. There were only two clouds on the horizon—the so-called Freedom of the Seas and the Prime Minister's election pledges on the Indemnity. The first, to the general surprise, was never raised by the President, a silence which, presumably, was the price he deemed it judicious to pay for British co-operation on other more vital issues; the second was more important.

The co-operation, which was thus rendered possible, was largely realised in practice. The individual members of the British and American delegations were united by bonds of fraternal feeling and mutual respect, and constantly worked together and stood together for a policy of honest dealing and broad-minded humanity. And the Prime Minister, too, soon established himself as the President's friend and powerful ally against the Latins' alleged rapacity or lack of international idealism. Why then did not the joint forces of these two powerful and enlightened autocrats give us the Good Peace?

The answer is to be sought more in those intimate workings of the heart and character which make the tragedies and comedies of the domestic hearthrug than in the supposed ambitions of empires or philosophies of statesmen. The President, the Tiger, and the Welsh witch were shut up in a room together for six months and the Treaty was what came out. Yes, the Welsh *witch*—for the British Prime Minister contributed the female element to this triangular intrigue. I have called Mr. Wilson a nonconformist clergyman. Let the reader figure Mr. Lloyd George as a *femme fatale*. An old man of the world, a *femme fatale,* and a nonconformist clergyman—these are the characters of our drama. Even though the lady was very religious at times, the Fourteen Commandments could hardly expect to emerge perfectly intact.

I must try to silhouette the broomstick as it sped through the twilit air of Paris.

Mr. Lloyd George's devotion to duty at the Paris Conference was an example to all servants of the public. He took no relaxation, enjoyed no pleasures, had no life and no occupation save that of Prime Minister and England's spokesman. His labours were immense and he spent his vast stores of spirit and of energy without stint on the formidable task he had put his hand to. His advocacy of the League of Nations was sincere; his support of a fair application of the principle of Self-Determination to Germany's eastern frontiers was disinterested. He had no wish to impose a Carthaginian Peace; the crushing of Germany was no part of his purpose. His hatred of war is real, and the strain of pacifism and radical idealism, which governed him during the Boer War, is a genuine part of his composition. He would have defended a Good Peace before the House of Commons with more heart than he did that which he actually brought back to them.

But in such a test of character and method as Paris provided, the Prime Minister's naturally good instincts, his industry, his inexhaustible nervous vitality were not serviceable. In that furnace other qualities were called for—a policy deeply grounded in permanent principle, tenacity, fierce indignation, honesty, loyal leadership. If Mr. Lloyd George had no good qualities, no charms, no fascinations, he would not be dangerous. If he were not a syren, we need not fear the whirlpools.

But it is not appropriate to apply to him the ordinary standards. How can I convey to the reader, who does not know him, any just impression of this extraordinary figure of our time, this syren, this goat-footed bard, this half-human visitor to our age from the hag-ridden magic and enchanted woods of Celtic antiquity? One catches in his company that flavour of final purposelessness, inner irresponsibility, existence outside or away from our Saxon good and evil, mixed with cunning, remorselessness, love of power, that lend fascination, enthralment, and terror to the fair-seeming magicians of North European folklore. Prince Wilson sailing out from the West in his barque *George Washington* sets foot in the enchanted castle of Paris to free from chains and oppression and an ancient curse the maid Europe, of eternal youth and beauty, his mother and his bride in one. There in the castle is the King with yellow parchment face, a million years old, and with him an enchantress with a harp singing the Prince's own words to a magical tune. If only the Prince could cast off the paralysis which creeps on him and, crying to heaven, could make the Sign of the Cross, with a sound of thunder and crashing glass the castle would dissolve, the magicians vanish, and Europe leap to his arms. But in this fairy-tale the forces of the half-world win and the soul of Man is subordinated to the spirits of the earth.

Lloyd George is rooted in nothing; he is void and without content; he lives and feeds on his immediate surroundings; he is an instrument and a player at the same time which plays on the company and is played on by them too; he is a prism, as I have heard him described, which collects light and distorts it and is most brilliant if the light comes from many quarters at once; a vampire and a medium in one.

Whether by chance or by design, the principal British war aims (with the exception of the Indemnity, if this was one of them) were dealt with in the earliest stages of the Conference. Clemenceau was criticised at the time for his tardiness in securing the primary demands of France. But events proved him to be right in not forcing the pace. The French demands, as I have pointed out, were much more controversial than those of the British; and it was essential to get the British well embroiled in a Peace of selfish interests before putting the professions of the Conference to a severer test. The British demands afforded an excellent *hors d'œuvre* to accustom the delicate palate of the President to the stronger flavours which were to come. This order of procedure laid the British Prime Minister open to the charge, whenever he seemed too critical of French demands, that, having first secured every conceivable thing that he wanted himself, he was now ready with characteristic treachery to abandon his undertakings to his French comrades. In the atmosphere of Paris this seemed a much more potent taunt than it really was. But it gained its real strength, in its influence on the Prime Minister, from three special attendant circumstances. In two respects the Prime Minister found himself unavoidably and inextricably on Clemenceau's side—in the matters of the Indemnity and of the Secret Treaties. If the President's morale was maintained intact, Mr. Lloyd George could not hope to get his way on these issues; he was, therefore, almost equally interested with Clemenceau in gradually breaking down this morale. But, besides, he had Lord Northcliffe and the British Jingoes on his heels, and complaints in the French Press were certain to find their echo in a certain section of the British also.

If, therefore, he were to take his stand firmly and effectively on the side of the President, there was needed an act of courage and faith which could only be based on fundamental beliefs and principles. But Mr. Lloyd George has none such, and political considerations pointed to a middle path.

Precisely, therefore, as the President had found himself pushed along the path of compromise, so also did the Prime Minister, though for very different reasons. But while the President failed because he was very bad at the game of compromise, the Prime Minister trod the way of ill-doing because he was far too good at it.

The reader will thus apprehend how Mr. Lloyd George came

to occupy an ostensibly middle position, and how it became his rôle to explain the President to Clemenceau and Clemenceau to the President and to seduce everybody all round. He was only too well fitted for the task, but much better fitted for dealing with the President than with Clemenceau. Clemenceau was much too cynical, much too experienced, and much too well educated to be taken in, at his age, by the fascinations of the lady from Wales. But for the President it was a wonderful, almost delightful, experience to be taken in hand by such an expert. Mr. Lloyd George had soon established himself as the President's only real friend. The President's very masculine characteristics fell a complete victim to the feminine entice-ments, sharpness, quickness, sympathy of the Prime Minister.

We have Mr. Lloyd George, therefore, in his middle position, but exercising more sway over the President than over Clemen-ceau. Now let the reader's mind recur to the metaphors. Let him remember the Prime Minister's incurable love of a deal; his readiness to surrender the substance for the shadow; his intense desire, as the months dragged on, to get a conclusion and be back to England again. What wonder that in the even-tual settlement the real victor was Clemenceau.

Even so, close observers never regarded it as impossible right up to the conclusion of the affair that the Prime Minister's better instincts and truer judgement might yet prevail—he knew in his heart that this Peace would disgrace him and that it might ruin Europe. But he had dug a pit for himself deeper than even he could leap out of; he was caught in his own toils, defeated by his own methods. Besides, it is a character-istic of his inner being, of his kinship with the trolls and the soulless simulacra of the earth, that at the great crises of his fortunes it is the lower instincts of the hour that conquer.

These were the personalities of Paris—I forbear to mention other nations or lesser men: Clemenceau, aesthetically the no-blest; the President, morally the most admirable; Lloyd George, intellectually the subtlest. Out of their disparities and weak-nesses the Treaty was born, child of the least worthy attributes of each of its parents, without nobility, without morality, with-out intellect.

MR. BONAR LAW

Mr. Bonar Law's breakdown[1] is a great misfortune, not less to his political opponents than to his own supporters. We shall not easily find another leader of the Conservative Party who is so *unprejudiced*. Mr. Bonar Law has been, before everything, a party man, deeply concerned for his party, obedient to its instincts, and at each crisis the nominee of its machine. On two crucial questions, Tariff Reform and the support of Ulster, he adopted with vehemence the extreme party view. Yet, in truth, he was almost devoid of Conservative principles. This Presbyterian from Canada has no imaginative reverence for the traditions and symbols of the past, no special care for vested interests, no attachment whatever to the Upper Classes, the City, the Army, or the Church. He is prepared to consider each question on its merits, and his candid acknowledgement of the case for a Capital Levy was a striking example of an habitual state of mind.

Mr. Bonar Law's Conservatism was not based on dogma, or prejudice, or a passion to preserve certain sides of English life. It proceeded from caution, scepticism, lack of faith, a distrust of any intellectual process which proceeded more than one or two steps ahead, or any emotional enthusiasm which grasped at an intangible object, and an extreme respect for all kinds of *Success*.

Mr. Bonar Law's great skill in controversy, both in private conversation and in public debate, was due not only to the acuteness of his mind and his retentive memory which have impressed all observers, but also to his practice of limiting the argument to the pieces, so to speak, actually on the board and to the two or three moves ahead which could be definitely foreseen. (Mr. Bonar Law avowedly carried his well-known passion for the technique of chess into the problems of politics; and it is natural to use chess metaphors to describe the workings of his mind.) Mr. Bonar Law was difficult to answer in debate because he nearly always gave the perfectly sensible reply, on the assumption that the pieces visible on the board constituted the whole premises of the argument, that any attempt to look far ahead was too hypothetical and difficult to be worth while, and that one was playing the game in question *in vacuo*, with no ulterior purpose except to make the right move in that particular game. This method of his gained him perhaps more credit for candour and sincerity, as compared with other people, than he really deserved. He has been at times just as sly as other politicians; not, as he once pointed out, quite so simple as he looks. But it has been much easier for him to express, on any given occasion, more or less the whole contents of his mind, and very nearly his *real* reasons without reserve or ulterior purpose, than for others, some of whose reasons were too remote to be easily expressed or were not solely connected with the particular matter in hand, or could not be conveniently introduced on that occasion. An opponent who was trying to look some considerable way ahead, or saw the immediate position in the vague outlines of its relation to the situation as a whole, or had ultimate ideals which it would be priggish to mention too often, would always find himself at a great disadvantage in arguing with Mr. Bonar Law. His quietness and sweet reasonableness and patient attention to the more tangible parts of what his opponent had just said would bring into strong relief anything hysterical or overdone in the opposition attitude.

No mind, amongst those who waged war for this country, was swifter on the surface of things than his; there was no one

who could be briefed quicker than he and put *au courant* with
the facts of the case in those hurried moments which a Civil
Servant gets with his chief before a Conference; and no one
who could remember so much from a previous acquaintance
with the question. But this swiftness of apprehension, not only
of facts and arguments but also of persons and their qualities,
even in combination with his objective, chessplaying mind, did
not save him from a quite decided anti-intellectualist bias.
Those who were present at Trinity Commem. some four years
ago will remember a charming little speech given to the undergraduates after dinner, in which he dismissed with sweet-tem-
pered cynicism everything a University stands for. Mr. Bonar
Law has liked to think of himself as a plain business man,
who could have made a lot of money if he had chosen to, with
a good judgement of markets rather than of long-period trends,
right on the short swing, handling wars and empires and revo-
lutions with the coolness and limited purpose of a first-class
captain of industry. This distrust of intellectualist probings into
unrealised possibilities leads him to combine great caution and
pessimism about the chances of the immediate situation with
considerable recklessness about what may happen eventually
—a characteristic running through his policy both during and
since the war. He would hold, for example, that it was an
almost hopeless proposition to prevent France from going into
the Ruhr, but that the consequences of her doing so, though
very bad, might not be quite so bad as some people anticipate.
This quality prevented him sometimes from being as good a
negotiator as might have been expected. He was not held back
from yielding a little too much either by cheerful optimism
about the prospects of pulling off a better bargain or by getting
frightened about the remoter consequences of giving way. Perhaps, after all, he might not have made a very successful business man—too pessimistic to snatch present profits and too
shortsighted to avoid future catastrophe.

Mr. Bonar Law's inordinate respect for Success is noteworthy. He is capable of respecting even an intellectualist who
turns out right. He admires self-made millionaires. He is not
easily shocked by the methods employed by others to attain

success. The great admiration in which he formerly held Mr. Lloyd George was largely based on the latter's success, and diminished proportionately when the success fell off.

Modest, gentle, unselfish ways have won for him affection from all who have worked near him. But the feeling of the public is due, perhaps, to their instinctive apprehension of a larger, rarer thing about him than these simple qualities. They feel him to have been a great public servant, whose life of austerity and duty served them rather than himself. Many politicians are too much enthralled by the crash and glitter of the struggle, their hearts obviously warmed by the swell and pomp of authority, enjoying their positions and their careers, clinging to these sweet delights, and primarily pleasing themselves. These are the natural target of envy and detraction and a certain contempt. They have their reward already and need no gratitude. But the public have liked to see a Prime Minister not enjoying his lot unduly. We have preferred to be governed by the sad smile of one who adopts towards the greatest office in the State the attitude that whilst, of course, it is nice to be Prime Minister, it is no great thing to covet, and who feels in office, and not merely afterwards, the vanity of things.

May 1923

LORD OXFORD

Those who only knew Lord Oxford in his later life must find it hard to credit either the appearance or the reputation which are reported to have been his thirty or more years ago. The ability and the reticence were there to be recognised, but the somewhat tight features, the alleged coldness of the aspiring lawyer from Balliol, were entirely transformed in the noble Roman of the war and post-war years, who looked the part of Prime Minister as no one has since Mr. Gladstone. His massive countenance and aspect of venerable strength were, in these later days, easily perceived to mask neither coldness nor egoism, but to clothe with an appropriate form a warm and tender heart easily touched to emotion, and a personal reserve which did not ask or claim anything for himself.

Lord Oxford possessed most of the needed gifts of a great statesman except ruthlessness towards others and insensitiveness for himself. One wonders whether in the conditions of the modern age a man so sensitive as he was will ever again be robust enough to expose himself to the outrages of public life. Lord Oxford protected his sensitiveness by silence, by totally refraining from retort or from complaint. He absolutely rejected the aid or the opportunities of the venal Press. He could be the leader of a Nation or of a Party; he would hasten to protect a friend or a colleague; but he disdained to protect himself to a degree which was scarcely compatible with the actual conditions of contemporary life. Yet it was probably this course of behaviour, this element of character, which, increasingly with years, moulded for him the aspect of dignity, the air of sweetness and calm, the gentle ruggedness of countenance, which those who knew him after he had finally left office will carry in their memories as characteristically his. He had, besides, a keen sense of the pleasure of simple things, and it was this capacity, perhaps, which helped him to face political disappointments, when they came, without self-pity.

It is natural to dwell at this moment on the qualities which made him lovable and were also those which events brought most to notice in the closing phase of his career—the phase after he had ceased to be Prime Minister, the last twelve years, which have contributed little or nothing to his constructive services to the State, yet have greatly added to the world's knowledge and appreciation of his own personality. But it was, of course, his powers of intellect and of rapid industry which carried him to great offices of State. Lord Oxford's intellect combined rapidity of apprehension, lucidity, critical sharpness, a copious and accurate memory, taste and discrimination, freedom both from prejudices and from illusion, with an absence of originality and creative power; and I am not sure that this want of originality was not one of the most necessary of the ingredients to produce the successful combination. His mind was built for the purpose of dealing with the given facts of the outside world; it was a mill or a machine, not a mine or a springing field. But this deficiency conserved the strength of his judgement. Lord Oxford had no intellectual fancies to lead him astray, no balloons of his own making to lift his feet off the ground. It was his business to hear and to judge; and the positions he occupied—Home Secretary, Chancellor of the Exchequer, Prime Minister—are positions best occupied, not by one ingenious to invent and to build, but by one whose business it is to hear and to judge. For this business there has been no man in this century by any means his equal. Few words and little time were necessary for him to apprehend perfectly the purport of what he was being told; and he would

bring his knowledge and experience to bear on it with an entire freedom from bias and *parti pris.*

His temperament was naturally conservative. With a little
stupidity and a few prejudices dashed in he would have been
Conservative in the political sense also. As it was, he was the
perfect Whig for carrying into execution those Radical projects
of his generation which were well judged. It is remarkable,
looking back on the Liberal legislation of the eight years before
the war, to see how abundant it was, yet how well chosen,
and how completely on the whole it has stood the test of events.
To Lord Oxford we owe, not the invention of any part of
that programme, but the wisdom of its selection and execution.
In the controversy as to the conduct of the war, which culminated in the downfall of the first Coalition Government at
the end of 1916, I believed then, and I believe now, that he
was largely in the right.

Few men can have accomplished in their lives more hard
work than Lord Oxford. But he worked, as a Prime Minister
must if he is to survive, with great economy of effort. He
could deal with printed and written matter with the rapidity
of a scholar. He never succumbed to the modern curse of
shorthand and the verbosity it breeds. Lord Oxford belonged
to the lineage of great men, which will, I pray, never die out,
who can take up a pen and do what is necessary in short
notes written in their own hand. Lord Oxford's fault, in relation to his work, lay, perhaps, in his willingness to relax his
attention from it when it was put by, not to carry it about
with him in his mind and on his tongue when the official
day's work was done. Certainly this was a source of strength
sometimes, but also, on occasion, of weakness. In combination
with his reserve, which made it difficult to broach with him an
awkward topic—in part the necessary equipment of any leading
statesman to keep the impertinent at bay, but practised by him
in an unusual degree—it would sometimes cut him off from
full knowledge of what was brewing in the political cauldron.
These habits of mind were also capable of facilitating an eva-
sion, especially of a personal issue. The discipline and the harsh
severity towards faithful friends and less faithful rivals alike

which the management of a Cabinet must needs entail were to him extraordinarily distasteful.

Lord Oxford was, therefore, at his best and at his happiest when there were great issues afoot which were entirely political and not at all personal; when he had behind him a body of supporters and lieutenants united at heart and in intention, and only differing in the degrees of their impulsiveness. On such occasions he would be able to use, and direct into the courses of wisdom, all that is most valuable in a great political party. The fight for Free Trade, the fight for the Parliament Act, the opening year of the War were opportunities of this kind, when Mr. Asquith could stand up as a leader with the full powers of his intellect and composure of spirit.

It is to be recorded of Lord Oxford that he loved learning and studious ways and the things which a University stands for. He was a real reader; he could handle books in a library with love. The classical and literary pursuits, his aptitude for which had gained him his first step on the ladder, were not discarded when they had ceased to be useful. I think that he liked these things, just as he liked great constitutional and political controversies, all the better because they were not too much mixed with the soiled clay of personal issues.

Those who knew Lord Oxford intimately cannot think of him except in the environment of a unique family. He was the solid core round which that brilliant circle revolved—the centre of the gayest and brightest world, the widest-flung yet the simplest hospitality of modern England. With an incomparable hostess opposite him, with wit and abundance, indiscretion and all that was most rash and bold flying round him, Lord Oxford would love to appear the dullest amidst so much light, to rest himself, and to enjoy the flow of reason and of unreason, stroking his chin, shrugging his shoulders, a wise and tolerant umpire.

February 1928.

EDWIN MONTAGU

Most of the newspaper accounts which I have read do less
than justice to the remarkable personality of Edwin Montagu.
He was one of those who suffer violent fluctuations of mood,
quickly passing from reckless courage and self-assertion to
abject panic and dejection—always dramatising life and his
part in it, and seeing himself and his own instincts either in
the most favourable or in the most unfavourable light, but
seldom with a calm and steady view. Thus it was easy for the
spiteful to convict him out of his own mouth, and to belittle
his name by remembering him only when his face was turned
towards the earth. At one moment he would be Emperor of
the East riding upon an elephant, clothed in rhetoric and
glory, but at the next a beggar in the dust of the road, crying for
alms but murmuring under his breath cynical and outrageous
wit which pricked into dustier dust the rhetoric and the glory.

That he was an Oriental, equipped, nevertheless, with the
intellectual technique and atmosphere of the West, drew him
naturally to the political problems of India, and allowed an
instinctive, mutual sympathy between him and its peoples. But
he was interested in all political problems and not least in the
personal side of politics and was most intensely a politician.
Almost everything else bored him. Some memoir-writers have
suggested that he was really a scientist, because with Nature

189

he could sometimes find escape from the footlights. Others, judging from his parentage and from his entering the City in the last two years of his life, make out that he was, naturally, a financier. This also is far from the truth. I saw him intimately in the Treasury and in the financial negotiations of the Peace Conference, and, whilst his general judgement was good, I do not think that he cared, or had great aptitude, for the problems of pure finance. Nor—though he loved money for what it could buy—was he interested in the details of money-making.

Mr. Lloyd George was, of course, the undoing of his political career—as, indeed, Montagu always said that he would be. He could not keep away from that bright candle. But he knew, poor moth, that he would burn his wings. It was from his tongue that I, and many others, have heard the most brilliant, true, and witty descriptions of that (in his prime) undescriba-ble. But whilst, behind the scenes, Montagu's tongue was mas-ter, his weaknesses made him, in action, the natural tool and victim; for, of all men, he was one of the easiest to use and throw on one side. It used to be alleged that a certain very Noble Lord had two footmen, of whom one was lame and the other swift of foot, so that letters of resignation carried by the one could be intercepted by the other before their fatal delivery at No. 10. Edwin Montagu's letters were not intercepted; but the subtle intelligencer of human weakness, who opened them, knew that by then the hot fit was over and the cold was blowing strong. They could be ignored or used against the writer—at choice.

I never knew a male person of big mind like his who was more addicted to gossip than Edwin Montagu. Perhaps this was the chief reason why he could not bear to be out of things. He was an inveterate gossip in the servants' hall of secretaries and officials. It was his delight to debate, at the Cabinet, affairs of State, and then to come out and deliver, to a little group, a brilliant and exposing parody, aided by mimicry, of what each of the great ones, himself included, had said. But he loved it better when he could push gossip over into intimacy. He never went for long without an intense desire to unbosom himself, even to exhibit himself, and to squeeze out of his confidant a drop of—perhaps reluctant—affection. And then again he would be silent and reserved beyond bearing, sitting stonily with his great hand across his mouth and a staring monocle.

November 1924.

Part III: Two Memoirs

INTRODUCTION

The two memoirs printed here were written by the late Lord Keynes to read to a small audience of old and intimate friends, of whom I was one. Over a long period, we met together two or three times a year, dined at a restaurant, and after dinner revived our memories of the past by listening to one, or more often two, memoirs read aloud by different members of our company.

In later years such meetings were frequently held in Lord Keynes' house—once, I remember, we met on a summer evening at Tilton under the South Downs. Very frequently we met at No. 46 Gordon Square.

Lydia would welcome us and usher us upstairs to the great room which Maynard had had constructed by throwing the drawing-rooms of Nos. 46 and 47 into one. Maynard would lie, half-reclining on a couch, to rest his heart, with a reading-lamp beside him and his head in shadow, joining in sometimes with his own memories of the events or persons spoken of by whoever was reading.

The first of these memoirs needs no introduction—the subject is of great historical importance. It provides an extremely clear analysis of the characters and the lives of the men responsible for continuing the food-blockade of Germany in 1919 for months after the signing of the Armistice. That policy appeared politically unwise to the best judges at the time; their view was afterwards confirmed by the fact that the continuance of the blockade was most effectively exploited by Hitler, and most useful to him in building up his position by propaganda against the Treaty and the Treatymakers of Versailles.

Both memoirs are printed here as they were written, with the allusions and personal jokes which were immediately understood by the circle to which they were read. I have not laboured to explain them all, but I have added a list of those names which were not mentioned in full, in order to prevent misunderstandings, or obscurities. But the reader of this book is asked to remember that he is privileged. He is hearing what was written only for the ears of those to whom the writer could speak entirely without reserve, and who would never mistake his meaning. Truth and wit are felt by many to be rather shocking virtues which should appear in public only if they are decently veiled. There are no veils here, but then these memoirs were not written for publication, and the reason they are published now is not because of their great interest or because of their literary merit—though they are, I think, among the best things that Lord Keynes ever wrote; they are published by his Executors in order to carry out an express desire in his will that these papers, and these alone of his unpublished writings, should be printed.

DAVID GARNETT.

DR. MELCHIOR [1]

I

None of the officials in London who were connected with the
Peace Conference knew when it was going to start. This was
in accordance with the Prime Minister's usual method. There
must be plenty of officials to hang about in case he might need
them; but the real business of the Conference was to be done
by himself and the other two (or perhaps three) "getting together," and the less the officials knew of what was going on,
the freer his hands would be. On a certain date, therefore,
which would not be announced beforehand, the Prime Minister
would leave for Paris; but the proceedings would begin with
informal conferences between the Great Ones, and when the
officials would be wanted or what they were to do either eventually or in the meantime was quite uncertain.

This left them in a most awkward dilemma. An early departure for Paris probably meant that there would be nothing
whatever to occupy them when they got there, while there was a
great deal of business to complete in their usual offices in London. On the other hand most of those who had managed to
get appointed to the Conference Staff had made themselves very
important on the subject, and it would not do at all for the
Conference to begin without them. Besides, as everyone's position was quite undefined in relation to the others and to the

work, there was great danger that those on the spot might "get in" first. Lastly, the rooms in the Hotel Majestic were reputed to be of unequal excellence, and he who arrived last might fare worst.

In the face of these problems I decided to compromise by sending on my secretary, Geoffrey Fray, to snatch rooms, for which, however, he showed no great competence, and my chief of staff, Dudley Ward, to absorb the atmosphere, report the gossip, defend the prerogatives of the Treasury, and telegraph immediately in case of real danger, for all of which, as I knew, he would be wholly reliable.

When I eventually reached Paris early in January 1919, it was as I had expected, and no one yet knew what the Conference was doing or whether it had started. But the peculiar atmosphere and routine of the Majestic were already compounded and established, the typists drank their tea in the lounge, the dining-room diners had distinguished themselves from the restaurant diners, the security officers from Scotland Yard burnt such of the waste paper as the French charwomen had no use for, much factitious work circulated in red boxes, and the feverish, persistent and boring gossip of that hellish place had already developed in full measure the peculiar flavour of smallness, cynicism, self-importance and bored excitement that it was never to lose.

But I arrived to find also that Dudley had nosed out one matter, which had, however, nothing to do with the Conference, of some interest and importance. When on the 11th November 1918 an Armistice had been concluded with Germany, it had been considered a matter for the naval and military only, and no civilian authorities were present or were consulted. Such matters as might need further discussion with the enemy on land were to be the affair of the military, that is to say Foch, and Foch alone, unaccompanied by any military representative of the other Allies; and those on sea equally the uncriticised prerogative of the British Admiralty, represented by Admiral Browning, a most surly and ignorant sea-dog with a real and large hook instead of a hand, in the highest nautical tradition, with no idea in his head but the extirpation and further humiliation of a despised and defeated enemy. When these arrangements were first made it was supposed, presumably, that the Armistice would be an affair of but a few weeks, and it was forgotten that the continuance of the Blockade, the occupation of enemy territory and many other matters must raise endless financial and economic problems which were the concern of the civilian departments. The French were quick to seize the possibilities of the situation.

What Dudley Ward had discovered, then, was that, under cover of the whole proceedings being in the charge of Foch, the French had appointed a financial representative who, without consultation with the other Allies, was carrying on direct financial negotiations with the Germans on matters of substantial importance under the nose and blind eye of Admiral Browning. The first to discover this had been the Americans, very suspicious as usual lest they should not be in the front rank of the stalls; and Ward had got it from them. Norman Davis, the American Treasury representative, and I decided therefore that it would be extremely amusing and perhaps useful if we stepped on board the Marshal's train on his journey a day or two later to Trèves, where he was to meet Erzberger and other Germans to discuss or dictate current business. I sent a note to Lord Hardinge, and telegraphed to the Chancellor of the Exchequer, and the matter was arranged. When the time came we boarded the Marshal's train. It was to his obvious disgust, and he had as little to do with us as he could.

I do not remember having ever seen a detailed account of Marshal Foch. His photograph everyone knows. But what, beyond his bare appearance, is the popular conception of him? The Marshal is a pious Catholic, he and his stout wife are a very bourgeois couple in their way of life—one is told this much, and it is interesting. I formed the following conception of him at the Council of Ten, at the Invalides and at Trèves.

Foch is of a French peasant type, rather short, with decidedly bandy legs; his moustache is badly kept, and he tugs it; in his own dingy office at the Invalides he sucks at a pipe; he has a trick, very characteristic, when he is listening to civilians who bore him, of pushing out a pendulous lower lip, probably by a movement of the tongue against false teeth, and letting it flap in the wind. He rises early, he lunches early and he retires early. He is not self-conscious and is without vanity. He has an air of authority. These qualities lend him a presence and a considerable dignity. Not knowing who he was, you would not notice him. But when you are told that it is the great Marshal, you are not entirely disappointed. I doubt if he is specially ambitious.

His narrow intellect is, in the strict sense, militarist. He believes that there is an absolute and a clear distinction between matters which are the affair of the military and those which are the affair of the civilians. The former are alone important, and with them no meddling by a civilian is tolerable. Civilians and their affairs, of which he is and professes to be wholly ignorant, he views with a polite contempt. Just as certain matters are the affair of the priests and the Jesuits, who justly resent the interference of laymen, so other matters are the affair of the military, who should be equally exempt from interference.

I am certain that Foch's mind and character are of an extreme simplicity—of an almost medieval simplicity. He is honest, fearless and tenacious. But nine-tenths of the affairs of mankind are blotted out from his vision, and his mind is not susceptible of attention to them. He is capable, therefore, in the appropriate circumstances of being as dangerous to the welfare of mankind as others have been who have added a narrow and impervious intellect to a strong and simple character. But this must not lead you to over-rate his importance. Though a real figure he is a small one—a peasant.

I know nothing of the Marshal's State papers or whether he writes them himself. But his powers of expressing himself by word of mouth are feeble. He is apt to sit in Council silent and expressionless for long periods, until called upon for his opinion, which he expresses uncompromisingly and unpersuasively in the style of the orders of the day. Sometimes General Weygand,[2] his attendant sprite, would speak in the Marshal's behalf. The Marshal was as without the arts of argument as those of persuasion. Except where he could gain the day by prestige or the exercise of military authority, his conduct as chairman was incompetent. He had, therefore, little conception of how to man-

age a meeting of civilian representatives of foreign governments; yet he remained good-tempered on the whole. On the first
occasion that I saw Foch, in the great room at the Quai d'Orsay,
I remember his feebly ringing a small bell amidst a universal
babel; but he seemed to feel more contempt at the disorder of
civilians than annoyance at it or surprise.

The journey to Trèves was the only period during the Peace
Conference when I played much bridge. There happened to be a
four on the train—Norman Davis, the American, Sheldon, another American concerned with food interests, Sir John Beale,
solicitor to the Midland Railway and Secretary of the Ministry
of Food, and myself. We played almost continuously day and
night during the whole of the journey and during the whole of
our three days' stop at Trèves, except when we were actually
in conference with the Germans.

Trèves, as you know, is in Germany. It seemed to all of us an
extraordinary adventure in January 1919 to step on German
soil. We wondered what the streets would look like, whether
the children's ribs would be sticking through their clothes and
what there would be in the shops. Dudley Ward sped through
the streets at electric speed, collecting odd bank-notes, paper
clothing and other souvenirs. But we saw little of Trèves, since
our train was our dwelling-place, and we seldom left the station.
One domestic scene remains in my memory. The town was at
that time within the American sphere of occupation and in the
hands of the American Army. The American representatives
asked accordingly that suitable apartments might be comman-
deered for them. Rather proud of their superior position, they
offered me also their hospitality. Accordingly we were taken
round by an American lieutenant—with charms and also a habit
of internal expectoration characteristic of his type, if only I had
time to expound them—to inspect one or two domiciles available for us. The first we entered was a typical upper middle-
class German household, bare but spotlessly clean. With dejected
but respectful faces the Frau of the house and her husband
showed the alien conquerors round. I felt very much ashamed
of the whole business. We talked loudly amongst ourselves,
enquired after the bathroom, inspected the mattresses, de-

clared that it would do on the whole and were given the latch-key. I think we really tried to be polite and regardful of their feelings. The manner of the American lieutenant was perfect. But gentlemen from Wall Street are not trained for such contingencies, and the essence of the situation was, indeed the point of it for the Americans since we were really much more comfortable in our *train de luxe,* that we were indulging our victorious rights to impose on these poor people for the sake of our own passing and trifling convenience. We civilians secured for ourselves just a slight imitation of the thrill, which I then realised, for the first time vividly, that the humblest units of a victorious army must feel when they plant themselves on a defeated and alien homeland. We were really committing an atrocity, and that was what was so enjoyable.

Half an hour later we had all realised that it would be a great bore to leave our train late at night and walk through wet streets simply for the sake of sleeping on the straw mattresses we had pillaged; and we never visited our quarters again. It was only as we were leaving Trèves that I discovered I still had the good lady's latchkey.

Meantime the Germans had met us. Our train arrived about breakfast time. Theirs from Berlin appeared a little later. Erzberger, fat and disgusting in a fur coat, walked down the platform to the Marshal's saloon. With him were a General and a Sea-Captain with an iron cross round his neck and an extraordinary resemblance of face and figure to the pig in *Alice in Wonderland.* They satisfied wonderfully, as a group, the popular conception of Huns. The personal appearance of that race is really extraordinarily against them. Who knows but that it was the real cause of the war! Compare these Germans with that stupid and callous militarist, our Admiral Browning! The commercial and military and diplomatic value of looking like a typical English gentleman, with the added spice of eccentricity and independence given by the old boy's whim of wearing a large meat hook instead of a hand and filling his pipe with it, is worth all the millions of Spandau and all the uniforms in the world.

We watched them as sightseers. They walked stiffly and uneasily, seeming to lift their feet like men in a photograph or a movie. The Marshal could be seen through the window of his railway carriage, tugging a ragged moustache and laying down his pipe.

A moment later we were called back to our own saloon, since the German financiers were announced. The railway carriage was small, and both we and they were numerous. How were we to behave? Ought we to shake hands? We crushed together at one end of the carriage with a small bridge-table between us and the enemy. They pressed into the carriage, bowing stiffly. We bowed stiffly also, for some of us had never bowed before. We nervously made a movement as though to shake hands and then didn't. I asked them in a voice intended to be agreeable, if they all spoke English.

A sad lot they were in those early days, with drawn, dejected faces and tired staring eyes, like men who had been hammered on the Stock Exchange. But from amongst them stepped forward into the middle place a very small man, exquisitely clean, very well and neatly dressed, with a high stiff collar which seemed cleaner and whiter than an ordinary collar, his round head covered with grizzled hair shaved so close as to be like in substance to the pile of a close-made carpet, the line where his hair ended bounding his face and forehead in a very sharply defined and rather noble curve, his eyes gleaming straight at us, with extraordinary sorrow in them, yet like an honest animal at bay. This was he with whom in the ensuing months I was to have one of the most curious intimacies in the world, and some very strange passages of experience—Dr. Melchior.

II

At the end of my first chapter, Dr. Melchior had entered the railway carriage at Trèves. Perhaps I had better explain what our meeting was about.

The Armistice of November 1918 specifically provided for the continuance of the Blockade, but added that "the Allies contemplated the provisioning of Germany to the extent that shall be deemed necessary." The supplementary Armistice of December 1918, which was negotiated by French and Belgian financial representatives, without the knowledge of England or America, prohibited Germany from disposing abroad of any of her gold, foreign securities or other liquid assets, on the ground that they were a pledge over which the Allies held a lien for the purposes of reparation. This provision was agreed to by the Germans a fortnight after the Revolution, at the lowest ebb of their fortunes and their vitality. You may be surprised that such a provision could have been added to the original Armistice terms. But the first three Armistice agreements were each of them for a period of a month only; and the French held that we were entitled on each occasion of its renewal to add to our terms any new condition, which, although forgotten in the original agreement, would now be useful to us, and to insist on its acceptance under threat of a suspension of the Armistice and a renewed invasion of Germany.

Consequently the Blockade was continued, and the remnant of Germany's financial resources for purchasing food from the neighbouring neutrals was immobilised. She could buy no food, the period was approaching when the fruits of her own harvest would run low, and the starvation which had defeated her was to be prolonged into a period when her vitality was gone, her Government overthrown, and the support of hope removed.

The Americans, under the influence of Mr. Hoover, in part humanitarian, in part imaginatively apprehensive of the consequences, maintained that this policy was an error; and during December the argument was debated in London. I hardly know why we, the English, decided to promote its continuance. I attribute it in part to the irresolution of Lord Reading, who was in charge of the business on our side; for he was intriguing at that time day and night to be one of the party for Paris and was terrified of identifying himself too decidedly with anything controversial. I recall him picking at the nail of his left thumb for minutes together in his room in the War Cabinet offices in Whitehall Gardens in an agony of doubt which way the cat was jumping; his top hat perfect; his whole face and person so chiselled and polished, reflecting pin-points of light from so many angles that one longed to wear him as a tie pin; tie pin on tie pin, till one hardly knew which was Earl and which was jewel; poor Earl!

But I attribute it more profoundly to a cause inherent in bureaucracy. The Blockade had become by that time a very perfect instrument. It had gaken four years to create and was Whitehall's finest achievement; it had evoked the qualities of the English at their subtlest. Its authors had grown to love it for its own sake; it included some recent improvements, which would be wasted if it came to an end; it was very complicated, and a vast organisation had established a vested interest. The experts reported, therefore, that it was our one instrument for imposing our Peace Terms on Germany, and that once suspended it could hardly be reimposed.

When therefore we reached Paris, some modification of this situation seemed to me to be the most important and pressing problem, and my position as the English financial representative on the Supreme Economic Council gave me an opportunity for interesting myself in it. The Peace negotiations might obviously last for months, and in the meantime to find some way of feeding Germany must be a principal object of policy. It was not obvious that it would do anyone any good if the structure of the German State were to collapse and if disorder under the opposed banners of Communism and Reaction were to plunder the rest of Europe on the other side of the Rhine. The project was not hopeless, for Lord Robert openly and the Prime Minister in his heart were of the same opinion; and only the French opposed it.

The game was begun at the Economic Council on the 12th January 1919, and was continued at the War Council on the next day. M. Klotz was the protagonist of opposition. He had no objection to England or America furnishing Germany with food, but he was determined that Germany should not pay for it out of assets which were available for Reparation and virtually belonged, therefore, to France. President Wilson, his spirit at that time unbroken, held forth in lofty and rhetorical strains. "So long as hunger continued to gnaw," he said, "the foundations of government would continue to crumble. . . ." He trusted the French Finance Department—I quote his words—

"would withdraw their objection, as we were faced with the great problems of Bolshevism and the forces of dissolution which now threatened society." M. Klotz rejoined, a little cowed, that he would gladly meet the President's wishes. But it was not altogether a question of food supplies. It was also a question of justice. He asked as a matter of justice why Germany should pay for food in preference to paying off debts incurred for the reparation of damage they had committed. The victory that day ended substantially with Kotz, for while he had to agree *en principe* that Germany should pay for the food, he succeeded in reserving the question as to *how* she should pay.

I have said that the President spoke in lofty strains, but the motives of men are mixed. Mr. Hoover was at his elbow, who, in his capacity of American Food Controller, had promised the American farmers a minimum price for their hogs; the promise had overstimulated the sows of that continent; the price was falling; and Congress had omitted to vote the money necessary to make Mr. Hoover's promise good. The following is an extract from a Report to the Chancellor of the Exchequer which I posted from Paris that evening:

"As regards bacon, it has been suggested by the Americans that we unload on Germany the large stocks of low-grade bacon which we now hold, and replace these by fresher stocks from America which would be more readily saleable. From the food point of view this would clearly be a good deal for us. . . . The situation is a curious one. The blockade on fats to neutral countries is being raised, and Germany is to receive fat supplies on a very generous scale. Bolshevism is to be defeated and the new era to begin. At the Supreme War Council, President Wilson was very eloquent on the subject of instant action on these lines. But really the underlying motive of the whole thing is Mr. Hoover's abundant stocks of low-grade pig products at high prices which must at all costs be unloaded on someone, enemies failing Allies. When Mr. Hoover sleeps at night visions of pigs float across his bedclothes and he frankly admits that at all hazards the nightmare must be dissipated."

This, therefore, was why I was at Trèves. We had managed to break down the French plan according to which only military personages were to talk with the Germans during the Armistice period; and we were there to make preliminary arrangements for the supply of food to Germany, and to explore with German civilian representatives their available means of payment.

Before we return to the railway carriage in Trèves station, there are two complications which I must explain to you at some length, because they are vital to the later developments of my plot.

Whilst some of us had come to Trèves about food and finance, there was also another business on hand. The original Armistice Agreement had left a good many things out which subsequent desire would have preferred in; and amongst these was the German Mercantile Marine. The Allies had every intention of taking these ships under the Peace Treaty, but in the meantime there was no provision for getting hold of them. Yet the supply of tonnage was very short, and the German ships would have been very useful. It was proposed, therefore, to make their immediate cession a condition of the second Armistice renewal; you will remember that it was this second renewal which Foch was now at Trèves to negotiate. But the business was not so simple as it sounded. It was certain that the Germans would strenuously resist the surrender of their ships; yet to threaten the suspension of the Armistice in the event of their refusal involved a considerable element of bluff, since it was doubtful how far the public opinion of the world, especially in America, would stand an invasion of Germany, simply on the ground that Germany refused to do something which she had not promised when she laid down her arms and which was not yet in a Treaty; besides the German Army was not then, as it is now, substantially demobilised and disarmed, so that invasion would have to be in force, which would postpone our own demobilisation and make the politicians unpopular.

The Admiralty, who had been asked to report on the possibility of the British Navy simply descending on the German ports and taking the German ships piratically, had replied that it would be an awkward undertaking.

There was room, therefore, for diplomacy; and the central

idea of our diplomatic plan was to link up the surrender of the ships with the supply of food. This, too, involved an element of bluff, since it was probably to our interest to supply Germany with food, whether or not she surrendered the ships. But a better face could be put on it before the world; because we could point out, quite truthfully, as indeed we did, that, *unless* Germany put her ships at our disposal, it would be very difficult for us to find enough ships to furnish her with food. Germany, by her submarines, had reduced shipping to a level at which all Europe risked starvation; if she wanted to be fed herself, it was only reasonable that she should lend us the ships laid up in her harbours to carry the food both to her and to her neighbours. Ships against food was, therefore, a reasonable bargain. The bluff was also far less dangerous, because Germany probably needed the food more urgently than we the ships.

There was another complication—a psychological one—the difficulty of getting the German representatives, bewildered, cowed, nerve-shattered and even hungry, to apprehend how the ground really lay. You will hear in the sequel what crude methods were eventually necessary to illuminate them. The situation was certainly difficult for them. They had two leading ideas in their heads. The first was that the ships might be one of their best bargaining counters in the Peace Negotiations, and must not be surrendered in advance except for a perfectly definite *quid pro quo;* the second was that they might reasonably hope to get their first instalments of food paid for, not out of their own resources, but by a loan from America. For at that time they believed very sincerely in the benevolent intentions of the President and in the humanitarian impulses of his countrymen. But neither idea was really a good one. For we were quite determined to take the ships anyhow as compensation for submarine losses, and their eventual bargaining value was trifling. And at that time anti-German feeling in the United States had been worked up to its greatest height, so that the political possibility of a loan to Germany (which would have had to be voted by Congress) was absolutely nil. Preoccupation with these two ideas prevented the Germans from seeing the real situation, which was that England and the United States really desired and intended to facilitate the food supply of Germany, that the game we had to play with the French prevented our saying so too openly or making categorical promises, that we could not, for domestic political reasons, lend them money, but were willing to allow them to use, for the purchase of food, assets which otherwise would certainly be pinched for reparation a little later on, and that they (the Germans) had nothing to gain by hanging on to the ships or gold which at this juncture they would be allowed to use for food, but which under the Treaty would be taken for reparation. Our relations with them were partly in good faith and partly in bad, and they, German-wise, were incapable of distinguishing which was which. We, on the other hand, rather over-estimated, I think, the urgency at that date of their requirements for imported cereals. Even then, I fancy, they had rather more up their sleeves than we had credited them with. It was a curious feature of the negotiations of the next three months that British anxiety over German food supplies was, so far as concerned its urgency in point of time, decidedly greater, to all appearances, than the anxiety of the Germans themselves. I was never quite clear in my own mind how far this was due to concealed reserves known to the Germans but not to us, how far to their under-estimation of the long period, well known to us, which must elapse between the date of setting on foot negotiations to purchase wheat overseas and the actual delivery of the wheat in Germany, and how far to the general fecklessness, failure of foresight, and absence of any plan whatever which had notably succeeded at that time in the minds of the authorities in Germany on the breakdown of the Great Plan, with which all other plans had been bound up. Even now Germans have by no means recovered their *Planmässigkeit,* and this has to be allowed for.

We bowed stiffly and sat down very crowded at opposite ends of the railway carriage with a small folding bridge-table between us, nine of us and six of them. We agreed to speak in English, which had the advantage of cutting out the French. For the Comte de C——, being able to speak English perfectly, could never bring himself to admit that he couldn't understand a word of it. So he was reduced to looking down his long nose, placing a long finger against it, and saying at inappropriate moments: "For my one self I protest," "For my one self I cannot be in *accord*". A foolish creature! I wonder what has become of him. I don't believe that I have ever in the aggregate been so rude to anyone. I met him first at lunch in the Café Royal when he and I were manipulating the Spanish exchange, and we got on well enough. In fact, in a sort of way we always did. He was a genteel Catholic, who in peacetime eked out a small estate with slightly shady finance. But he had lately become Foch's spy in the French Treasury and played his game in the agreeable, sly, half blundering mode of the Jesuit trained. I lunched with him once in his little flat in Paris. It was a small banquet. Three hired waiters of immense distinction in immaculate shirts and white cotton gloves; a new glass of a new wine with each course; exquisite food produced abundantly from nowhere, but every dish and the dressings of every dish conventionalised and stereotyped down to the shapes of the potatoes, the whole thing an exact replica of an official luncheon I once attended at the Élysée. Madame exchanged witticisms with me on the subject of my being a bachelor. Mr. Crosby, who, born in Louisiana of a French mother, had risen to great eminence as the only American who could talk French, rattled on with abundant fluency about the privations which the South suffered in his childhood after the Civil War. The graceless and confined discomfort of the apartment's exactitudes, which I still feel though I could describe none, impressed on me deeply the grasping sterility of France; or of that part of France, which in spite of what Clive and Roger may say, *is* France.

Dr. Melchior was their spokesman in moving, persuasive, almost perfect English. Of the others I now visualise two only—Dr. Kaufmann, the representative of the Reichsbank, elderly, broken, with hungry, nervous eyes, deeply middle class, looking somehow like an old, broken umbrella, who lost the thread of the conference at the outset and never recovered it, but was eager to affirm whatever Melchior indicated; the other a representative of the Foreign Office, his face cut to pieces with duelling, a sort of Corps student type, sly and rather merry, over-anxious to catch the eyes of one or other of us with a cheerful grin. Melchior spoke always deliberately but without pause, in a way which gave one an extraordinary impression that he was truthful. His hardest task, now as on later occasions, was to keep his companions in check, eager to jump in with little undignified misplaced appeals, or foolish *ad hominem* insincerities which couldn't have deceived the stupidest American. This Jew, for such, though not by appearance, I afterwards learnt him to be, and he only, upheld the dignity of defeat.

This first Conference led to little of substance. We wasted some time over an attempt of the French to get the gold in the Reichsbank transferred to the occupied territory on the pretext that it would be safer from Bolshevism. It was not difficult for me to carry out Mr. Bonar Law's instructions that the project should not be encouraged. Melchior vainly pleaded for a loan, being ingenious in the variant forms he proposed for it. I bent my efforts, speaking coldly and very clearly, to an endeavour to impress it on them that they must banish this idea from their heads as politically impossible, and that they would waste precious time if they pursued it. We could make little progress with the food against ships project, since the proposal was new to the Germans, they were without instructions from Weimar, and their shipping representatives had not arrived at Trèves. But we did reach a useful provisional agreement by which they handed over to us immediately a sum of about £5,000,000 in gold and foreign currencies, in exchange for an immediate supply of fats and condensed milk. On a small scale, the supply of food for them had started, and the organisation for supplying it was being built up. I drafted the arrangements, endeavouring to be strictly fair in details. They were pleased, I think; felt the atmosphere not wholly unfriendly; and began to think (not indeed to be deceived so far as the food supply was in question) that there was a chance of being treated fairly.

In the afternoon the Shipping Representatives arrived, representatives of the Government and also of the leading German Lines. For they had just heard by telegram that the surrender of their Marine was to be a condition of the renewal of the Armistice. This Conference was no affair of mine. I attended it out of curiosity. The great shipowners of Hamburg were too numerous for the railway carriage; so the meeting was fixed in a public house just outside Trèves railway station. We, the Allies, congregated in the parlour. They, the defeated, had no room given them, but collected uneasily in the bar, which continued, however, its usual business with the working men of Trèves drifting in and out. The chair was taken by Mr. B——, a vain and almost imbecile American who had made a fortune by purchasing for nothing from the inventor of it a small contrivance essential to the modern laundry machine. The Germans were summoned to the parlour. When their leading representative had spoken, the little French boy interpreter began "Thees mann sez" . . . when the German snapped out in English "Thees mann! Say, if you pleese, thees gentlemann." Thus did these sea lords, about to die, salute their fate, and in the back parlour of the public house the German Mercantile Marine passed from her.

By the time we were back in Paris, I was feeling extremely unwell and took to my bed two days later. High fever followed, and Dr. Beecham announced that some poisonous germ had infected me in the uncleanliness of Trèves railway station. I lay in my suite in the Majestic, nearly delirious, and the image of the raised pattern of the *nouveau art* wall-paper so preyed on my sensibilities in the dark that it was a relief to switch on the light and, by perceiving the reality, to be relieved for a moment from the yet more hideous pressure of its imagined outlines. When the fever left me I was weak and unequal to the turmoils of controversy; events in Paris moved slowly; so I slipped away from it to the Riviera and spent a fortnight sitting in the sun of Simon Bussy's veranda.

When a telegram from Dudley Ward called me back, a month had passed since Trèves, the temporary renewal of the Armistice was again lapsing, and another conference was impending. On the 13th February I stepped on a train again, following the Marshal to Germany. For, in spite of superficial appearances to the contrary, the first Conference of Trèves had settled very little. Although we had persuaded Melchior to offer us £4,000,000 of

gold in payment for food, our acceptance of this was not
absolute, but subject to the approval of the Supreme Council.
For Klotz's embargo on the employment of gold for this purpose still held good. And while we could reckon on his con-
ceding the acceptance of this small sum, there was as yet no
financial provision in sight for the main German food programme plus imported cereals. Prolonged discussions with
Melchior as to the possibility of other means of payment than
gold had produced very little result. And as for the ships, whilst
the Germans, with vehement protest and under duress, had
agreed to the addition of the following clause to the Armistice
terms "In order to ensure the revictualling of Germany and
the rest of Europe, the German Government will take all
necessary steps to put, for the duration of the Armistice, the
whole German merchant fleet under the control and under the
flags of the Allied Powers and the United States, assisted by a
German Delegate. This agreement does not prejudice in any
way the final disposition of these vessels"; yet no definite date
was fixed and preliminary details were left to be fixed by a
separate Convention. An abortive conference for this purpose
had been held, without settling anything, while I was in the
South of France; so that I came back a month later to find
that there was still no provision for the finance of German
food imports and that no steps had been taken for the surrender of the ships.

The Marshal did his best to give us the slip. Our train was
supposed to be following him across France. But we were told
that this Conference was to be at Luxembourg and that the
Germans would meet us there. We arrived to find no one.
Luxembourg was a boring place; melting snow was on the
ground; we trudged about in a disconsolate body trying to find
someone who could give us news. At last a telephone message
indicated that the Marshal and the Germans were at Trèves,
and we pointed our engine's nose in that direction.

The second Conference of Trèves was not very interesting
and did little more than develop and focus the situation created by the first. The shipping representatives sparred over details and got no nearer securing the ships. We, the financiers,

pursued with Melchior and his associates in great detail the various possible modes in which Germany could pay for the food. It became evident that no considerable sum could be available quickly, except in the form of gold or by a loan from the Allies. The Germans pressed for the latter and I made a formal declaration as to its impossibility. Finally, the Germans took their stand on what was probably the best ground open to them. Excellenz von Braun on the 15th February made a declaration on behalf of the German Government as follows:

"After extended consideration of Germany's financial position, we have come to the conclusion that it will . . . be impossible to cover the provision of food supplies for Germany without the granting of credit. Mr. Keynes has explained to us the psychological and financial reasons why no credit can be granted to Germany by America or the Entente. We, however, are of the opinion that the provision of food supplies for Germany is one of the conditions of the Armistice. As far back as the first Armistice . . . Article 26 agreed to the supplying of foodstuffs for the German people in such measure as might be recognised to be necessary. . . . The Agreement of the 15th January demanded the temporary handing over of the German mercantile fleet for the express purpose 'of assuring the supply of foodstuffs to Germany.' We are, therefore, of the opinion . . . that the agreements as to the handing over of the mercantile fleet, the supply of foodstuffs and the financing represent an indivisible whole, that no single agreement of the three can be carried out before the other, and that the guaranteeing of Germany's food supply is a condition precedent on the handing over of the mercantile fleet."

He added that if in the view of the Germans the food could not be financed without a credit, and in the view of the Allies such a credit was not feasible, then the Germans must refuse to deliver the ships. He concluded with an appeal, as he expressed it, "not so much to your humanitarian sentiments as to the political conscience of the world. We are firmly convinced that the collapse of Germany by the action of Bolshevism and the flooding of Bolshevism over the whole of Europe cannot be prevented if we terminate these negotiations with the result foreshadowed by your former statements. It is to the interest of all civilised peoples that this development should be arrested."

The atmosphere was tense and sombre, the declaration was made seriously and we all believed it true. I recall the heavy, stupid face of Excellenz von Braun, with the lips of his nose slightly eaten away, like a chipped Chinese mask. He had raised questions far beyond our competence at that moment, and we turned our train towards Paris.

On the basis of what we and they had promised, the declaration of von Braun was partly well-founded but partly sophistical. Our two undertakings, that in spite of the Blockade Germany should be allowed food supplies, and that our purpose in taking her ships was in part to convey such food supplies, precluded us from placing obstacles in the way of her purchasing food abroad. Our undertakings were in substance broken, if, having given them, we then forbade Germany to employ her liquid assets to pay for her purchases. But it cannot well be contended that they committed us to pay for the food ourselves. When the Armistice negotiators wrote the words "The Allies and the United States contemplate the provisioning of Germany," they certainly meant that they would permit such provisioning, not that they themselves would furnish and pay for the food. Von Braun had at the best but a verbal case which he pushed too far and too late in the day.

But the point which the French and our own naval and shipping authorities fixed on was, of course, the refusal of the Germans to surrender their ships in accordance with their undertaking of January. The demand that the details of their food supply should be definitely assured them *in advance* of the surrender of the ships went beyond anything in the Armistice articles. It was a typical piece of German chicane; they were at their old tricks; we should now take a firm line and refuse to discuss anything whatever until the ships were in our hands; etc., etc. You know the style.

On the financial side I was more than ever convinced that the only possible solution lay in the use of the German gold. It had become evident that they had no other liquid assets in adequate quantity; and the gold, once we had agreed the principle, could be used immediately. On the other hand the German plan of a credit from us to them was really hopeless; for it required legislation, and in the state of opinion at that time it was not to be thought for a moment that either the President would ask Congress for it or Lloyd George, Parliament.

Meanwhile time passed, and the breakdown of Germany's food organisation was daily nearer. Endless discussions on the Supreme Economic Council availed nothing, since under the constitution of the body there was no way through French obstruction. Nothing would really be done until the attention of the Big Five was attracted. But they were otherwise engaged. They had just spent three afternoons debating how many votes Brazil should have on a sub-commission on which questions were not decided by voting; and they had in front of them a long programme of interesting deputations; Copts, Armenians, Slovaks, Arabs and Zionists crowded the ante-rooms of the Quai d'Orsay, and each of them was permitted to make in the presence of the Great Ones a set oration in an unknown tongue. It was about this time that the Emir Feisal, so it was alleged, recited in M. Pichon's cabinet, unabashed by the naked charms of Rubens's Marie de Medici, a chapter of the Koran, whilst Colonel Lawrence, in his capacity of the Emir's interpreter, propounded an ingenious *politik* for the creation of an Arab hegemony from the Mediterranean to the Persian Gulf, over Damascus and Mosul and Bagdad.

Yet by the mere passage of time some progress, nevertheless, proceeded under the surface. The President and the Prime Minister were firmly with us; and it seemed that French opposition to the employment of gold must break down in the end, though their faces would have to be saved. The food authorities were getting forward with the details, and had concerted their plans for a rapid shipment of 200,000 tons of bread stuffs and 70,000 tons of pork products, as soon as the finance was arranged. Besides some sort of a reply had had to be concocted to the declaration of von Braun. It contained various minor concessions and facilitated various minor methods by which Germany might get food from abroad. But it granted no loan and released no gold; and the whole of it was conditional on the surrender of the mercantile marine.

Thus barely a fortnight later we were on our train again, destined this time for Spa. The party was differently constituted. As there was no question this time of renewing the Armistice, we were quit of the Marshal's sour presence and unfriendly courtesies. The main topic being ships, Rear-Admiral Hope was our head, a gentle, intelligent, decidedly deaf sailor, with pink, deceptively youthful cheeks, and the most peculiar irises I have ever seen—a circular band of tortoiseshell on a blue background. I liked him and trusted him; he, for his part, was a little unfamiliar with the business and obviously wanted to lean on me. Our offer to the Germans was, of course, far too nearly the same as last time; but while we were still precluded from any formal agreement to the release of gold for food finance, Hope and I were given to understand that it was the firm policy of the British Government to see Germany fed, and that they could rely on our seeing the matter through somehow if only they would put themselves in order by delivering the ships in accordance with their undertaking.

Spa, once a fashionable watering place on the frontier of Belgium, had been in the later stages of the war the Grand Headquarters of the German Army. It was now the seat of the Armistice Commission, a body of Allied and of German military officers which, primarily entrusted with the daily executive details of the Armistice conventions, was also the sole channel of communication between the German Government and Paris. This body met daily and had established sensible relations. Our representative, General Haking, prepared each day a general report on the situation, which was by far the most impartial and valuable review of what was happening in Germany which reached us from any of our sources of so-called information. He sent these reports, however, to no one but Sydney Waterlow, and for a considerable time, indeed until Dudley Ward in his usual fashion got wind of them, Sydney kept them to himself.

General Haking asked Hope and myself to stay with him, and we left the rest of the party sleep as usual in the train, drawn up by a side platform of the station.

The General had had assigned to him the villa which a few months before had been the quarters of Ludendorff. Up on one side of the semicircle of pine-clad hills which surround the watering place, the lords of Germany had suffered, in physical seclusion, the decisions of fate. A few steps away was the Kaiser's villa and a little farther up the hill Hindenburg's. There, far from the guns and armies, away from the mechanism of Berlin, far also from the starved cities and growling mob, the three despots had dwelt in a surrounding network of telephones. It was not merely sentimental to feel that the ground was haunted. The air was still charged with the emotions of that vast collapse. The spot was melancholy with the theatrical Teutonic melancholy of black pinewoods. As one walked on the villa's terrace the horizon was bounded by the black line of woods, the sun sank behind them, and the trees behind the house sighed like a love-sick Prussian. When Ludendorff's nerves began to break, he got no comfort from nature, and the buzz of the telephones in the back room off the hall mingled with the voice of the trees to suggest to him the conventional symbols of a German's despair.

The house itself was built, I suppose, not long before the war, as the summer resort of some minor magnate of industry, who hoped at the same time to enjoy the fruits of his success and moderate the dimensions of his person by the breezes of the hill and the waters of the valley. Spick and span, semi-baronial, yet hardly larger than Charleston,[3] decorated with vast and hideous imitations of the late German medieval in tapestry and mural decoration, stiff and bare almost to the point of meanness.

One can believe sometimes that no greater responsibility for the war lies on any one man than on Wagner. Evidently the Kaiser's conception of himself was so moulded. And what was Hindenburg but the bass and Ludendorff but the fat tenor of third-rate Wagnerian opera? How else did they see themselves in their dreams and in their bath? And what else had planted them in their villas at Spa but that these were the likest the neighbourhood could furnish to third-rate operatic scenery? [4]

General Haking, having been allotted the villa, had summoned to it his English wife and his two marriageable English daughters, his A.D.C. from the Yeomanry, and his clever Staff-Captain, whom I suspected, unjustly I fancy to the General, of writing the clever reports which Sydney kept to himself. It was all very domestic and we sat down, with a passing pleasantry at the expense of the mural decorations and the more than life-size portraits of the proprietor and his wife, to an English dinner of which every item had been imported from England, served by two genial and slightly comical English Tommies. *The Times* arrived regularly and in good time; and the sporting A.D.C. had clubbed together with his brother subalterns to import a pack of hounds and was hunting the country as usual eight weeks after his arrival there. But outside on the terrace I could hear Ludendorff unbuckling his bright breastplate and calling in a thick voice on the trees to strike up with their soughings to prelude his passing monody. Miss Bates had vanquished Brünnhilde, and Mr. Weston's foot was firmly planted on the neck of Wotan.

Next morning, Hope and I descended the hill to the building of the German Armistice Commission, where we were to hold our conference. Hope, by whom I sat, presided and for the Germans von Braun, by whom sat Melchior. It was soon evident that there would be trouble. Weimar, having got over its internal problem for the moment, was attending to foreign affairs; the surrender of the ships threatened trouble with the seamen of Hamburg (for one of our most disputed demands was that the German crews should be removed); and von Braun's instructions were inelastic. They were also on their dignity and refused to talk or understand anything but German, which had to be interpreted phrase by phrase first from or into English and then French. There was one absurd moment when von Braun having spoken for a minute or two paused in the middle of his sentence for the interpretation. But the interpreter was defeated —von Braun hadn't reached the verb. Nor could the Frenchman, once wound up to oratory, his pregnancy consummated,

and the motions of evacuation set in train, interrupt the processes of Nature half-way or restrain the stream half-cock, until
he had far overpassed the retentiveness of the interpreter's
vessel.

We were plainly wasting our time, getting to grips neither
with one another nor with the situation. Their instructions were
incompatible with ours; ours there was no means of modifying
except by returning to Paris, and unless they could soften theirs
by telephonic communications with Weimar, a rupture was in
sight. As the time to adjourn drew near, I was in despair.
Two months had passed since Trèves, and we were now in the
middle of March. Our Food people declared on their honour
that, unless the supplies could be set in motion immediately,
they couldn't possibly arrive in time. Haking's reports from
Germany, about the imminent collapse of organisation unless
physical privation was soon relieved, were dark and convincing. After dinner the night before, he had given us his personal
impressions of the state of mind of the Germans, whom he met
every day at the Armistice Commission, and he had begged us
to be reasonable and accommodating. As far as a soldier could
judge, he told us, Paris seemed to have lost its reason. You
mustn't drive these fellows too hard.

I looked across the table at Melchior. He seemed to feel as I
did. Staring, heavy-lidded, helpless, looking, as I had seen him
before, like an honourable animal in pain. Couldn't we break
down the empty formalities of this Conference, the threebarred
gate of triple interpretations, and talk about the truth and the
reality like sane and sensible persons? The Conference adjourned. We drifted out towards the urinal to put our coats
on. I pulled Hope on one side. "May I speak to Melchior
privately?" I murmured. "It seems the only possible chance of
getting on." He glanced at me with his odd irises, startled but
not shocked. "Do what you like," he answered. I hung about
in the hall until the French were out of sight; then stood uneasily a few steps up the central staircase; persons I did not
know were hurrying or drifting about. I saw someone coming
down the stairs whom I recognised as a German secretary. "I
want to speak to Dr. Melchior for a moment," I said to him,

"about this afternoon's arrangements." "If you'll come upstairs," he replied, "I'll try to find him." I waited for some minutes on the landing and then saw Melchior approaching. "May I speak to you privately?" I asked him. He led me along the passage and entered one of the rooms. At the farther end of it were three young Germans; one was strumming loudly on a piano, one a fat ungainly creature in his shirt-sleeves bellowed a raucous tenor, the third sprawled on a table. "Excuse me," said Melchior, "but I'd be much obliged if for a few minutes I could have this room for a private conference." They roared at him vulgarly. Did he not know that this was the hour of the day when music was permitted in that place? And had he forgotten—pointing to his cigarette—that smoking was prohibited there before five o'clock? We went farther down the passage. With a shrug of his shoulders, "Here," he said, "you have a picture of Germany in revolution. These are my clerks."

At last we were by ourselves in a small room. I was quivering with excitement, terrified out of my wits at what I was doing, for the barriers of permitted intercourse had not then begun to crumble, and somewhat emotional. Melchior wondered what I wanted. My memory of the interview is blurred. I tried to convey to him what I was feeling, how we believed his prognostications of pessimism, how we were impressed, not less than he, with the urgency of starting food supplies, how personally I believed that my Government and the American Government were really determined that the food should come, but that in the giving of formal undertakings our hands were tied; that if they, the Germans, adhered to their attitude of the morning a fatal delay was inevitable; that they must make up their minds to the handing over of the ships; and that, if only he could secure a little latitude from Weimar, we could between us concoct a formula which would allow the food supplies to move in practice and would evade the obstructions of the French. It was so greatly to our own interest that the German Government should survive, that we did really intend to furnish the food. I allowed that our recent actions had not been such as to lead him to trust in our sincerity; but I begged him to believe that I, at least, at that moment, was sincere and truthful. He was as much moved as I was, and I think he believed me. We both stood all through the interview. In a sort of way I was in love with him. He would do his best, he said, but had little hope of success. He would speak with Weimar on the telephone and would urge them to give him some discretion. But they did not understand the position, and he had little expectation of this Conference effecting anything. He spoke with the passionate pessimism of a Jew. German honour and organisation and morality were crumbling; he saw no light anywhere; he expected Germany to collapse and civilisation to grow dim; we must do what we could; but dark forces were passing over us. We pressed hands, and I hurried quickly into the street where Hope had sent his motor car back for me.

I gave him a summary of what had passed. The afternoon's conference was brief. Hope made a formal declaration to von Braun that the morning's discussion furnished no basis for a settlement, and requested him to ask his Government for further discretion to negotiate. Unless he was granted such discretion, it was useless to continue the Conference and we proposed to return to Paris to report to the Supreme Council. The French derived great satisfaction from the firm tone of the Admiral. This was quite the right way to treat the beastly Bosch. Von Braun agreed to report to his Government by telephone and would let us know the result later in the day or next morning.

I strolled through the pinewoods and dined with the Haking family. General Sir Walter Lawrence, Haig's Chief of Staff, passing that way on an inspection, was one of the party in the evening. I liked him and we talked eagerly, until at about eleven o'clock when we were thinking of bed a missive arrived from the Germans. Von Braun regretted that Weimar could not modify its fundamental position, but he hoped nevertheless that the Conference would be resumed in the morning, as had been arranged provisionally, since there were some points of detail on which he thought we might make progress.

It was evident that Melchior had failed and that every day which passed before we reported at Paris and he at Weimar was time wasted. We must bring matters to a head and attract the attention of the Great Ones. For this purpose a dramatic move was essential. Let there be a public rupture of the Conference, which the Great Ones would read about in the newspapers. I begged Hope, therefore, to break off the Conference that moment, and to order our train to return to Paris that night, so that when the Germans woke in the morning it would be to find us flitted. He fell in with the notion; the General's car was ordered, and carried down Hope and me to join our colleagues in the railway station; a hurried conference was called in the restaurant car with the French, Americans and Italians, some of them in their pyjamas; and by 1 A.M. our train was puffing for Paris, with the approval of everyone but the French, especially the Comte de C——, who were alarmed at the precipitate turn which matters had taken and had begun to feel doubtful whether such a dramatic situation was going to work out to their advantage.

We were back in Paris on the 6th March. Our reports won over the Prime Minister, and those of our American colleagues, whom I have failed to describe but who were a most important section of the party and with whom we worked in close collusion, equally impressed Mr. Lansing and Colonel House. (By this time the President was absent.) It was clear that a solution must be found immediately, and on the afternoon of the 8th March a meeting of the Supreme War Council was summoned for the purpose. This was in the days before the creation of the Council of Four. There were fifty-nine persons present.

The meeting was held, not in the great Conference Chamber of the Quai d'Orsay, but in Pichon's personal cabinet. The room was panelled in pale oak, in which were set in a vast array surrounding the room tapestry representations of the great Rubens series of Henri Quatre and Marie de Medici. The Delegates sat in a steep horseshoe with their advisers crowded behind them. Inside the horseshoe was Clemenceau. In the middle of it facing the fireplace sat Foch. To the left of Foch were ranged in order the Japanese, the Italians, ourselves and the Americans, and on his other side facing us were the French.

It is not to be supposed that ours was the only business. It may give you an idea of how the Supreme Council occupied itself at this time if I mention the business that preceded it.

First, the raising of the Blockade of the Adriatic was agreed to—five months after the Armistice. Next, a Committee of Generals was appointed to proceed to Laibach to report on the character of certain incidents which had occurred there, for which the responsibility was disputed. The Commission on Belgian Affairs under the Treaty of 1839 then presented its report. Next came the *pièce de résistance* of the afternoon. M. Jules Cambon stated that he had presided at a meeting of the Small Powers to elect their representatives on the Commissions which were to draw up the Economic and Financial Provisions of the Peace Treaty. Unfortunately an understanding had been reached beforehand by the Latin American states to form a combination, with the result that the five seats on the Financial Committee fell to Peru, Brazil, Bolivia, Panama and Portugal and the five seats on the Economic Commission to Brazil, China, Cuba, Siam and Ecuador. The small European powers, thus finding themselves outvoted, had refused to take any further part in the proceedings. Belgium, for instance, had found herself entirely excluded from a voice, in matters profoundly affecting her, in favour of China and Peru. Serbia had had to yield its place to Panama. It was a most awkward affair, and in the meantime the Commissions could not meet. After a long discussion, M. Pichon was authorised to prepare a draft solution for the following Monday's session.

At last our business was reached. Lord Robert Cecil, as Chairman of the Supreme Economic Council, sat in the front row with the Prime Minister and Mr. Balfour. Admiral Hope and I crouched behind the Prime Minister's chair. Lord Robert, speaking for the Economic Council, opened the argument. The surrender of the ships was one thing; the supply of food was another. The Germans had undertaken the former. But under the Armistice we had given undertakings about the latter. There were also the obligations of humanity and the grave danger of Germany drifting into Bolshevism unless food were sent her. He, therefore, proposed that Germany be informed that she is bound to deliver the ships, that we categorically undertake to furnish the food as soon as she begins to deliver the ships, that she be permitted to use her liquid assets, including gold, to pay for the food, and that the Blockade be raised to the extent of allowing Germany to export goods (with some exceptions) and to purchase food in neutral countries. He had to add that his French colleagues had not yet agreed to the use of the gold. This was, of course, in its definiteness a great improvement on anything we had been authorised to offer at Spa. But everything turned on the gold; for, in the absence of other liquid assets, without this all the rest would be a dead letter. I had got this clearly and definitely into the Prime Minister's head.

M. Clémentel on the French side of the room straightway raised difficulties. We ought not to enter into any undertaking more than a month ahead. In the opinion of the French Government those who wanted to eat should work and the Germans should be given the ultimatum that they would only receive food in return for raw materials. M. Klotz interposed to suggest that Marshal Foch's views should be heard. The debate dragged on. A few words from the Marshal and from Clemenceau on the French side; a speech from Hoover to emphasise the report of us delegates from Spa that in our judgment the Germans would never surrender the ships except in return for a categorical assurance about food. But the debate was not going favourably; the issue was getting confused; and it looked as if once again the French would succeed, while appearing to give way a little, in getting some qualification inserted which would allow them in practice to obstruct the whole thing. There was no passion in the proceedings—debating points, technical objections, the whole real issue was being niggled away. Lord Robert had taken a deliberately prosaic line and had almost said that, while of course the obligations of humanity and the fear of Bolshevism were at the back of all our heads, he recognised that it would not be in the best of taste to rub such points in too crudely.

But meantime Lloyd George was rousing himself. He can be amazing when one agrees with him. Never have I more admired his extraordinary powers than in the next half-hour of this conference. So far he had said nothing, but I could see

from behind that he was working himself up, shaking himself
and frowning as he does on these occasions. Now he spoke; the
creeping lethargy of the proceedings was thrown off, and he
launched his words with rage. This is the sort of thing he said,
in this commonplace diction but with an air which swept away
the spiders and their cobwebs. He wished to urge with all his
might that steps should at once be taken to revictual Germany.
The honour of the Allies was involved. Under the terms of the
Armistice the Allies did imply that they meant to let food into
Germany. The Germans had accepted our Armistice conditions,
which were sufficiently severe, and they had complied with the
majority of those conditions. But so far not a single ton of food
had been sent into Germany. The fishing fleet had even been
prevented from going out to catch a few herrings. The Allies
were now on top, but the memories of starvation might one
day turn against them. The Germans were being allowed to
starve whilst at the same time hundreds of thousands of tons
of food were lying at Rotterdam. These incidents constituted
far more formidable weapons for use against the Allies than
any of the armaments which it was sought to limit. The Allies
were sowing hatred for the future: they were piling up agony,
not for the Germans, but for themselves. The British troops
were indignant about our refusal to revictual Germany. General Plumer had said that he could not be responsible for his
troops if children were allowed to wander about the streets
half-starved. The British soldiers (with a characteristic shake of
the head) would not stand that. . . . As long as order was
maintained in Germany, a breakwater would exist between the
countries of the Allies and the waters of revolution beyond.
Once that breakwater was swept away, he could not speak for
France, but he trembled for his own country. He was there that
afternoon to reinforce the appeal which had come to him from
the men who had helped the Allies to conquer the Germans,
the soldiers, who said that they refused to continue to occupy
a territory in order to maintain the population in a state of
starvation. Meanwhile the Conference continued to haggle.
They had heard the same arguments about gold six weeks before. When he came to the word gold, he used the intonation

which was to be repeated in the climax a few minutes later. It had been a superb farrago of sense and sentiment, of spontaneous rhetoric and calculated art. By the conclusion, he had moved himself at least as much as the audience, and turning round to us behind him we heard him threaten half-audibly that if this sort of thing went on he would order the British Army of Occupation back to England tomorrow.

No one but Clemenceau could speak next, and the old man saw that he must needs concede a good deal. Still he stood his ground considerably. In the Armistice, he said, no promise had ever been made to feed Germany, at which Mr. Balfour interposed in a silver voice that "almost a promise" had been made. His information tended to show, Clemenceau went on, that the Germans were using Bolshevism as a bogey with which to frighten the Allies. The main point was that the Germans had promised to surrender their ships and had not done so. However, he agreed that, subject to suitable conditions, the Germans must be fed. He would waive his objection to the use of the gold provided the Germans would work for their food. This demand, the old atheist oddly added, would be found to be in agreement with the teachings of Christianity. As for his colleagues, M. Loucheur, M. Klotz and M. Clémentel were ever ready to be guided by feelings of humanity.

The debate dragged on, but the French were losing ground. Suddenly a secretary hurried in with a sealed envelope for the Prime Minister. It contained another telegram from Plumer received whilst the Conference was in session. The Prime Minister read it out immediately in a sensational manner. "Please inform the Prime Minister," the General telegraphed, "that in my opinion food must be sent into this area by the Allies without delay. . . . The mortality amongst women, children and sick is most grave, and sickness due to hunger is spreading. The attitude of the population is becoming one of despair, and the people feel that an end by bullets is preferable to death by starvation. . . . I request therefore that a definite date be fixed for the arrival of the first supplies." A considerable effect was produced; it became very difficult for the French to raise petty obstructionisms. I learnt afterwards that the whole thing had been stage-managed and that Plumer's telegram had been sent in response to a request from Paris, conveyed to him that morning in preparation for the afternoon.

The French were now collapsing, but were not yet finished. It was agreed that food should be furnished. But before the Germans were told this, they must formally acknowledge their obligation to surrender the ships. This was agreed. Very well, said Clemenceau, Marshal Foch shall meet the Germans and communicate the message to them. It was said innocently; but Lloyd George was quick enough to see the trap. Evidently the Marshal might contrive to deliver this ultimatum in such a way that the Germans would inevitably reject it. No, said Lloyd George, discarding the rhetorical for his bantering and humorous method, this has to do with ships, with sea not with land, and whilst he would defer to no man in his admiration of the Marshal on land, no, not to any man (stretching his hands towards Foch), was the Marshal equally at home on the sea? He, Lloyd George, had never crossed the Channel with him and so could not say for certain (smiling); but he would certainly get into terrible trouble in England if he did not retain for an Admiral the prerogative in such a matter as this. Admiral Wemyss, our First Sea Lord, was the man to deliver the message. The Marshal did not quite follow what was being said, but saw that he was being flattered and bantered; so he grinned and tugged his moustache. The Prime Minister appeared to be wreathed in good humour; everyone was pleased that the strain and tension were broken; and it was agreed at once that the Admiral should carry the ultimatum. It had been a ticklish moment, and Lloyd George's comic hint that the Marshal was a sea-sick subject was an inspiration in the creation of atmosphere.

But Klotz was not yet beaten. He still withheld the gold. The Germans should be allowed to pay in any other way, but not in gold. He had shown, he declared, a very conciliatory spirit and had made great sacrifices, but it was impossible for him to go further without compromising his country's interests, which (puffing himself out and attempting an appearance of dignity) had been placed in his charge.

Never have I seen the equal of the onslaught with which that poor man was overwhelmed. Do you know Klotz by sight? —a short, plump, heavy-moustached Jew, well groomed, well kept, but with an unsteady, roving eye, and his shoulders a little bent in an instinctive deprecation. Lloyd George had always hated him and despised him; and now saw in a twinkling that he could kill him. Women and children were starving, he cried, and here was M. Klotz prating and prating of his "goold." He leant forward and with a gesture of his hands indicated to everyone the image of a hideous Jew clutching a money bag. His eyes flashed and the words came out with a contempt so violent that he seemed almost to be spitting at him. The anti-Semitism, not far below the surface in such an assemblage as that one, was up in the heart of everyone. Everyone looked at Klotz with a momentary contempt and hatred; the poor man was bent over his seat, visibly cowering. We hardly knew what Lloyd George was saying, but the words "goold" and Klotz were repeated, and each time with exaggerated contempt. Then, turning, he called on Clemenceau to put a stop to these obstructive tactics, otherwise, he cried, M. Klotz would rank with Lenin and Trotsky among those who had spread Bolshevism in Europe. The Prime Minister ceased. All round the room you could see each one grinning and whispering to his neighbour "Klotzky."

Clemenceau did what he could to save the face of his minister, blustering for a few minutes how his country had been ruined and ravaged; what guarantees had France in return for this?—merely a few pieces of gold, a few securities, which it was now proposed to take from them. In a word, he was being asked to betray his country, and that he refused to do.

But it was really all over. Colonel House had supported the Prime Minister. So now did the Italians. The six Japs had sat, and still sat, silent, rigid and seemingly unapprehending, attendants at the drama of another planet. It was tea-time. Loucheur and I were told to go into the next room to prepare a formula. The gold was to be used after all.

Four days later I was on a train again, bound for Brussels with the staff of Admiral Wemyss. This time, surely, we should come to business. But there was one obstacle. The French had got their way on the point that the Germans were to give an unqualified acceptance to the surrender of the ships, *before* they were told our intentions about feeding them. In this way they must be taught that they were going to have to keep their engagements whatever we might do. But in the irritable, enraged and suspicious mood which they had shown at Spa might they not possibly refuse, and insist on our showing our hand about the food before they engaged themselves about the ships?

Rosie Wemyss, the First Sea Lord, was a new kind of admiral, unlike Browning of Trèves or Hope of Spa. The descendant of one of William IV's illegitimate children, with a comical, quizzical face and a single eye-glass, middle-aged, pleasure-loving, experienced and lazy, Rosie had still got a good many of the instincts of the flirtatious midshipman, and we had a very agreeable dinner in the restaurant car on that basis of relationship. Our level of wit may be measured by his great amusement that I, a University Professor, should, before we had finished the soup, have used the word "bloody"; he'd never before sat next a Professor at dinner, so he said, and was greatly surprised. The Germans next day were to be wonderfully perplexed by him; was he half-witted and imbecile? Or was he playing a game with them far cleverer than anything conceivable? They never made up their minds which; and to the end of history, I expect, the character of the English Rosie of the day will confound the understanding of Central Europe. There was one moment at the end of the Conference when the presiding German began to raise some financial point, of the answer to which Rosie hadn't the faintest conception. I was sitting three places down the table. So without any attempt at concealment from them sitting opposite, he hoisted a signal of distress and, turning my way with a comical, sea-sick-porpoise look, as good as said "For God's sake be quick and tell me what to say in answer to this silly ass' question." I wrote the reply on the paper table-cloth and tearing it off passed it down to him; he, all the time I was writing, keeping up a look of mock despair, like that with which the Provost (Durnford) often likes to catch my eye at a College Meeting which is being addressed by Macaulay. But the Germans were simply astonished—at his total abandonment of the faintest attempt to keep up appearances of knowing what this Conference was about, coupled with his supreme self-possession and unassailable, as it were social, superiority, like a humorous and good-natured duchess presiding over the financial business of a local charity—which somehow made *them,* so serious and pompous, seem to be a little absurd.

Later in the evening, when I had returned to my sleeping-car and was preparing for bed, Captain Jack Grant, R.N., the Admiral's Chief of Staff, came down the train to say that the Admiral wanted to see me in his saloon. "Well," said the Admiral. "Is this business going to go all right, d'you think? Will they give us the ships?" "Our proposals taken as a whole," I answered, "are very favourable to them and very nearly what they demanded at Spa. But if they are in the same temper and with the same instructions as at Spa, they may make trouble about the preliminary declaration. That's the difficult part of your job to-morrow." "Yes," he went on, "but there's got to be no mistake about this, d'you understand? Those are my instructions from the Prime Minister." There was a pause. "You've had something to do with these fellows, haven't you?" he added, looking at me rather oddly; evidently Hope had told him about my escapade with Melchior. "Yes," I said, "a little." "D'you think you could see to it that they don't make any unnecessary trouble? There's got to be no mistake about this, you know." I tumbled to his meaning, looked him in the eyes, and we both smiled. "Yes," I replied, "I might." "Well, you and Jack here had better see to it together." And without any more words I went back to my sleeping-car.

We reached Brussels and attended the Admiral at an official call at the British Legation. Then Captain Jack Grant and I slipped away from the rest and made off in a motor car for the hotel where the Germans were staying. We entered the lounge and could see them through a glass door with their paper napkins under their chins eating a heavy and an early lunch. We hung about awkwardly, until I saw the secretary with the cut-about face crossing the lounge. I accosted him. "The Allied

Delegation has just arrived," I said, "and I want to see Dr. Melchior for a moment about the time of this afternoon's meeting." Melchior was fetched out, and the three of us went up in the lift to Melchior's bedroom. The bed was unmade, an unemptied chamberpot was on the floor, something which seemed like a chemise lay across the bed; it must have been the wrong room or these were the debris of the guest of the previous night. But Melchior took no notice. "I want to tell you," I began, "the order of the afternoon's proceedings. At the beginning Excellenz von Braun will be called upon to make the following declaration about the ships, and until he has made it no further business can be proceeded with." Melchior's face fell. "But," I went on, looking at him, "for your own most private information I think it is desirable that you should know what will follow. If von Braun feels able to make this declaration freely and without qualification, the Allied representatives will then proceed to undertake to revictual Germany on the following conditions. Can you assure me that von Braun will do this?" Melchior started; looked round from me and saw on his other side, Captain Jack Grant, R.N. This was evidently more than a personal impulse on my part; and the situation was clear to him. After only a moment's pause he looked at me again with his solemn eyes. "Yes," he replied, "there shall be no difficulty about that." No more was said. I have recorded very nearly, I think, the *whole* of what passed between us. Jack Grant and I got up to go, and a few minutes later we were lunching at the Hotel Britannique with our own Delegation. The Admiral at the head of the table goggled his eyes at me. "I fancy it will be all right this afternoon," I murmured to him. And so it was; all went according to programme. The Admiral in as stern a voice as he could muster called on the Excellenz to make the declaration about the ships. The French waited eagerly. "Certainly," replied von Braun calmly and without a pause, "we have always been prepared to keep all of our engagements strictly, and I am entirely ready to repeat them in the manner requested."

There were many technical details to settle and we sat in conference with Melchior and the food experts for a long day.

But all was settled now and the food trains started for Germany.

I was to see Dr. Melchior a good many times more before I left Paris for good. The Brussels Conference gave rise to much detailed business, which could only be settled face to face. Yet frequent visits to Trèves or Spa were terribly wasteful of our time, and were becoming inconsistent with our other duties at the Peace Conference. I succeeded, therefore, without the knowledge of Foch, in getting off a telegram inviting Melchior and his colleagues to take up their residence in France. They agreed, and we kept them locked up for our convenience in the Chateau Villette near Compiègne, within a motor drive of Paris, where I visited them once a week for the transaction of current business. Later on when the rest of the German Delegation was invited to Versailles, Melchior removed there also, and our later meetings were held in the great Hotel bordering on the Park where in the autumn of 1914 I had visited my brother Geoffrey.

But I pass over these meetings to record the third and last occasion when I was alone with him. In October 1919, after I had returned to Cambridge, some Dutch financiers invited me to visit Amsterdam to discuss the situation with them; and on the 12th October I arrived in Holland. Melchior had resigned from his position sooner than be a party to the Peace Treaty. Since that time he had twice refused to become Minister of Finance in the new German State, and had quietly gone back to his banking business at Hamburg. I longed to see him again; and this was an opportunity. So from Amsterdam I caused a telegram to be sent to him saying that I should be there for a few days and would like to see him. Three days later he had arrived.

Amsterdam swarms with spies and busybodies, and it was thought better that we should not meet in an hotel. Accordingly my friend Dr. Vissering, the Governor of the Bank of the Netherlands, placed his study at our disposal. He lived on the Keizersgracht, one of those canals which, situated in concentric circles, give to Amsterdam its peculiarity. Before his house was one canal and behind his garden was another. The house, one of the merchant mansions of Dutch glory, had a narrow front, but immense depth, and was so placed that, bales being drawn up into the attics from barges, it could be residence and warehouse in one. Earlier in his career Dr. Vissering had been Governor of the Bank of Java, and in his long study, running back from the window over the canal into darkness, Chino-Javanese lamps and images and cabinets, and all the ungainly bric-à-brac of a middle-class merchant from the East, overlaid the comfortable dignity of seventeenth-century Holland. No one was there; it was drizzling heavily; and I looked out over the canal. I began to wonder at the impulse which had caused me to send for Melchior, for no such idea had entered my head before I left England, and what possible purpose this interview could serve. All the same I wanted to see him immensely. At last the door opened and he came in.

It was extraordinary to meet without barriers, we two who had faced one another so often in opposition and etiquette and constraint. Those Paris negotiations seemed to be absurd and to belong to a dream; and after a moment's emotional embarrassment we settled down to a long rambling gossip as two ordinary people. He told me of the last days at Weimar, and the struggle over the signature of the Treaty, his own resignation, how these days had been the most dreadful of all, how Erzberger had deliberately betrayed to an agent of the English Government the decision of a secret Cabinet Meeting between Noske, David and himself, in which it had been decided that in any event they must sign, and how he, Melchior, believed that it was out of a knowledge of this decision that Lloyd George finally decided to abandon his efforts towards moderation. Melchior's emotions were towards Germany and the falsehood and humiliation which his own people had brought on themselves, rather than towards us. I also understood most clearly, then for the first time, how dwellers in Eastern Germany look to the East and not Westwards. The war for him had been a war against Russia; and it was the thought of the dark forces which might now issue from the Eastwards, which most obsessed him. I also understood better than before, what a

precisian he was, a strict and upright moralist, a worshipper of
the Tablets of the Law, a Rabbi. The breach of promise, the
breach of discipline, the decay of honourable behaviour, the
betrayal of undertakings by the one party and the insincere
acceptance by the other of impossible conditions which it was
not intended to carry out, Germany almost as guilty to accept
what she could not fulfil as the Allies to impose what they were
not entitled to exact—it was these offences against The Word
which so much wounded him.

As we talked on, the morning passed and it began to seem
ridiculous to me that we should not lunch together openly,
like any other couple. So I asked him to my hotel, where a
German American Jew, Paul Warburg, brother of Melchior's
Hamburg partner, but one of the leading financiers of the
United States and formerly the chief spirit of the Federal Reserve Board, was also to be my guest. We strolled out through
Amsterdam, and Melchior, who knew it well, took me on our
way to see a courtyard of ancient almshouses, which conveyed
to him, he said, most perfectly the intimate atmosphere of the
town. It was a charming spot, indicative of order and of retirement.

My book was not then out, and I had with me the manuscript of my chapter on the President. After lunch I read it to
them. We went upstairs for privacy, this time to my bedroom
not Melchior's. I noted its effect on the two Jews. Warburg, for
personal reasons, hated the President and felt a chuckling delight at his discomfiture; he laughed and giggled and thought
it an awfully good hit. But Melchior, as I read, grew ever more
solemn, until at the end he appeared almost to be in tears.
This, then, was the other side of the curtain; neither profound
causes, nor inevitable fate, nor magnificent wickedness. The
Tablets of the Law, it was Melchior's thought at that moment,
had perished meanly.

Introductory note: MY EARLY BELIEFS

The paper which follows was written as the result of a memoir of mine which was read in Lord Keynes's absence, owing, I think, to his illness. It was afterwards sent to him to read. I am not sure of the date when my paper was read, but the envelope in which it is contained shows that it was returned by him from Tilton at the end of August 1938. His paper, which is printed here, was written at the beginning of September, when my paper was fresh in his mind. The subject of my memoir was the story of my introducing several of my friends to D. H. Lawrence, his intense dislike of them, and my bitter disappointment, which led me to stop seeing Lawrence. Keynes was one of my friends whom Lawrence most disliked. His feeling about them was, in essence, religious intolerance. He was a prophet who hated all those whose creeds protected them from ever becoming his disciples. I brought this out in my memoir and thus led Keynes to the re-examination of his early beliefs which follows.

I had got to know Lawrence and Frieda in 1912 owing to my father's friendship with him.

I was extremely fond of him and have no doubt that he liked me. I have never met a writer who appeared to have such genius. I greatly admired, and still admire, his short stories, his poems and several of his novels, particularly his first novel *The White Peacock*. But I was a rationalist and a scientist, and I was repelled by his intuitive and dogmatic philosophy, whereas the ideas of my friends from Cambridge interested and attracted me.

It was thus inevitable that sooner or later Lawrence should spew me out of his mouth, since I could never take his philosophy seriously. The breach was merely hastened by his meeting my friends. After my last visit to stay with Lawrence he wrote to Lady Ottoline Morrell, to whom I had also introduced him, in a letter included in his published correspondence:

We had David Garnett and Francis Birrell here for the weekend. When Birrell comes, tired and a bit lost and wandering— I love him. But, my God, to hear him talk sends me mad. To hear these young people talk really fills me with black fury: they talk endlessly, but endlessly—and never, never a good thing said. They are cased each in a hard little shell of his own and out of this they talk words. There is never for one second any outgoing of feeling and no reverence, not a crumb or grain of reverence. I cannot stand it. I will not have people like this —I had rather be alone. They made me dream of a beetle that bites like a scorpion. But I killed it—a very large beetle. I scotched it and it ran off—but I came on it again, and killed it. It is this horror of little swarming selves I can't stand.

On the same day, the 19th April, 1915, Lawrence wrote to me:

My dear David,
Never bring Birrell to see me any more. There is something nasty about him like black beetles. He is horrible and unclean. I feel I should go mad when I think of your set, Duncan Grant and Keynes and Birrell. It makes me dream of beetles. In Cambridge I had a similar dream. I had felt it slightly before in the Stracheys. But it came full upon me in Keynes and in Duncan Grant. And yesterday I knew it again in Birrell . . . you must leave these friends, these beetles, Birrell and Duncan Grant are done for forever. Keynes I am not sure . . . when I saw Keynes that morning in Cambridge it was one of the crises of my life. It sent me mad with misery and hostility and rage. . . .

I replied to this letter, which was really an ultimatum telling me to break with him or with my friends, as I thought suitably and I only once saw Lawrence again, by accident, on Armistice Night, the 11th November 1918, in Montague Shearman's rooms in the Adelphi. The breach would no doubt have been healed had Lawrence been more often in England. I continued to see Frieda when she visited England periodically, and in 1928 I wrote to Lawrence to tell him how much I admired *Lady Chatterley's Lover* in a letter which pleased him, and he wrote me a warm and friendly letter in return.

The reader is now in possession of the facts which led Maynard Keynes to re-examine his beliefs and those of his closest friends when they were undergraduates at Cambridge.

DAVID GARNETT

MY EARLY BELIEFS

I can visualise very clearly the scene of my meeting with D. H. Lawrence in 1914 (Bunny seems to suggest 1915, but my memory suggests that it may have been earlier than that) of which he speaks in the letter from which Bunny quoted at the last meeting of the Club. But unfortunately I cannot remember any fragment of what was said, though I retain some faint remains of what was felt.

It was at a breakfast party given by Bertie Russell in his rooms in Nevile's Court. There were only the three of us there. I fancy that Lawrence had been staying with Bertie and that there had been some meeting or party the night before, at which Lawrence had been facing Cambridge. Probably he had not enjoyed it.[1] My memory is that he was morose from the outset and said very little, apart from indefinite expressions of irritable dissent, all the morning. Most of the talk was between Bertie and me, and I haven't the faintest recollection of what it was about. But it was not the sort of conversation we should have had if we had been alone. It was *at* Lawrence and with the intention, largely unsuccessful, of getting him to participate. We sat round the fireplace with the sofa drawn across. Lawrence sat on the right-hand side in rather a crouching position with his head down. Bertie stood up by the fireplace, as I think I did, too, from time to time. I came away

feeling that the party had been a failure and that we had
failed to establish contact, but with no other particular impression. You know the sort of situation when two familiar
friends talk *at* a visitor. I had never seen him before, and I
never saw him again. Many years later he recorded in a letter,
which is printed in his published correspondence, that I was the
only member of Bloomsbury who had supported him by sub-
scribing for *Lady Chatterley*.

That is all I *remember*. But Bunny's story suggests some inferences to me. In the passage of his life which Bunny has
described I think that Lawrence was influenced by two causes
of emotional disturbance. One of them centred round Ottoline.
As always, Ottoline was keeping more than one world. Except
for Bertie, the Cambridge and Bloomsbury world was only just
beginning to hold her. Lawrence, Gertler, Carrington were a
different strand in her furbelows. Lawrence was jealous of the
other lot; and Cambridge rationalism and cynicism, then at
their height, were, of course, repulsive to him. Bertie gave him
what must have been, I think, his first glimpse of Cambridge.
It overwhelmed, attracted and repulsed him—which was the
other emotional disturbance. It was obviously a civilisation,
and not less obviously uncomfortable and unattainable for
him—very repulsive and very attractive. Now Bunny had
come into his life quite independently, neither through Ottoline nor from Cambridge and Bloomsbury; he was evidently
very fond of Bunny; and when he saw *him* being seduced by
Cambridge, he was yet more jealous, just as he was jealous
of Ottoline's new learnings that way. And jealousy apart, it
is impossible to imagine moods more antagonistic than those
of Lawrence and of pre-war Cambridge.

But when all that has been said, was there something true
and right in what Lawrence felt? There generally was. His
reactions were incomplete and unfair, but they were not usually
baseless. I have said that I have forgotten what the conversation was about. But I expect it was pretty brittle stuff—not so
brittle as Frankie Birrell's—but pretty brittle all the same. And
although it was silly to take it, or to estimate it, at its face
value, did the way of responding to life which lay behind it

lack something important? Lawrence was oblivious of anything valuable it may have offered—it was a *lack* that he was violently apprehending. So Bunny's memoir has thrown my mind back to reflections about our mental history in the dozen years before the war; and if it will not shock the club too much, I should like in this contribution to its proceedings to introduce for once, mental or spiritual, instead of sexual, adventures, to try and recall the principal impacts on one's virgin mind and to wonder how it has all turned out, and whether one still holds by that youthful religion.

I went up to Cambridge at Michaelmas 1902, and Moore's *Principia Ethica* came out at the end of my first year. I have never heard of the present generation having read it. But, of course, its effect on *us,* and the talk which preceded and followed it, dominated, and perhaps still dominate, everything else. We were at an age when our beliefs influenced our behaviour, a characteristic of the young which it is easy for the middle-aged to forget, and the habits of feeling formed then still persist in a recognisable degree. It is those habits of feeling, influencing the majority of us, which make this Club a collectivity and separate us from the rest. They overlaid, somehow, our otherwise extremely different characters—Moore himself was a puritan and precisian, Strachey (for that was his name at that time) a Voltairean, Woolf a rabbi, myself a nonconformist, Sheppard a conformist and (as it now turns out) an ecclesiastic, Clive a gay and amiable dog, Sydney-Turner a quietist, Hawtrey a dogmatist and so on. Of those who had come just before, only MacCarthy and Ainsworth, who were much influenced by their personal feelings for Moore, came under his full influence. We did not see much of Forster at that time; who was already the elusive colt of a dark horse. It was only for us, those who were active in 1903, that Moore completely ousted McTaggart, Dickinson, Russell. The influence was not only overwhelming; but it was the extreme opposite of what Strachey used to call *funeste;* it was exciting, exhilarating, the beginning of a renaissance, the opening of a new heaven on a new earth, we were the forerunners of a new dispensation, we were not afraid of anything. Perhaps it was because we were so brought up that even at our gloomiest and worst we have never lost a certain resilience which the younger generation seem never to have had. They have enjoyed, at most, only a pale reflection of something, not altogether superseded, but faded and without illusions.

Now what we got from Moore was by no means entirely what he offered us. He had one foot on the threshold of the new heaven, but the other foot in Sidgwick and the Benthamite calculus and the general rules of correct behaviour. There was one chapter in the *Principia* of which we took not the slightest notice. We accepted Moore's religion, so to speak, and discarded his morals. Indeed, in our opinion, one of the greatest advantages of his religion, was that it made morals unnecessary—meaning by "religion" one's attitude towards oneself and the ultimate and by "morals" one's attitude towards the outside world and the intermediate. To the consequences of having a religion and no morals I return later.

Even if the new members of the Club know what the religion was (do they?), it will not do any of us any harm to try and recall the crude outlines. Nothing mattered except states of mind, our own and other people's of course, but chiefly our own. These states of mind were not associated with action or achievement or with consequences. They consisted in timeless, passionate states of contemplation and communion, largely unattached to "before" and "after." Their value depended, in accordance with the principle of organic unity, on the state of affairs as a whole which could not be usefully analysed into parts. For example, the value of the state of mind of being in love did not depend merely on the nature of one's own emotions, but also on the worth of their object and on the reciprocity and nature of the object's emotions; but it did not depend, if I remember rightly, or did not depend much, on what happened, or how one felt about it, a year later, though I myself was always an advocate of a principle of organic unity through time, which still seems to me only sensible. The appropriate subjects of passionate contemplation and communion were a beloved person, beauty and truth, and one's prime objects in life were love, the creation and enjoyment of aesthetic experience and the pursuit of knowledge. Of these love came a long way first. But in the early days under Moore's influence the public treatment of this and its associated acts was, on the whole, austere and platonic. Some of us might argue that physical enjoyment could spoil and detract from the state of mind as a whole. I do not remember at what date Strachey issued his edict that certain Latin technical terms of sex were the correct words to use, that to avoid them was a grave error, and, even in mixed company, a weakness, and the use of other synonyms a vulgarity. But I should certainly say that this was later. In 1903 those words were not even esoteric terms of common discourse.

Our religion closely followed the English puritan tradition of being chiefly concerned with the salvation of our own souls. The divine resided within a closed circle. There was not a very intimate connection between "being good" and "doing good"; and we had a feeling that there was some risk that in practice the latter might interfere with the former. But religions proper, as distinct from modern "social service" pseudo-religions, have always been of that character; and perhaps it was a sufficient offset that our religion was altogether unworldly—with wealth, power, popularity or success it had no concern whatever, they were thoroughly despised.

How did we know what states of mind were good? This was a matter of direct inspection, of direct unanalysable intuition about which it was useless and impossible to argue. In that case who was right when there was a difference of opinion? There were two possible explanations. It might be that the two parties were not really talking about the same thing, that they were not bringing their intuitions to bear on precisely the same object, and, by virtue of the principle of organic unity, a very small difference in the object might make a very big difference in the result. Or it might be that some people had an acuter sense of judgement, just as some people can judge a vintage port and others cannot. On the whole, so far as I remember, this explanation prevailed. In practice, victory was with those who could speak with the greatest appearance of clear, undoubting conviction and could best use the accents

of infallibility. Moore at this time was a master of this method
—greeting one's remarks with a gasp of incredulity—*Do* you
really think *that,* an expression of face as if to hear such a
thing said reduced him to a state of wonder verging on imbecility, with his mouth wide open and wagging his head in
the negative so violently that his hair shook. *Oh!* he would say,
goggling at you as if either you or he must be mad; and
no reply was possible. Strachey's methods were different; grim
silence as if such a dreadful observation was beyond comment
and the less said about it the better, but almost as effective
for disposing of what he called deathpackets. Woolf was fairly
good at indicating a negative, but he was better at producing
the effect that it was useless to argue with *him* than at crushing *you*. Dickinson knew how to shrug his shoulders and retreat unconvinced, but it was retreat all the same. As for
Sheppard and me we could only turn like worms, but worms
who could be eventually goaded into voluble claims that worms
have at least the *right* to turn. Yet after all the differences
were about details. Broadly speaking we all knew for certain
what were good states of mind and that they consisted in
communion with objects of love, beauty and truth.

I have called this faith a religion, and some sort of relation
of neo-platonism it surely was. But we should have been very
angry at the time with such a suggestion. We regarded all this
as entirely rational and scientific in character. Like any other
branch of science, it was nothing more than the application of
logic and rational analysis to the material presented as sense-
data. Our apprehension of good was exactly the same as our
apprehension of green, and we purported to handle it with
the same logical and analytical technique which was appropriate
to the latter. Indeed we combined a dogmatic treatment as to
the nature of experience with a method of handling it which
was extravagantly scholastic. Russell's *Principles of Mathematics*
came out in the same year as *Principia Ethica;* and the former,
in spirit, furnished a method for handling the material provided
by the latter. Let me give you a few examples of the sort
of things we used to discuss.

If A was in love with B and believed that B reciprocated

his feelings, whereas in fact B did not, but was in love with C, the state of affairs was certainly not so good as it would have been if A had been right, but was it worse or better than it would become if A discovered his mistake? If A was in love with B under a misapprehension as to B's qualities, was this better or worse than A's not being in love at all? If A was in love with B because A's spectacles were not strong enough to see B's complexion, did this altogether, or partly, destroy the value of A's state of mind? Suppose we were to live our lives backwards, having our experiences in the reverse order, would this affect the value of our successive states of mind? If the states of mind enjoyed by each of us were pooled and then redistributed, would this affect their value? How did one compare the value of a good state of mind which had bad consequences with a bad state of mind which had good consequences? In valuing the consequences did one assess them at their actual value as it turned out eventually to be, or their probable value at the time? If at their probable value, how much evidence as to possible consequences was it one's duty to collect before applying the calculus? Was there a separate objective standard of beauty? Was a beautiful thing, that is to say, by definition that which it was good to contemplate? Or was there an actual objective quality "beauty," just like "green" and "good"? And knowledge, too, presented a problem. Were all truths equally good to pursue and contemplate?—as for example the number of grains in a given tract of sea-sand. We were disposed to repudiate very strongly the idea that useful knowledge could be preferable to useless knowledge. But we flirted with the idea that there might be some intrinsic quality —though not, perhaps, quite on a par with "green" and "good" and "beautiful"—which one could call "interesting," and we were prepared to think it just possible that "interesting" knowledge might be better to pursue than "uninteresting" knowledge. Another competing adjective was "important," provided it was quite clear that "important" did not mean "useful." Or to return again to our favourite subject, was a violent love affair which lasted a short time better than a more tepid one which endured longer? We were inclined to think it was. But

I have said enough by now to make it clear that the problems of mensuration, in which we had involved ourselves, were somewhat formidable.

It was all under the influence of Moore's method, according to which you could hope to make essentially vague notions clear by using precise language about them and asking exact questions. It was a method of discovery by the instrument of impeccable grammar and an unambiguous dictionary. "What *exactly* do you mean?" was the phrase most frequently on our lips. If it appeared under cross-examination that you did not mean *exactly* anything, you lay under a strong suspicion of meaning nothing whatever. It was a stringent education in dialectic; but in practice it was a kind of combat in which strength of character was really much more valuable than subtlety of mind. In the preface to his great work, bespattered with the numerous italics through which the reader who knew him could actually hear, as with Queen Victoria, the vehemence of his utterance, Moore begins by saying that error is chiefly "the attempt to answer questions, without first discovering precisely *what* question it is which you desire to answer. . . . Once we recognise the exact meaning of the two questions, I think it also becomes plain exactly what kind of reasons are relevant as arguments for or against any particular answer to them." So we spent our time trying to discover *precisely what* questions we were asking, confident in the faith that, if only we could ask precise questions, everyone would know the answer. Indeed Moore expressly claimed as much. In his famous chapter on "The Ideal" he wrote:

Indeed, once the meaning of the question is clearly understood, the answer to it, in its main outlines, appears to be so obvious, that it runs the risk of seeming to be a platitude. By far the most valuable things, which we know or can imagine, are certain states of consciousness, which may be roughly described as the pleasures of human intercourse and the enjoyment of beautiful objects. No one, probably, who has asked himself the question, has ever doubted that personal affection and the appreciation of what is beautiful in Art or Nature, are good in themselves; nor if we consider strictly what things are worth having *purely for their own sakes,* does it appear probable that any one will think that anything else has *nearly* so great a value as the things which are included under these two heads.

And then there was the question of pleasure. As time wore on towards the nineteen-tens, I fancy we weakened a bit about pleasure. But, in our prime, pleasure was nowhere. I would faintly urge that if two states of mind were similar in all other respects except that one was pleasurable and the other was painful there *might* be a little to be said for the former, but the principle of organic unities was against me. It was the general view (though not quite borne out by the *Principia*) that pleasure had nothing to do with the case and, on the whole, a pleasant state of mind lay under grave suspicion of lacking intensity and passion.

In those days X. had not taken up women, nor Woolf monkeys, and they were not their present blithe selves. The two of them, sunk deep in silence and in basket chairs on opposite sides of the fireplace in a room which was at all times pitch dark, would stop sucking their pipes only to murmur that all good states of mind were extremely painful and to imply that all painful states of mind were extremely good. Strachey seconded them—it was only in his second childhood that Lytton took up pleasure—though his sorrow was more fitful than their settled gloom. But with Sheppard and myself cheerfulness could not but break through, and we were in great disgrace about it. There was a terrible scene one evening when we turned insubordinate and reckless and maintained that there was nothing wrong in itself in being cheerful. It was decided that such low habits were particularly characteristic of King's as opposed to the austerity of Trinity.

Socrates had persuaded Protarchus that pure hedonism was absurd. Moore himself was only prepared to accept pleasure as an enhancement of a state of affairs otherwise good. But Moore hated evil and he found a place in his religion for vindictive punishment. "Not only is the pleasantness of a state *not* in proportion to its intrinsic worth; it may even add positively to its vileness. . . . The infliction of pain on a person whose state of mind is bad may, if the pain be not too intense, create a state of things that is better *on the whole* than if the evil state of mind had existed unpunished. Whether such a state of affairs can ever constitute a *positive* good is another question." I call attention to the qualification "if the pain be not too intense." Our Ideal was a merciful God.

Thus we were brought up—with Plato's absorption in the good in itself, with a scholasticism which outdid St. Thomas, in calvinistic withdrawal from the pleasures and successes of Vanity Fair, and oppressed with all the sorrows of Werther. It did not prevent us from laughing most of the time and we enjoyed supreme self-confidence, superiority and contempt towards all the rest of the unconverted world. But it was hardly a state of mind which a grown-up person in his senses could sustain literally. When MacCarthy came down for a week-end, he would smile affectionately, persuade Moore to sing his German Lieder at the piano, to hear which we all agreed was a very good state of mind indeed, or incite Bob Trevy to deliver a broken oration which was a frantic travesty of the whole method, the charm of it lying in the impossibility of deciding whether Bob himself meant it, half at least, seriously or not.

It seems to me looking back, that this religion of ours was a very good one to grow up under. It remains nearer the truth than any other that I know, with less irrelevant extraneous matter and nothing to be ashamed of; though it is a comfort to-day to be able to discard with a good conscience the calculus and the mensuration and the duty to know *exactly* what one means and feels. It was a purer, sweeter air by far than Freud cum Marx. It is still my religion under the surface. I read again last week Moore's famous chapter on "The Ideal." It is remarkable how wholly oblivious he managed to be of the qualities of the life of action and also of the pattern of life as a whole. He was existing in a timeless ecstasy. His way of translating his own particular emotions of the moment into the language of generalised abstraction is a charming and beautiful comedy. Do you remember the passage in which he discusses whether, granting that it is mental qualities which one should chiefly love, it is important that the beloved person should also be good-looking? In the upshot good looks win a modest victory over "mental qualities." I cannot forbear to quote this sweet and lovely passage, so sincere and passionate and careful:

I think it may be admitted that wherever the affection is most valuable, the appreciation of mental qualities must form a large part of it, and that the presence of this part makes the whole far more valuable than it could have been without it. But it seems very doubtful whether this appreciation, by itself, can possess as much value as the whole in which it is combined with an appreciation of the appropriate *corporeal* expression of the mental qualities in question. It is certain that in all actual cases of valuable affection, the bodily expressions of character, whether by looks, by words, or by actions, do form a part of the object towards which the affection is felt, and that the fact of their inclusion appears to heighten the value of the whole state. It is, indeed, very difficult to imagine what the cognition of mental qualities *alone,* unaccompanied by *any* corporeal expression, would be like; and, in so far as we succeed in making this abstraction, the whole considered certainly appears to have less value. I therefore conclude that the importance of an admiration of admirable mental qualities lies chiefly in the immense superiority of a whole, in which it forms a part, to one in which it is absent, and not in any high degree of intrinsic value which it possesses by itself. It even appears to be doubtful, whether, in itself, it possesses so much value as the appreciation of mere corporeal beauty undoubtedly does possess; that is to say, whether the appreciation of what has great intrinsic value is so valuable as the appreciation of what is merely beautiful.
But further if we consider the nature of admirable mental qualities, by themselves, it appears that a proper appreciation of them involves a reference to purely material beauty in yet another way. Admirable mental qualities do, if our previous conclusions are correct, consist very largely in an emotional contemplation of beautiful objects; and hence the appreciation of them will consist essentially in the contemplation of such contemplation. It is true that the most valuable appreciation of persons appears to be that which consists in the appreciation of their appreciation of other persons: but even here a reference to material beauty appears to be involved, *both* in respect of the fact that what is appreciated in the last instance may be the contemplation of what is merely beautiful, *and* in respect of the fact that the most valuable appreciation of a person appears to *include* an appreciation of his corporeal expression. Though, therefore, we may admit that the appreciation of a person's attitude towards other persons, or, to take one instance,

the love of love, is far the most valuable good we know, and far more valuable than the mere love of beauty, yet we can only admit this if the first be understood to *include* the latter, in various degrees of directness.

The New Testament is a handbook for politicians compared with the unworldliness of Moore's chapter on "The Ideal." I know no equal to it in literature since Plato. And it is better than Plato because it is quite free from *fancy*. It conveys the beauty of the literalness of Moore's mind, the pure and passionate intensity of his vision, *un*fanciful and *un*dressed-up. Moore had a nightmare once in which he could not distinguish propositions from tables. But even when he was awake, he could not distinguish love and beauty and truth from the furniture. They took on the same definition of outline, the same stable, solid, objective qualities and common-sense reality.

I see no reason to shift from the fundamental intuitions of *Principia Ethica;* though they are much too few and too narrow to fit actual experience which provides a richer and more various content. That they furnish a justification of experience wholly independent of outside events has become an added comfort, even though one cannot live to-day secure in the undisturbed individualism which was the extraordinary achievement of the early Edwardian days, not for our little lot only, but for everyone else, too.

I am still a long way off from D. H. Lawrence and what he might have been justified in meaning when he said that we were "done for." And even now I am not quite ready to approach that theme. First of all I must explain the other facet of our faith. So far it has been a question of our attitude to ourselves and one another. What was our understanding of the outside world and our relation to it?

It was an important object of Moore's book to distinguish between goodness as an attribute of states of mind and rightness as an attribute of actions. He also has a section on the justification of general rules of conduct. The large part played by considerations of probability in his theory of right conduct was, indeed, an important contributory cause to my spending all the leisure of many years on the study of that subject: I was writing under the joint influence of Moore's *Principia Ethica* and Russell's *Principia Mathematica*. But for the most part, as I have said, we did not pay attention to this aspect of the book or bother much about it. We were living in the specious present, nor had begun to play the game of consequences. We existed in the world of Plato's *Dialogues;* we had not reached the *Republic,* let alone the *Laws.*

This brought us one big advantage. As we had thrown hedonism out of the window and, discarding Moore's so highly problematical calculus, lived entirely in present experience, since social action as an end in itself and not merely as a lugubrious duty had dropped out of our Ideal, and, not only social action, but the life of action generally, power, politics, success, wealth, ambition, with the economic motive and the economic criterion less prominent in our philosophy than with St. Francis of Assisi, who at least made collections for the birds, it follows that we were amongst the first of our generation, perhaps alone amongst our generation, to escape from the Benthamite tradition. In practice, of course, at least so far as I was concerned, the outside world was not forgotten or forsworn. But I am recalling what our Ideal was in those early days when the life of passionate contemplation and communion was supposed to oust all other purposes whatever. It can be no part of this memoir for me to try to explain why it was such a big advantage for us to have escaped from the Benthamite tradition. But I do now regard that as the worm which has been gnawing at the insides of modern civilisation and is responsible for its present moral decay. We used to regard the Christians as the enemy, because they appeared as the representatives of tradition, convention and hocus-pocus. In truth it was the Benthamite calculus, based on an over-valuation of the economic criterion, which was destroying the quality of the popular Ideal.

Moreover, it was this escape from Bentham, joined with the unsurpassable individualism of our philosophy, which has served to protect the whole lot of us from the final *reductio ad absurdum* of Benthamism known as Marxism. We have completely failed, indeed, to provide a substitute for these economic bogus-faiths capable of protecting or satisfying our successors. But we ourselves have remained—am I not right in saying *all* of us?—altogether immune from the virus, as safe in the citadel of our ultimate faith as the Pope of Rome in his.

This is what we gained. But we set on one side, not only that part of Moore's fifth chapter on "Ethics in relation to Conduct" which dealt with the obligation so to act as to produce by causal connection the most probable maximum of eventual good through the whole procession of future ages (a discussion which was indeed riddled with fallacies), but also the part which discussed the duty of the individual to obey general rules. We entirely repudiated a personal liability on us to obey general rules. We claimed the right to judge every individual case on its merits, and the wisdom, experience and self-control to do so successfully. This was a very important part of our faith, violently and aggressively held, and for the outer world it was our most obvious and dangerous characteristic. We repudiated entirely customary morals, conventions and traditional wisdom. We were, that is to say, in the strict sense of the term, immoralists. The consequences of being found out had, of course, to be considered for what they were worth. But we recognised no moral obligation on us, no inner sanction, to conform or to obey. Before heaven we claimed to be our own judge in our own case. I have come to think that this is, perhaps, rather a Russian characteristic. It is certainly not an English one. It resulted in a general, widespread, though partly covert, suspicion affecting ourselves, our motives and our behaviour. This suspicion still persists to a certain extent, and it always will. It has deeply coloured the course of our lives in relation to the outside world. It is, I now think, a justifiable suspicion. Yet so far as I am concerned, it is too late to change. I remain, and always will remain, an immoralist.

I am not now concerned, however, with the fact that this aspect of our code was shocking. It would have been not less so, even if we had been perfectly right. What matters a great deal more is the fact that it was flimsily based, as I now think, on an *a priori* view of what human nature is like, both other people's and our own, which was disastrously mistaken.

I have said that we were amongst the first to escape from Benthamism. But of another eighteenth-century heresy we were the unrepentant heirs and last upholders. We were among the last of the Utopians, or meliorists as they are sometimes called, who believe in a continuing moral progress by virtue of which the human race already consists of reliable, rational, decent people, influenced by truth and objective standards, who can be safely released from the outward restraints of convention and traditional standards and inflexible rules of conduct, and left, from now onwards, to their own sensible devices, pure motives and reliable intuitions of the good. The view that human nature is reasonable had in 1903 quite a long history behind it. It underlay the ethics of self-interest—rational self-interest as it was called—just as much as the universal ethics of Kant or Bentham which aimed at the general good; and it was because self-interest was *rational* that the egoistic and altruistic systems were supposed to work out in practice to the same conclusions.

In short, we repudiated all versions of the doctrine of original sin, of there being insane and irrational springs of wickedness in most men. We were not aware that civilisation was a thin and precarious crust erected by the personality and the will of a very few, and only maintained by rules and conventions skilfully put across and guilefully preserved. We had no respect for traditional wisdom or the restraints of custom. We lacked reverence, as Lawrence observed and as Ludwig with justice also used to say—for everything and everyone. It did not occur to us to respect the extraordinary accomplishment of our predecessors in the ordering of life (as it now seems to me to have been) or the elaborate framework which they had devised to protect this order. Plato said in his *Laws* that one of the best of a set of good laws would be a law forbidding any young man to enquire which of them are right or wrong, though an old man remarking any defect in the laws might communicate this observation to a ruler or to an equal in years when no young man was present. That was a *dictum* in which we should have been unable to discover any point or significance whatever. As cause and consequence of our general state of mind we completely misunderstood human nature, including our own. The rationality which we attributed to it led to a superficiality, not only of judgement, but also of feeling. It was not only that intellectually we were pre-Freudian, but we had lost something which our predecessors had without replacing it. I still suffer incurably from attributing an unreal rationality to other people's feelings and behaviour (and doubtless to my own, too). There is one small but extraordinarily silly manifestation of this absurd idea of what is "normal," namely the impulse to *protest*—to write a letter to *The Times,* call a meeting in the Guildhall, subscribe to some fund when my presuppositions as to what is "normal" are not fulfilled. I behave as if there really existed some authority or standard to which I can successfully appeal if I shout loud enough—perhaps it is some hereditary vestige of a belief in the efficacy of prayer.

I have said that this pseudo-rational view of human nature led to a thinness, a superficiality, not only of judgement, but also of feeling. It seems to me that Moore's chapter on "The Ideal" left out altogether some whole categories of valuable emotion. The attribution of rationality to human nature, instead of enriching it, now seems to me to have impoverished it. It ignored certain powerful and valuable springs of feeling. Some of the spontaneous, irrational outbursts of human nature can have a sort of value from which our schematism was cut off. Even some of the feelings associated with wickedness can have value. And in addition to the values arising out of spontaneous, volcanic and even wicked impulses, there are many objects of valuable contemplation and communion beyond those we knew of—those concerned with the order and pattern of life amongst communities and the emotions which they can inspire. Though one must ever remember Paley's *dictum* that "although we speak of communities as of sentient beings and ascribe to them happiness and misery, desires, interests and passions, nothing really exists or feels but *individ-*

uals," yet we carried the individualism of our individuals too far.

And as the years wore on towards 1914, the thinness and superficiality, as well as the falsity, of our view of man's heart became, as it now seems to me, more obvious; and there was, too, some falling away from the purity of the original doctrine. Concentration on moments of communion between a pair of lovers got thoroughly mixed up with the, once rejected, pleasure. The pattern of life would sometimes become no better than a succession of permutations of short sharp superficial "intrigues," as we called them. Our comments on life and affairs were bright and amusing, but brittle—as I said of the conversation of Russell and myself with Lawrence—because there was no solid diagnosis of human nature underlying them. Bertie in particular sustained simultaneously a pair of opinions ludicrously incompatible. He held that in fact human affairs were carried on after a most irrational fashion, but that the remedy was quite simple and easy, since all we had to do was to carry them on rationally. A discussion of practical affairs on these lines was really very boring. And a discussion of the human heart which ignored so many of its deeper and blinder passions, both good and bad, was scarcely more interesting. Indeed it is only states of mind that matter, provided we agree to take account of the pattern of life through time and give up regarding it as a series of independent, instantaneous flashes, but the ways in which states of mind can be valuable, and the objects of them, are more various, and also much richer, than we allowed for. I fancy we used in old days to get round the rich variety of experience by expanding illegitimately the field of aesthetic appreciation (we would deal, for example, with all branches of the tragic emotion under this head), classifying as aesthetic experience what is really human experience and somehow sterilising it by this mis-classification.

If, therefore, I altogether ignore our merits—our charm, our intelligence, our unworldliness, our affection—I can see us as water-spiders, gracefully skimming, as light and reasonable as air, the surface of the stream without any contact at all with the eddies and currents underneath. And if I imagine us as coming under the observation of Lawrence's ignorant, jealous, irritable, hostile eyes, what a combination of qualities we offered to arouse his passionate distaste; this thin rationalism skipping on the crust of the lava, ignoring both the reality and the value of the vulgar passions, joined to libertinism and comprehensive irreverence, too clever by half for such an earthy character as Bunny, seducing with its intellectual *chic* such a portent as Ottoline, a regular skin-poison. All this was very unfair to poor, silly, well-meaning us. But that is why I say that there may have been just a grain of truth when Lawrence said in 1914 that we were "done for."

9th September 1938.

Part IV: Additional Essays

THE COUNCIL OF FOUR, PARIS, 1919

Clemenceau was by far the most eminent member of the Council of Four, and he had taken the measure of his colleagues. He alone both had an idea and had considered it in all its consequences. His age, his character, his wit, and his appearance joined to give him objectivity and a defined outline in an environment of confusion. One could not despise Clemenceau or dislike him, but only take a different view as to the nature of civilised man, or indulge, at least, a different hope.

The figure and bearing of Clemenceau are universally familiar. At the Council of Four he wore a square-tailed coat of very good, thick black broadcloth, and on his hands, which were never uncovered, grey suède gloves; his boots were of thick black leather, very good, but of a country style, and sometimes fastened in front, curiously, by a buckle instead of laces. His seat in the room in the President's house, where the regular meetings of the Council of Four were held (as distinguished from their private and unattended conferences in a smaller chamber below), was on a square brocaded chair in the middle of the semicircle facing the fire-place, with Signor Orlando on his left, the President next by the fire-place, and the Prime Minister opposite on the other side of the fire-place on his right. He carried no papers and no portfolio, and was unattended by any personal secretary, though several French ministers and officials appropriate to the particular matter in hand would be present round him. His walk, his hand, and his voice were not lacking in vigour, but he bore, nevertheless, especially after the attempt upon him, the aspect of a very old man conserving his strength for important occasions. He spoke seldom, leaving the initial statement of the French case to his ministers or officials; he closed his eyes often and sat back in his chair with an impassive face of parchment, his grey-gloved hands clasped in front of him. A short sentence, decisive or cynical, was generally sufficient, a question, an unqualified abandonment of his ministers, whose face would not be saved, or a display of obstinacy reinforced by a few words in a piquantly delivered English.[1] But speech and passion were not lacking when they were wanted, and the sudden outburst of words, often followed by a fit of deep coughing from the chest, produced their impression rather by force and surprise than by persuasion.

Not infrequently, Mr. Lloyd George, after delivering a speech in English, would, during the period of its interpretation into French, cross the hearthrug to the President to reinforce his case by some *ad hominem* argument in private conversation, or to sound the ground for a compromise—and this would sometimes be the signal for a general upheaval and disorder. The President's advisers would press round him, a moment later the British experts would dribble across to learn the result or see that all was well, and next the French would be there, a little suspicious lest the others were arranging something behind them, until all the room were on their feet and conversation was general in both languages. My last and most vivid impression is of such a scene—the President and the Prime Minister as the centre of a surging mob and a babel of sound, a welter of eager, impromptu compromises and counter-compromises, all sound and fury signifying nothing, on what was an unreal question anyhow, the great issues of the morning's meeting forgotten and neglected; and Clemenceau, silent and aloof on the outskirts—for nothing which touched the security of France was forward—throned, in his grey gloves, on the brocade chair, dry in soul and empty of hope, very old and tired, but surveying the scene with a cynical and almost impish air; and when at last silence was restored and the company had returned to their places, it was to discover that he had disappeared.

He felt about France what Pericles felt of Athens—unique value in her, nothing else mattering; but his theory of politics was Bismarck's. He had one illusion—France; and one disillusion—mankind, including Frenchmen and his colleagues not least. His principles for the Peace can be expressed simply. In the first place, he was a foremost believer in the view of German psychology that the German understands and can understand nothing but intimidation, that he is without generosity or remorse in negotiation, that there is no advantage he will not take of you, and no extent to which he will not demean himself for profit, that he is without honour, pride, or mercy. Therefore you must never negotiate with a German or conciliate him; you must dictate to him. On no other terms will he respect you, or will you prevent him from cheating you. But it is doubtful how far he thought these characteristics peculiar to Germany, or whether his candid view of some other nations was fundamentally different. His philosophy had, therefore, no place for "sentimentality" in international relations. Nations are real things, of which you love one and feel for the rest indifference—or hatred. The glory of the nation you love is a desirable end—but generally to be obtained at your neighbour's expense. The politics of power are inevitable, and there is nothing very new to learn about this war or the end it was fought for; England had destroyed, as in each preceding century, a trade rival; a mighty chapter had been closed in the secular struggle between the glories of Germany and of France. Prudence required some measure of lip service to the "ideals" of foolish Americans and hypocritical Englishmen; but it would be stupid to believe that there is much room in the world, as it really is, for such affairs as the League of Nations, or any sense in the principle of self-determination except as an ingenious formula for rearranging the balance of power in one's own interests.

These, however, are generalities. In tracing the practical details of the Peace which he thought necessary for the power and the security of France, we must go back to the historical causes which had operated during his lifetime. Before the Franco-German war the populations of France and Germany were approximately equal; but the coal and iron and shipping of Germany were in their infancy and the wealth of France was greatly superior. Even after the loss of Alsace-Lorraine there was no great discrepancy between the real resources of the two countries. But in the intervening period the relative position had changed completely. By 1914 the population of Germany was nearly 70 per cent in excess of that of France; she had become one of the first manufacturing and trading nations of the world; her technical skill and her means for the production of future wealth were unequalled. France, on the other hand, had a stationary or declining population, and, relatively to others, had fallen seriously behind in wealth and in the power to produce it.

In spite, therefore, of France's victorious issue from the present struggle (with the aid, this time, of England and America), her future position remained precarious in the eyes of one who took the view that European civil war is to be regarded as a normal, or at least a recurrent, state of affairs for the future, and that the sort of conflicts between organised Great Powers which have occupied the past hundred years will also engage the next. According to this vision of the future, European history is to be a perpetual prize-fight, of which France has won this round, but of which this round is certainly not the last. From the belief that essentially the old order does not change, being based on human nature which is always the same, and from a consequent scepticism of all that class of doctrine which the League of Nations stands for, the policy of France and of Clemenceau followed logically. For a Peace of magnanimity or of fair and equal treatment, based on such "ideology" as the Fourteen Points of the President, could only have the effect of shortening the interval of Germany's recovery and hastening the day when she will once again hurl at France her greater numbers and her superior resources and technical skill. Hence the necessity of "guarantees"; and each guarantee that was taken, by increasing irritation and thus the probability of a subsequent *revanche* by Germany, made necessary yet further provisions to crush. Thus, as soon as this view of the world is adopted and the other discarded, a demand for a Carthaginian Peace is inevitable, to the full extent of the momentary power to impose it. For Clemenceau made no pretence of considering himself bound by the Fourteen Points, and left chiefly to others such concoctions as were necessary from time to time to save the scruples or the face of the President.

So far as possible, therefore, it was the policy of France to set the clock back and to undo what, since 1870, the progress of Germany had accomplished. By loss of territory and other measures her population was to be curtailed; but chiefly the economic system, upon which she depended for her new strength, the vast fabric built upon iron, coal, and transport, must be destroyed. If France could seize, even in part, what Germany was compelled to drop, the inequality of strength between the two rivals for European hegemony might be remedied for many generations. Hence sprang those cumulative provisions of the Treaty for the destruction of highly organised economic life.

This is the policy of an old man, whose most vivid impressions and most lively imagination are of the past and not of the future. He sees the issue in terms of France and Germany, not of humanity and of European civilisation struggling forwards to a new order. The war has bitten into his consciousness somewhat differently from ours, and he neither expects nor hopes that we are at the threshold of a new age.

It happens, however, that it is not only an ideal question that is at issue. The Carthaginian Peace is not *practically* right or possible. Although the school of thought from which it springs is aware of the economic factor, it overlooks, nevertheless, the deeper economic tendencies which are to govern the future. The clock cannot be set back. You cannot restore Central Europe to 1870 without setting up such strains in the European structure and letting loose such human and spiritual forces as, pushing beyond frontiers and races, will overwhelm not only you and your "guarantees," but your institutions, and the existing order of your Society.

By what legerdemain was this policy substituted for the Fourteen Points, and how did the President come to accept it? The answer to these questions is difficult and depends on elements of character and psychology and on the subtle influence of surroundings, which are hard to detect and harder still to describe. But, if ever the action of a single individual matters, the collapse of the President has been one of the decisive moral events of history; and I must make an attempt to explain it. What a place the President held in the hearts and hopes of the world when he sailed to us in the *George Washington*! What a great man came to Europe in those early days of our victory!

In November 1918 the armies of Foch and the words of Wilson had brought us sudden escape from what was swallowing up all we cared for. The conditions seemed favourable beyond any expectation. The victory was so complete that fear need play no part in the settlement. The enemy had laid down his arms in reliance on a solemn compact as to the general character of the Peace, the terms of which seemed to assure a settlement of justice and magnanimity and a fair hope for a restoration of the broken current of life. To make assurance certain the President was coming himself to set the seal on his work.

When President Wilson left Washington he enjoyed a prestige and a moral influence throughout the world unequalled in history. His bold and measured words carried to the peoples of Europe above and beyond the voices of their own politicians. The enemy peoples trusted him to carry out the compact he had made with them; and the allied peoples acknowledged him not as a victor only but almost as a prophet. In addition to this moral influence, the realities of power were in his hands. The American armies were at the height of their numbers, discipline, and equipment. Europe was in complete dependence on the food supplies of the United States; and financially she was even more absolutely at their mercy. Europe not only already owed the United States more than she could pay; but only a large measure of further assistance could save her from starvation and bankruptcy. Never had a philosopher held such weapons wherewith to bind the princes of this world. How the crowds of the European capitals pressed about the carriage of the President! With what curiosity, anxiety, and hope we sought a glimpse of the features and bearing of the man of destiny who, coming from the West, was to bring healing to the wounds of the ancient parent of his civilisation and lay for us the foundations of the future!

The disillusion was so complete that some of those who had trusted most hardly dared speak of it. Could it be true? they asked of those who returned from Paris. Was the Treaty really as bad as it seemed? What had happened to the President? What weakness or what misfortune had led to so extraordinary, so unlooked-for a betrayal?

Yet the causes were very ordinary and human. The President was not a hero or a prophet; he was not even a philosopher; but a generously intentioned man, with many of the weaknesses of other human beings, and lacking that dominating intellectual equipment which would have been necessary to cope with the subtle and dangerous spell-binders whom a tremendous clash of forces and personalities had brought to the top as triumphant masters in the swift game of give and take, face to face in Council—a game of which he had no experience at all.

We had indeed quite a wrong idea of the President. We knew him to be solitary and aloof, and believed him very strong-willed and obstinate. We did not figure him as a man of detail, but the clearness with which he had taken hold of certain main ideas would, we thought, in combination with his tenacity, enable him to sweep through cobwebs. Besides these qualities he would have the objectivity, the cultivation, and the wide knowledge of the student. The great distinction of language which had marked his famous Notes seemed to indicate a man of lofty and powerful imagination. His portraits indicated a fine presence and a commanding delivery. With all this he had attained and held with increasing authority the first position in a country where the arts of the politician are not neglected. All of which, without expecting the impossible, seemed a fine combination of qualities for the matter in hand.

The first impression of Mr. Wilson at close quarters was to impair some but not all of these illusions. His head and features were finely cut and exactly like his photographs, and the muscles of his neck and the carriage of his head were distinguished. But, like Odysseus, the President looked wiser when he was seated; and his hands, though capable and fairly strong, were wanting in sensitiveness and finesse. The first glance at the President suggested not only that, whatever else he might be, his temperament was not primarily that of the student or the scholar, but that he had not much even of that culture of the world which marks M. Clemenceau and Mr. Balfour as exquisitely cultivated gentlemen of their class and generation. But more serious than this, he was not only insensitive to his surroundings in the external sense, he was not sensitive to his environment at all. What chance could such a man have against Mr. Lloyd George's unerring, almost medium-like, sensibility to everyone immediately round him? To see the British Prime Minister watching the company, with six or seven senses not available to ordinary men, judging character, motive, and subconscious impulse, perceiving what each was thinking and even what each was going to say next, and compounding with telepathic instinct the argument or appeal best suited to the vanity, weakness, or self-interest of his immediate auditor, was to realise that the poor President would be playing blind-man's-buff in that party. Never could a man have stepped into the parlour a more perfect and predestined victim to the finished accomplishments of the Prime Minister. The Old World was tough in wickedness, anyhow; the Old World's heart of stone might blunt the sharpest blade of the bravest knight-errant. But this blind and deaf Don Quixote was entering a cavern where the swift and glittering blade was in the hands of the adversary.

But if the President was not the philosopher-king, what was he? After all, he was a man who had spent much of his life at a University. He was by no means a business man or an ordinary party politician, but a man of force, personality, and importance. What, then, was his temperament?

The clue, once found, was illuminating. The President was

like a Nonconformist minister, perhaps a Presbyterian. His thought and his temperament were essentially theological, not intellectual, with all the strength and the weakness of that manner of thought, feeling, and expression. It is a type of which there are not now in England and Scotland such magnificent specimens as formerly; but this description, nevertheless, will give the ordinary Englishman the distinctest impression of the President.

With this picture of him in mind we can return to the actual course of events. The President's programme for the world, as set forth in his speeches and his Notes, had displayed a spirit and a purpose so admirable that the last desire of his sympathisers was to criticise details—the details, they felt, were quite rightly not filled in at present, but would be in due course. It was commonly believed at the commencement of the Paris Conference that the President had thought out, with the aid of a large body of advisers, a comprehensive scheme not only for the League of Nations but for the embodiment of the Fourteen Points in an actual Treaty of Peace. But in fact the President had thought out nothing; when it came to practice, his ideas were nebulous and incomplete. He had no plan, no scheme, no constructive ideas whatever for clothing with the flesh of life the commandments which he had thundered from the White House. He could have preached a sermon on any of them or have addressed a stately prayer to the Almighty for their fulfilment, but he could not frame their concrete application to the actual state of Europe.

He not only had no proposals in detail, but he was in many respects, perhaps inevitably, ill-informed as to European conditions. And not only was he ill-informed—that was true of Mr. Lloyd George also—but his mind was slow and unadaptable. The President's slowness amongst the Europeans was noteworthy. He could not, all in a minute, take in what the rest were saying, size up the situation with a glance, frame a reply, and meet the case by a slight change of ground; and he was liable, therefore, to defeat by the mere swiftness, apprehension, and agility of a Lloyd George. There can seldom have been a statesman of the first rank more incompetent than the President in the agilities of the council chamber. A moment often arrives when substantial victory is yours if by some slight appearance of a concession you can save the face of the opposition or conciliate them by a restatement of your proposal helpful to them and not injurious to anything essential to yourself. The President was not equipped with this simple and usual artfulness. His mind was too slow and unresourceful to be ready with *any* alternatives. The President was capable of digging his toes in and refusing to budge, as he did over Fiume. But he had no other mode of defence, and it needed as a rule but little manœuvring by his opponents to prevent matters from coming to such a head until it was too late. By pleasantness and an appearance of conciliation the President would be manœuvred off his ground, would miss the moment for digging his toes in, and, before he knew where he had been got to, it was too late. Besides, it is impossible month after month in intimate and ostensibly friendly converse between close associates to be digging the toes in all the time. Victory would only have been possible to one who had always a sufficiently lively apprehension of the position as a whole to reserve his fire and know for certain the rare exact moments for decisive action. And for that the President was far too slow-minded and bewildered.

He did not remedy these defects by seeking aid from the collective wisdom of his lieutenants. He had gathered round him for the economic chapters of the Treaty a very able group of business men; but they were inexperienced in public affairs and knew (with one or two exceptions) as little of Europe as he did, and they were only called in irregularly as he might need them for a particular purpose. Thus the aloofness which had been found effective in Washington was maintained, and the abnormal reserve of his nature did not allow near him anyone who aspired to moral equality or the continuous exercise of influence. His fellow-plenipotentiaries were dummies; and even the trusted Colonel House, with vastly more knowledge of men and of Europe than the President, from whose sensitiveness the President's dullness had gained so much, fell into the background as time went on. All this was encouraged by his colleagues on the Council of Four, who, by the break-up of the

Council of Ten, completed the isolation which the President's own temperament had initiated. Thus day after day and week after week he allowed himself to be closeted, unsupported, unadvised, and alone, with men much sharper than himself, in situations of supreme difficulty, where he needed for success every description of resource, fertility, and knowledge. He allowed himself to be drugged by their atmosphere, to discuss on the basis of their plans and of their data, and to be led along their paths.

These and other various causes combined to produce the following situation. The reader must remember that the processes which are here compressed into a few pages took place slowly, gradually, insidiously, over a period of about five months.

As the President had thought nothing out, the Council was generally working on the basis of a French or British draft. He had to take up, therefore, a persistent attitude of obstruction, criticism, and negation if the draft was to become at all in line with his own ideas and purpose. If he was met on some points with apparent generosity (for there was always a safe margin of quite preposterous suggestions which no one took seriously), it was difficult for him not to yield on others. Compromise was inevitable, and never to compromise on the essential very difficult. Besides, he was soon made to appear to be taking the German part, and laid himself open to the suggestion (to which he was foolishly and unfortunately sensitive) of being "pro-German."

After a display of much principle and dignity in the early days of the Council of Ten, he discovered that there were certain very important points in the programme of his French, British, or Italian colleague, as the case might be, of which he was incapable of securing the surrender by the methods of secret diplomacy. What then was he to do in the last resort? He could let the Conference drag on an endless length by the exercise of sheer obstinacy. He could break it up and return to America in a rage with nothing settled. Or he could attempt an appeal to the world over the heads of the Conference. These were wretched alternatives, against each of which a great deal could be said. They were also very risky—especially for a politician. The President's mistaken policy over the Congressional election had weakened his personal position in his own country, and it was by no means certain that the American public would support him in a position of intransigency. It would mean a campaign in which the issues would be clouded by every sort of personal and party consideration, and who could say if right would triumph in a struggle which would certainly not be decided on its merits. Besides, any open rupture with his colleagues would certainly bring upon his head the blind passions of "anti-German" resentment with which the public of all allied countries were still inspired. They would not listen to his arguments. They would not be cool enough to treat the issue as one of international morality or of the right governance of Europe. The cry would simply be that for various sinister and selfish reasons the President wished "to let the Hun off." The almost unanimous voice of the French and British Press could be anticipated. Thus, if he threw down the gage publicly he might be defeated. And if he were defeated, would not the final Peace be far worse than if he were to retain his prestige and endeavour to make it as good as the limiting conditions of European politics would allow him? But above all, if he were defeated, would he not lose the League of Nations? And was not this, after all, by far the most important issue for the future happiness of the world? The Treaty would be altered and softened by time. Much in it which now seemed so vital would become trifling, and much which was impracticable would for that very reason never happen. But the League, even in an imperfect form, was permanent; it was the first commencement of a new principle in the government of the world; Truth and Justice in international relations could not be established in a few months—they must be born in due course by the slow gestation of the League. Clemenceau had been clever enough to let it be seen that he would swallow the League at a price.

At the crisis of his fortunes the President was a lonely man. Caught up in the toils of the Old World, he stood in great need of sympathy, of moral support, of the enthusiasm of masses. But buried in the Conference, stifled in the hot and poisoned atmosphere of Paris, no echo reached him from the outer world, and no throb of passion, sympathy, or encouragement from his silent constituents in all countries. He felt that the blaze of popularity which had greeted his arrival in Europe was already dimmed; the Paris Press jeered at him openly; his political opponents at home were taking advantage of his absence to create an atmosphere against him; England was cold, critical, and unresponsive. He had so formed his *entourage* that he did not receive through private channels the current of faith and enthusiasm of which the public sources seemed dammed up. He needed, but lacked, the added strength of collective faith. The German terror still overhung us, and even the sympathetic public was very cautious; the enemy must not be encouraged, our friends must be supported, this was not the time for discord or agitations, the President must be trusted to do his best. And in this drought the flower of the President's faith withered and dried up.

Thus it came to pass that the President countermanded the *George Washington*, which, in a moment of well-founded rage, he had ordered to be in readiness to carry him from the treacherous halls of Paris back to the seat of his authority, where he could have felt himself again. But as soon, alas, as he had taken the road of compromise the defects, already indicated, of his temperament and of his equipment were fatally apparent. He could take the high line; he could practise obstinacy; he could write Notes from Sinai or Olympus; he could remain unapproachable in the White House or even in the Council of Ten and be safe. But if he once stepped down to the intimate equality of the Four, the game was evidently up.

Now it was that what I have called his theological or Presbyterian temperament became dangerous. Having decided that some concessions were unavoidable, he might have sought by firmness and address and the use of the financial power of the United States to secure as much as he could of the substance, even at some sacrifice of the letter. But the President was not capable of so clear an understanding with himself as this implied. He was too conscientious. Although compromises were now necessary, he remained a man of principle and the Fourteen Points a contract absolutely binding upon him. He would do nothing that was not honourable; he would do nothing that was not just and right; he would do nothing that was contrary to his great profession of faith. Thus, without any abatement of the verbal inspiration of the Fourteen Points, they became a document for gloss and interpretation and for all the intellectual apparatus of self-deception, by which, I dare say, the President's forefathers had persuaded themselves that the course they thought it necessary to take was consistent with every syllable of the Pentateuch.

The President's attitude to his colleagues had now become: I want to meet you so far as I can; I see your difficulties and I should like to be able to agree to what you propose, but I can do nothing that is not just and right, and you must first of all show me that what you want does really fall within the words of the pronouncements which are binding on me. Then began the weaving of that web of sophistry and Jesuitical exegesis that was finally to clothe with insincerity the language and substance of the whole Treaty. The word was issued to the witches of all Paris:

> Fair is foul, and foul is fair,
> Hover through the fog and filthy air.

The subtlest sophisters and most hypocritical draftsmen were set to work, and produced many ingenious exercises which might have deceived for more than an hour a cleverer man than the President.

Thus instead of saying that German Austria is prohibited from uniting with Germany except by leave of France (which would be inconsistent with the principle of self-determination), the Treaty, with delicate draftsmanship, states that "Germany acknowledges and will respect strictly the independence of Austria, within the frontiers which may be fixed in a Treaty between that State and the Principal Allied and Associated Powers; she agrees that this independence shall be inalienable, except with the consent of the Council of the League of Nations," which sounds, but is not, quite different. And who knows but that the President forgot that another part of the

Treaty provides that for this purpose the Council of the League must be *unanimous.*

Instead of giving Danzig to Poland, the Treaty establishes Danzig as a "Free" City, but includes this "Free" City within the Polish Customs frontier, entrusts to Poland the control of the river and railway system, and provides that "the Polish Government shall undertake the conduct of the foreign relations of the Free City of Danzig as well as the diplomatic protection of citizens of that city when abroad."

In placing the river system of Germany under foreign control, the Treaty speaks of declaring international those "river systems which naturally provide more than one State with access to the sea, with or without transhipment from one vessel to another."

Such instances could be multiplied. The honest and intelligible purpose of French policy, to limit the population of Germany and weaken her economic system, is clothed, for the President's sake, in the august language of freedom and international equality.

But perhaps the most decisive moment, in the disintegration of the President's moral position and the clouding of his mind, was when at last, to the dismay of his advisers, he allowed himself to be persuaded that the expenditure of the Allied Governments on pensions and separation allowances could be fairly regarded as "damage done to the civilian population of the Allied and Associated Powers by German aggression by land, by sea, and from the air," in a sense in which the other expenses of the war could not be so regarded. It was a long theological struggle in which, after the rejection of many different arguments, the President finally capitulated before a masterpiece of the sophist's art.[2]

At last the work was finished, and the President's conscience was still intact. In spite of everything, I believe that his temperament allowed him to leave Paris a really sincere man; and it is probable that to his death he was genuinely convinced that the Treaty contained practically nothing inconsistent with his former professions.

But the work was too complete, and to this was due the last tragic episode of the drama. The reply of Brockdorff-Rantzau naturally took the line that Germany had laid down her arms on the basis of certain assurances, and that the Treaty in many particulars was not consistent with these assurances. But this was exactly what the President could not admit; in the sweat of solitary contemplation and with prayers to God he had done *nothing* that was not just and right; for the President to admit that the German reply had force in it was to destroy his self-respect and to disrupt the inner equipoise of his soul, and every instinct of his stubborn nature rose in self-protection. In the language of medical psychology, to suggest to the President that the Treaty was an abandonment of his professions was to touch on the raw a Freudian complex. It was a subject intolerable to discuss, and every subconscious instinct plotted to defeat its further exploration.

Thus it was that Clemenceau brought to success what had seemed to be, a few months before, the extraordinary and impossible proposal that the Germans should not be heard. If only the President had not been so conscientious, if only he had not concealed from himself what he had been doing, even at the last moment he was in a position to have recovered lost ground and to have achieved some very considerable successes. But the President was set. His arms and legs had been spliced by the surgeons to a certain posture, and they must be broken again before they could be altered. To his horror, Mr. Lloyd George, desiring at the last moment all the moderation he dared, discovered that he could not in five days persuade the President of error in what it had taken five months to prove to him to be just and right. After all, it was harder to de-bamboozle this old Presbyterian than it had been to bamboozle him, for the former involved his belief in and respect for himself.

Thus in the last act the President stood for stubbornness and a refusal of conciliations.

TROTSKY ON ENGLAND

A contemporary reviewing this book [1] says: "He stammers out platitudes in the voice of a phonograph with a scratched record." I should guess that Trotsky dictated it. In its English dress it emerges in a turbid stream with a hectoring gurgle which is characteristic of modern revolutionary literature translated from the Russian. Its dogmatic tone about our affairs, where even the author's flashes of insight are clouded by his inevitable ignorance of what he is talking about, cannot commend it to an English reader. Yet there is a certain style about Trotsky. A personality is visible through the distorting medium. And it is not all platitudes.

The book is, first of all, an attack on the official leaders of the British Labour Party because of their "religiosity," and because they believe that it is useful to prepare for Socialism without preparing for Revolution at the same time. Trotsky sees, what is probably true, that our Labour Party is the direct offspring of the Radical Nonconformists and the philanthropic bourgeois, without a tinge of atheism, blood, and revolution. Emotionally and intellectually, therefore, he finds them intensely unsympathetic. A short anthology will exhibit his state of mind:

The doctrine of the leaders of the Labour Party is a kind of amalgam of Conservatism and Liberalism partially adapted to the needs of trade unions. . . . The Liberal and semi-Liberal leaders of the Labour Party still think that the social revolution is the mournful privilege of the European Continent.

"In the realm of feeling and conscience," MacDonald begins, "in the realm of spirit, Socialism forms the religion of service to the people." In those words is immediately betrayed the benevolent bourgeois, the left Liberal, who "serves" the people, coming to them from one side, or more truly from above. Such an approach has its roots entirely in the dim past, when the radical intelligentsia went to live in the working-class districts of London in order to carry on cultural and educational work.

Together with theological literature, Fabianism is perhaps the most useless, and in any case the most boring form of verbal creation. . . . The cheaply optimistic Victorian epoch, when it seemed that to-morrow would be a little better than to-day, and the day after to-morrow still better than to-morrow, found its most finished expression in the Webbs, Snowden, MacDonald, and other Fabians. . . . These bombastic authorities, pedants, arrogant and ranting poltroons, systematically poison the Labour Movement, befog the consciousness of the proletariat, and paralyse its will. . . . The Fabians, the I.L.P.ers, the Conservative bureaucrats of the trade unions represent at the moment the most counterrevolutionary force in Great Britain, and perhaps of all the world's development. . . . Fabianism, MacDonaldism, Pacifism, is the chief rallying-point of British imperialism and of the European, if not the world, bourgeoisie. At any cost, these self-satisfied pedants, these gabbling eclectics, these sentimental careerists, these upstart liveried lackeys of the bourgeoisie, must be shown in their natural form to the workers. To reveal them as they are will mean their hopeless discrediting.

Well, that is how the gentlemen who so much alarm Mr. Winston Churchill strike the real article. And we must hope that the real article, having got it off his chest, feels better. How few words need changing, let the reader note, to permit the attribution of my anthology to the philo-fisticuffs of the Right. And the reason for this similarity is evident. Trotsky is concerned in these passages with an attitude towards public affairs, not with ultimate aims. He is just exhibiting the temper of the band of brigand-statesmen to whom Action means War, and who are irritated to fury by the atmosphere of sweet reasonableness, of charity, tolerance, and mercy in which, though the wind whistles in the East or in the South, Mr. Baldwin and

Lord Oxford and Mr. MacDonald smoke the pipe of peace.
"They smoke Peace where there should be no Peace," Fascists
and Bolshevists cry in a chorus, "canting, imbecile emblems of
decay, senility, and death, the antithesis of Life and the Life-
Force which exist only in the spirit of merciless struggle." If
only it was so easy! If only one could accomplish by roaring,
whether roaring like a lion or like any sucking dove!

The roaring occupies the first half of Trotsky's book. The
second half, which affords a summary exposition of his political philosophy, deserves a closer attention.

First proposition. The historical process necessitates the
change-over to Socialism if civilisation is to be preserved.
"Without a transfer to Socialism all our culture is threatened
with decay and decomposition."

Second proposition. It is unthinkable that this change-over
can come about by peaceful argument and voluntary surrender. Except in response to force, the possessing classes will surrender nothing. The strike is already a resort to force. "The
class struggle is a continual sequence of open or masked forces,
which are regulated in more or less degree by the State, which
in turn represents the organised apparatus of force of the
stronger of the antagonists, in other words, the ruling class."
The hypothesis that the Labour Party will come into power by
constitutional methods and will then "proceed to the business
so cautiously, so tactfully, so intelligently, that the bourgeoisie
will not feel any need for active opposition," is "facetious"—
though this "is indeed the very rock-bottom hope of MacDonald and company."

Third proposition. Even if, sooner or later, the Labour Party
achieve power by constitutional methods, *the reactionary parties will at once proceed to force*. The possessing classes will do
lip-service to parliamentary methods so long as they are in control of the parliamentary machine, but if they are dislodged,
then, Trotsky maintains, it is absurd to suppose that they will
prove squeamish about a resort to force on their side. Suppose,
he says, that a Labour majority in Parliament were to decide
in the most legal fashion to confiscate the land without compensation, to put a heavy tax on capital, and to abolish the

Crown and the House of Lords, "there cannot be the least doubt that the possessing classes will not submit without a struggle, the more so as all the police, judiciary, and military apparatus is entirely in their hands." Moreover, they control the banks and the whole system of social credit and the machinery of transport and trade, so that the daily food of London, including that of the Labour Government itself, depends on the great capitalist combines. It is obvious, Trotsky argues, that these terrific means of pressure "will be brought into action with frantic violence in order to dam the activity of the Labour Government, to paralyse its exertions, to frighten it, to effect cleavages in its parliamentary majority, and, finally, to cause a financial panic, provision difficulties, and lock-outs." To suppose, indeed, that the destiny of Society is going to be determined by whether Labour achieves a parliamentary majority and not by the actual balance of material forces at the moment is an "enslavement to the fetishism of parliamentary arithmetic."

Fourth proposition. In view of all this, whilst it may be good strategy to aim also at constitutional power, it is silly not to organise on the basis that material force will be the determining factor in the end.

In the revolutionary struggle only the greatest determination is of avail to strike the arms out of the hands of reaction to limit the period of civil war, and to lessen the number of its victims. If this course be not taken it is better not to take to arms at all. If arms are not resorted to, it is impossible to organise a general strike; if the general strike is renounced, there can be no thought of any serious struggle.

Granted his assumptions, much of Trotsky's argument is, I think, unanswerable. Nothing can be sillier than to *play* at revolution—if that is what he means. But what are his assumptions? He assumes that the moral and intellectual problems of the transformation of Society have been already solved—that a plan exists, and that nothing remains except to put it into operation. He assumes further that Society is divided into two parts—the proletariat who are converted to the plan, and the rest who for purely selfish reasons oppose it. He does not understand that no plan could win until it had first convinced many people, and that, if there really were a plan, it would draw support from many different quarters. He is so much occupied with means that he forgets to tell us what it is all for. If we pressed him, I suppose he would mention Marx. And there we will leave him with an echo of his own words—"together with theological literature, perhaps the most useless, and in any case the most boring form of verbal creation."

Trotsky's book must confirm us in our conviction of the uselessness, the empty-headedness of Force at the present stage of human affairs. Force would settle nothing—no more in the Class War than in the Wars of Nations or in the Wars of Religion. An understanding of the historical process, to which Trotsky is so fond of appealing, declares not for, but against, Force at this juncture of things. We lack more than usual a coherent scheme of progress, a tangible ideal. All the political parties alike have their origins in past ideas and not in new ideas—and none more conspicuously so than the Marxists. It is not necessary to debate the subtleties of what justifies a man in promoting his gospel by force; for no one has a gospel. The next move is with the head, and fists must wait.

March 1926.

NEWTON, THE MAN [1]

It is with some diffidence that I try to speak to you in his own home of Newton *as he was himself.* I have long been a student of the records and had the intention to put my impressions into writing to be ready for Christmas Day 1942, the tercentenary of his birth. The war has deprived me both of leisure to treat adequately so great a theme and of opportunity to consult my library and my papers and to verify my impressions. So if the brief study which I shall lay before you to-day is more perfunctory than it should be, I hope you will excuse me.

One other preliminary matter. I believe that Newton was different from the conventional picture of him. But I do not believe he was less great. He was less ordinary, more extraordinary, than the nineteenth century cared to make him out. Geniuses *are* very peculiar. Let no one here suppose that my object to-day is to lessen, by describing, Cambridge's greatest son. I am trying rather to see him as his own friends and contemporaries saw him. And they without exception regarded him as one of the greatest of men.

In the eighteenth century and since, Newton came to be thought of as the first and greatest of the modern age of scientists, a rationalist, one who taught us to think on the lines of cold and untinctured reason.

I do not see him in this light. I do not think that any one who has pored over the contents of that box which he packed up when he finally left Cambridge in 1696 and which, though partly dispersed, have come down to us, can see him like that. Newton was not the first of the age of reason. He was the last of the magicians, the last of the Babylonians and Sumerians, the last great mind which looked out on the visible and intellectual world with the same eyes as those who began to build our intellectual inheritance rather less than 10,000 years ago. Isaac Newton, a posthumous child born with no father on Christmas Day, 1642, was the last wonderchild to whom the Magi could do sincere and appropriate homage.

Had there been time, I should have liked to read to you the contemporary record of the child Newton. For, though it is well known to his biographers, it has never been published *in extenso*, without comment, just as it stands. Here, indeed, is the makings of a legend of the young magician, a most joyous picture of the opening mind of genius free from the uneasiness, the melancholy and nervous agitation of the young man and student.

For in vulgar modern terms Newton was profoundly neurotic of a not unfamiliar type, but—I should say from the records—a most extreme example. His deepest instincts were occult, esoteric, semantic—with profound shrinking from the world, a paralyzing fear of exposing his thoughts, his beliefs, his discoveries in all nakedness to the inspection and criticism of the world. "Of the most fearful, cautious and suspicious temper that I ever knew," said Whiston, his successor in the Lucasian Chair. The too well-known conflicts and ignoble quarrels with Hooke, Falmsteed, Leibnitz are only too clear an evidence of this. Like all his type he was wholly aloof from women. He parted with and published nothing except under the extreme pressure of friends. Until the second phase of his life, he was a wrapt, consecrated solitary, pursuing his studies by intense introspection with a mental endurance perhaps never equalled.

I believe that the clue to his mind is to be found in his unusual powers of continuous concentrated introspection. A case can be made out, as it also can with Descartes, for regarding him as an accomplished experimentalist. Nothing can be more charming than the tales of his mechanical contrivances when he was a boy. There are his telescopes and his optical experiments. These were essential accomplishments, part of his un-equalled all-round technique, but not, I am sure, his *peculiar* gift, especially amongst his contemporaries. His peculiar gift was the power of holding continuously in his mind a purely mental problem until he had seen straight through it. I fancy his pre-eminence is due to his muscles of intuition being the strongest and most enduring with which a man has ever been gifted. Anyone who has ever attempted pure scientific or philo-sophical thought knows how one can hold a problem momen-tarily in one's mind and apply all one's powers of concentration to piercing through it, and how it will dissolve and escape and you find that what you are surveying is a blank. I believe that Newton could hold a problem in his mind for hours and days and weeks until it surrendered to him its secret. Then be-ing a supreme mathematical technician he could dress it up, how you will, for purposes of exposition, but it was his intuition which was pre-eminently extraordinary—"so happy in his con-jectures," said de Morgan, "as to seem to know more than he could possibly have any means of proving." The proofs, for what they are worth, were, as I have said, dressed up after-wards—they were not the instrument of discovery.

There is the story of how he informed Halley of one of his most fundamental discoveries of planetary motion. "Yes," re-plied Halley, "but how do you know that? Have you proved it?" Newton was taken aback—"Why, I've known it for years," he replied. "If you'll give me a few days, I'll certainly find you a proof of it"—as in due course he did.

Again, there is some evidence that Newton in preparing the *Principia* was held up almost to the last moment by lack of proof that you could treat a solid sphere as though all its mass was concentrated at the centre, and only hit on the proof a year before publication. But this was a truth which he had known for certain and had always assumed for many years.

Certainly there can be no doubt that the peculiar geometrical form in which the exposition of the *Principia* is dressed up bears no resemblance at all to the mental processes by which Newton actually arrived at his conclusions.

His experiments were always, I suspect, a means, not of discovery, but always of verifying what he knew already.

Why do I call him a magician? Because he looked on the whole universe and all that is in it *as a riddle,* as a secret which could be read by applying pure thought to certain evidence, certain mystic clues which God had laid about the world to allow a sort of philosopher's treasure hunt to the esoteric brotherhood. He believed that these clues were to be found partly in the evidence of the heavens and in the constitution of elements (and that is what gives the false suggestion of his being an experimental natural philosopher), but also partly in certain papers and traditions handed down by the brethren in an unbroken chain back to the original cryptic revelation in Babylonia. He regarded the universe as a cryptogram set by the Almighty—just as he himself wrapt the discovery of the calculus in a cryptogram when he communicated with Leibnitz. By pure thought, by concentration of mind, the riddle, he believed, would be revealed to the initiate.

He *did* read the riddle of the heavens. And he believed that by the same powers of his introspective imagination he would read the riddle of the Godhead, the riddle of past and future events divinely fore-ordained, the riddle of the elements and their constitution from an original undifferentiated first matter, the riddle of health and of immortality. All would be revealed to him if only he could persevere to the end, uninterrupted, by himself, no one coming into the room, reading, copying, testing—all by himself, no interruption for God's sake, no disclosure, no discordant breakings in or criticism, with fear and shrinking as he assailed these half-ordained, half-forbidden things, creeping back into the bosom of the Godhead as into his mother's womb. "Voyaging through strange seas of thought *alone,*" not as Charles Lamb "a fellow who believed nothing unless it was as clear as the three sides of a triangle."

And so he continued for some twenty-five years. In 1687, when he was forty-five years old, the *Principia* was published.

Here in Trinity it is right that I should give you an account of how he lived amongst you during these years of his greatest achievement. The east end of the Chapel projects farther eastwards than the Great Gate. In the second half of the seventeenth century there was a walled garden in the free space between Trinity Street and the building which joins the Great Gate to the Chapel. The south wall ran out from the turret of the Gate to a distance overlapping the Chapel by at least the width of the present pavement. Thus the garden was of modest but reasonable size, as is well shown in Loggan's print of the College in 1690. This was Newton's garden. He had the Fellow's set of rooms between the Porter's Lodge and the Chapel —that, I suppose, now occupied by Professor Broad. The garden was reached by a stairway which was attached to a veranda raised on wooden pillars projecting into the garden from the range of buildings. At the top of this stairway stood his telescope—not to be confused with the observatory erected on the top of the Great Gate during Newton's lifetime (but after he had left Cambridge) for the use of Roger Cotes and Newton's successor, Whiston. This wooden erection was, I think, demolished by Whewell in 1856 and replaced by the stone bay of Professor Broad's bedroom. At the Chapel end of the garden was a small two-storied building, also of wood, which was his laboratory. When he decided to prepare the *Principia* for publication he engaged a young kinsman, Humphrey Newton, to act as his amanuensis (the MS. of the *Principia,* as it went to the press, is clearly in the hand of Humphrey). Humphrey remained with him for five years—from 1684 to 1689. When Newton died his nephew-in-law Conduitt wrote to Humphrey for his reminiscences, and among the papers I have is Humphrey's reply.

During these twenty-five years of intense study mathematics and astronomy were only a part, and perhaps not the most absorbing, of his occupations. Our record of these is almost wholly confined to the papers which he kept and put in his box when he left Trinity for London.

Let me give some brief indications of their subject. They are enormously voluminous—I should say that upwards of 1,000,-

ooo words in his handwriting still survive. They have, beyond doubt, no substantial value whatever except as a fascinating sidelight on the mind of our greatest genius.

Let me not exaggerate through reaction against the other Newton myth which has been so sedulously created for the last two hundred years. There was extreme method in his madness. All his unpublished works on esoteric and theological matters are marked by careful learning, accurate method and extreme sobriety of statement. They are just as *sane* as the *Principia*, if their whole matter and purpose were not magical. They were nearly all composed during the same twenty-five years of his mathematical studies. They fall into several groups.

Very early in life Newton abandoned orthodox belief in the Trinity. At this time the Socinians were an important Arian sect amongst intellectual circles. It may be that Newton fell under Socinian influences, but I think not. He was rather a Judaic monotheist of the school of Maimonides. He arrived at this conclusion, not on so-to-speak rational or sceptical grounds, but entirely on the interpretation of ancient authority. He was persuaded that the revealed documents give no support to the Trinitarian doctrines which were due to late falsifications. The revealed God was one God.

But this was a dreadful secret which Newton was at desperate pains to conceal all his life. It was the reason why he refused Holy Orders, and therefore had to obtain a special dispensation to hold his Fellowship and Lucasian Chair and could not be Master of Trinity. Even the Toleration Act of 1689 excepted anti-Trinitarians. Some rumours there were, but not at the dangerous dates when he was a young Fellow of Trinity. In the main the secret died with him. But it was revealed in many writings in his big box. After his death Bishop Horsley was asked to inspect the box with a view to publication. He saw the contents with horror and slammed the lid. A hundred years later Sir David Brewster looked into the box. He covered up the traces with carefully selected extracts and some straight fibbing. His latest biographer, Mr. More, has been more candid. Newton's extensive anti-Trinitarian pamphlets are, in my judgement, the most interesting of his unpublished papers. Apart from his more serious affirmation of belief, I have a completed pamphlet showing up what Newton thought of the extreme dishonesty and falsification of records for which St. Athanasius was responsible, in particular for his putting about the false calumny that Arius died in a privy. The victory of the Trinitarians in England in the latter half of the seventeenth century was not only as complete, but also as extraordinary, as St. Athanasius's original triumph. There is good reason for thinking that Locke was a Unitarian. I have seen it argued that Milton was. It is a blot on Newton's record that he did not murmur a word when Whiston, his successor in the Lucasian Chair, was thrown out of his professorship and out of the University for publicly avowing opinions which Newton himself had secretly held for upwards of fifty years past.

That he held this heresy was a further aggravation of his silence and secrecy and inwardness of disposition.

Another large section is concerned with all branches of apocalyptic writings from which he sought to deduce the secret truths of the Universe—the measurements of Solomon's Temple, the Book of Daniel, the Book of Revelations, an enormous volume of work of which some part was published in his later days. Along with this are hundreds of pages of Church History and the like, designed to discover the truth of tradition.

A large section, judging by the handwriting amongst the earliest, relates to alchemy—transmutation, the philosopher's stone, the elixir of life. The scope and character of these papers have been hushed up, or at least minimized, by nearly all those who have inspected them. About 1650 there was a considerable group in London, round the publisher Cooper, who during the next twenty years revived interest not only in the English alchemists of the fifteenth century, but also in translations of the medieval and post-medieval alchemists.

There is an unusual number of manuscripts of the early English alchemists in the libraries of Cambridge. It may be that there was some continuous esoteric tradition within the University which sprang into activity again in the twenty years from 1650 to 1670. At any rate, Newton was clearly an unbridled addict. It is this with which he was occupied "about 6

weeks at spring and 6 at the fall when the fire in the elaboratory scarcely went out" at the very years when he was com-
posing the *Principia*—and about this he told Humphrey Newton not a word. Moreover, he was almost entirely concerned,
not in serious experiment, but in trying to read the riddle of
tradition, to find meaning in cryptic verses, to imitate the alleged but largely imaginary experiments of the initiates of past
centuries. Newton has left behind him a vast mass of records of
these studies. I believe that the greater part are translations and
copies made by him of existing books and manuscripts. But
there are also extensive records of experiments. I have glanced
through a great quantity of this—at least 100,000 words, I should
say. It is utterly impossible to deny that it is wholly magical and
wholly devoid of scientific value; and also impossible not to admit that Newton devoted years of work to it. Some time it might
be interesting, but not useful, for some student better equipped
and more idle than I to work out Newton's exact relationship
to the tradition and MSS. of his time.

In these mixed and extraordinary studies, with one foot in
the Middle Ages and one foot treading a path for modern science, Newton spent the first phase of his life, the period of life
in Trinity when he did all his real work. Now let me pass to the
second phase.

After the publication of the *Principia* there is a complete
change in his habit and way of life. I believe that his friends,
above all Halifax, came to the conclusion that he must be
rooted out of the life he was leading at Trinity which must
soon lead to decay of mind and health. Broadly speaking, of
his own motion or under persuasion, he abandons his studies.
He takes up University business, represents the University in
Parliament; his friends are busy trying to get a dignified and
remunerative job for him—the Provostship of King's, the
Mastership of Charterhouse, the Controllership of the Mint.

Newton could not be Master of Trinity because he was a
Unitarian and so not in Holy Orders. He was rejected as Provost of King's for the more prosaic reason that he was not an
Etonian. Newton took this rejection very ill and prepared a long
legalistic brief, which I possess, giving reasons why it was not

unlawful for him to be accepted as Provost. But, as ill-luck had it, Newton's nomination for the Provostship came at the moment when King's had decided to fight against the right of Crown nomination, a struggle in which the College was successful.

Newton was well qualified for any of these offices. It must not be inferred from his introspection, his absentmindedness, his secrecy and his solitude that he lacked aptitude for affairs when he chose to exercise it. There are many records to prove his very great capacity. Read, for example, his correspondence with Dr. Covell, the Vice-Chancellor, when, as the University's representative in Parliament, he had to deal with the delicate question of the oaths after the revolution of 1688. With Pepys and Lowndes he became one of the greatest and most efficient of our civil servants. He was a very successful investor of funds, surmounting the crisis of the South Sea Bubble, and died a rich man. He possessed in exceptional degree almost every kind of intellectual aptitude—lawyer, historian, theologian, not less than mathematician, physicist, astronomer.

And when the turn of his life came and he put his books of magic back into the box, it was easy for him to drop the seventeenth century behind him and to evolve into the eighteenth-century figure which is the traditional Newton.

Nevertheless, the move on the part of his friends to change his life came almost too late. In 1689 his mother, to whom he was deeply attached, died. Somewhere about his fiftieth birthday on Christmas Day 1692, he suffered what we should now term a severe nervous breakdown. Melancholia, sleeplessness, fears of persecution—he writes to Pepys and to Locke and no doubt to others letters which lead them to think that his mind is deranged. He lost, in his own words, the "former consistency of his mind." He never again concentrated after the old fashion or did any fresh work. The breakdown probably lasted nearly two years, and from it emerged, slightly "gaga," but still, no doubt, with one of the most powerful minds of England, the Sir Isaac Newton of tradition.

In 1696 his friends were finally successful in digging him out of Cambridge, and for more than another twenty years he reigned in London as the most famous man of his age, of Europe, and—as his powers gradually waned and his affability increased—perhaps of all time, so it seemed to his contemporaries.

He set up house with his niece Catharine Barton, who was beyond reasonable doubt the mistress of his old and loyal friend Charles Montague, Earl of Halifax and Chancellor of the Exchequer, who had been one of Newton's intimate friends when he was an undergraduate at Trinity. Catharine was reputed to be one of the most brilliant and charming women in the London of Congreve, Swift and Pope. She is celebrated not least for the broadness of her stories, in Swift's *Journal to Stella*. Newton puts on rather too much weight for his moderate height. "When he rode in his coach one arm would be out of his coach on one side and the other on the other." His pink face, beneath a mass of snow-white hair, which "when his peruke was off was a venerable sight," is increasingly both benevolent and majestic. One night in Trinity after Hall he is knighted by Queen Anne. For nearly twenty-four years he reigns as President of the Royal Society. He becomes one of the principal sights of London for all visiting intellectual foreigners, whom he entertains handsomely. He liked to have clever young men about him to edit new editions of the *Principia*—and sometimes merely plausible ones as in the case of Fatio de Duillier.

Magic was quite forgotten. He has become the Sage and Monarch of the Age of Reason. The Sir Isaac Newton of orthodox tradition—the eighteenth-century Sir Isaac, so remote from the child magician born in the first half of the seventeenth century—was being built up. Voltaire returning from his trip to London was able to report of Sir Isaac—" 'twas his peculiar felicity, not only to be born in a country of liberty, but in an Age when all scholastic impertinences were banished from the World. Reason alone was cultivated and Mankind cou'd only be his Pupil, not his Enemy." Newton, whose secret heresies and scholastic superstitions it had been the study of a lifetime to conceal!

But he never concentrated, never recovered "the former consistency of his mind." "He spoke very little in company." "He had something rather languid in his look and manner."

And he looked very seldom, I expect, into the chest where, when he left Cambridge, he had packed all the evidences of what had occupied and so absorbed his intense and flaming spirit in his rooms and his garden and his elaboratory between the Great Gate and Chapel.

But he did not destroy them. They remained in the box to shock profoundly any eighteenth- or nineteenth-century prying eyes. They became the possession of Catharine Barton and then of her daughter, Lady Lymington. So Newton's chest, with many hundreds of thousands of words of his unpublished writings, came to contain the "Portsmouth Papers."

In 1888 the mathematical portion was given to the University Library at Cambridge. They have been indexed, but they have never been edited. The rest, a very large collection, were dispersed in the auction room in 1936 by Catharine Barton's descendant, the present Lord Lymington. Disturbed by this impiety, I managed gradually to reassemble about half of them, including nearly the whole of the biographical portion, that is, the "Conduitt Papers," in order to bring them to Cambridge which I hope they will never leave. The greater part of the rest were snatched out of my reach by a syndicate which hoped to sell them at a high price, probably in America, on the occasion of the recent tercentenary.

As one broods over these queer collections, it seems easier to understand—with an understanding which is not, I hope, distorted in the other direction—this strange spirit, who was tempted by the Devil to believe, at the time when within these walls he was solving so much, that he could reach *all* the secrets of God and Nature by the pure power of mind—Copernicus and Faustus in one.

THE GREAT VILLIERS CONNECTION

Mr. Gun[1] has set himself to carry forward the fascinating subject which Galton invented—the collection of hereditary titbits connecting the famous and the moderately famous—quite a different subject from the scientific compilation of complete family trees of definitely determinable characteristics such as blue eyes, round heads, six toes, and the like. His method, like Galton's, is to take in turn each of a number of distinguished "connections" and to exhibit to us what a surprising number of celebrities are some sort of a cousin to one another.

One of the most striking of Mr. Gun's connections is by no means a novel one, yet not too hackneyed to be worth repeating —the cousinship of Dryden, Swift, and Horace Walpole. All three were descended from John Dryden of Canons Ashby, Northamptonshire, Dean Swift being a second cousin once removed, and Horace Walpole a first cousin three times removed of John Dryden the poet (Horace being descended on his mother's side—and therefore irrespective of doubts as to his paternity—from Dryden's aunt Elizabeth). Mr. Gun is disposed to trace this magnificent display to the wife of the original John Dryden—Elizabeth Cope, daughter of Erasmus's friend and great-granddaughter of Sir Ralph Verney, which brings a good many others into the same connection, including Robert Harley. A representative to-day of this great Verney connection is Lady Ottoline Morrell.[2] If, on the other hand, we remember that Lady Ottoline is not only descended from Verney the mercer, but also from Sir William Pierrepont (and through his wife from Henry VII.'s Empson, son of Empson the sieve-maker), we establish her cousinship with Francis Beaumont, Lord Chesterfield, and Lady Mary Wortley Montagu. Our families themselves lose track of their own ramifications; we wonder if Lady Ottoline herself knows that she can call cousin Beaumont, Dryden, Swift, Walpole, Harley, and Chesterfield. Birds of a feather? Perhaps one can perceive in the consanguinity a certain persistent element.

Mr. Gun's analysis of the descendants of John Reid, who fell at Flodden Field in 1515, is more novel, at least to the present writer. Here there is a remarkable versatility—and perhaps also a common quality? In the eighteenth century Mr. John Reid was responsible for Boswell, Robertson the historian, Robert Adam the architect, and Brougham. Amongst his living descendants are Mr. Bertrand Russell, Mr. Harold Nicolson, Mr. Bruce Lockhart, and General Booth-Tucker of the Salvation Army. More birds of a feather?

Mr. Gun is at pains to show how many of the well-known writers of to-day have old blood in their veins. He reminds us that Prof. G. M. and Mr. R. C. Trevelyan and Miss Rose Macaulay are descendants of the Highlander Aulay Macaulay (and therefore near connections of T. B. Macaulay), of whose son Kenneth's book Dr. Johnson said: "Very well written except some foppery about liberty and slavery"; that Mr. Hugh Walpole, Mr. Lytton Strachey, Mr. Compton Mackenzie, Mr. Maurice Baring, and (he should surely have added) Mrs. Virginia Woolf can claim distinction for several generations; and that Mr. Aldous Huxley is not only the grandson of his grandfather, but the nephew of Mrs. Humphry Ward, who was the niece of Matthew Arnold.

There remains for mention the most remarkable family of all—the great Villiers connection from whom are descended all the ambitious fascinators, with so much charm of countenance and voice and so hard a little nut somewhere inside, who were the favourites and mistresses of our monarchs in the seventeenth century and of the parliamentary democracy ever since. There cannot have been a Cabinet for two hundred years —save, perhaps, the two Labour Cabinets—which did not contain descendants of Sir George Villiers and Sir John St. John, two country gentlemen in the reign of James I., of whom the son of the former married the daughter of the latter. The famous progeny of these two families is far too extensive to follow out here in detail. But a simple list is impressive—the first Duke of Buckingham, favourite of James I.; Barbara, Countess of Castlemaine and Duchess of Cleveland, mistress of Charles II.; Arabella Churchill, mistress of James II.; Elizabeth, Countess of Orkney, mistress of William III.; (whom Swift called "the wisest woman he had ever known"); the second Duke of Buckingham; Lord Rochester; Lord Sandwich; the Duke of Berwick; the Duke of Marlborough; the third Duke of Grafton (George III.'s Premier); the two Pitts; Charles James Fox; Charles Townshend; Lord Castlereagh; the Napiers; the Herveys; the Seymours, Marquises of Hertford; the Butes; the Jerseys; the Lansdownes; the Cavendishes, Dukes of Devonshire; Lady Hester Stanhope; Lady Mary Wortley Montagu; Fielding, and, amongst many living contemporaries of the same blood, Mr. Winston Churchill and Viscount Grey of Fallodon. This is, indeed, the real bloodroyal of England.

What are we to conclude? Is it that all Englishmen would be found cousins within four centuries if we could all trace our trees? Or is it true that certain small "connections" have produced eminent characters out of all proportion to their size? Mr. Gund does not help us to a scientific conclusion, but it will be a very cautious and sceptical reader who does not leave his book with a bias for the latter conclusion.

MARY PALEY MARSHALL

1850-1944

Mary Marshall deserves a record of piety and remembrance, not only as the wife of Alfred Marshall, without whose understanding and devotion his work would not have fulfilled its fruitfulness, but for her place in the history of Newnham, now nearly three-quarters of a century ago, as the first woman lecturer on Economics in Cambridge, and for her part in the development of the Marshall Library of Economics in Cambridge in the last twenty years of her life.

She came of that high lineage from which most of virtue and value in this country springs—yeoman farmers owning their own land back to the sixteenth century and beyond, turning in the eighteenth century into thrifty parsons and scholars. The Paleys had been thus settled at Giggleswick in Yorkshire for many generations. Her great-great-grandfather took his degree at Christ's College, Cambridge, in 1733, and was headmaster of Giggleswick Grammar School for fifty-four years. Her great-grandfather, born just over two hundred years ago, was William Paley, fellow and tutor of Christ's and "the delight of combination rooms," Archdeacon of Carlisle, author of the *Principles of Moral and Political Philosophy*, which anticipated Bentham, and of what is generally known as "Paley's Evidences"

(*Natural Theology, or Evidence of the Existence and Attributes of the Deity collected from the Appearances of Nature*),
the reading of which a generation later by another Christ's man,
Charles Darwin, put him on the right track. She has bequeathed
to the writer of these pages the small picture of the great Archdeacon which always hung in her room, and she once showed
him a small packet, in an embroidered case, of the love-letters
of this most unromantic of the philosophers. One of the Archdeacon's grandsons was F. A. Paley, Greek scholar of the mid-
nineteenth century, another was Mary Marshall's father, Rector
of Ufford near Stamford, an evangelical clergyman of the strait-
est Simeonite sect. Her mother was a member of the Yorkshire
family of Wormald.

In the last years of her life Mary Marshall put together short
biographical notes which she called *What I Remember*. She kept
them by her chair down to her last days, and would, from time
to time, add new passages as she sat there alone and another
echo from the past came back to her. It will be published, for
there is no more tender and humorous record of the early days
of Newnham and the newly-married Cambridge which blos-
somed from the desert when the ban on marriage was removed
in 1882. Meanwhile I will steal from it here and there in what
follows as much as is permissible, perhaps more, though much
less than would be in place if the Notes themselves were not due
to be soon published as she wrote them.

In these Notes she recalls her upbringing in the country Rectory, where she was born on October 24, 1850. "These twenty
years were spent in a rambling old house, its front covered with
red and white roses and looking out on a lawn with forest trees
as a background, and a garden with long herbaceous borders
and green terraces. I did not realise the beauty of the place until
I visited it years later, as an old woman." Reading her memories
of those years in the same week as Coulton's records of his upbringing in Norfolk not much later (he, too, from yeoman
farmers in Yorkshire, with records back to the sixteenth century, turned parsons and lawyers), is to understand what the
world has lost in the atmosphere of plain living and high thinking and strictly restrained beauty and affection, which is the

only education worth much. Perhaps no one who was not brought up as an evangelical or a nonconformist is entitled to think freely in due course—which means that before long no one will be so entitled, as is, indeed, obvious to see. Mary Marshall, by living for ninety-four years without decay of the grace and dignity and humour of character and sensibility which nurture as well as nature had given her, was able to show to the youngest student in her Library the beauty, the behaviour and the reserve of an age of civilisation which has departed.

But what a very odd, and sometimes terrible, thing are strict principles! Why can an age only be great if it believes, or at least is bred up in believing, what is preposterous? The Simeonite rector's beliefs were so strict that he could not even be intimate with any neighbouring clergyman; he thought Dickens a writer of doubtful morality (perhaps he was); when his dear Mary escaped from the narrow doctrine, it was a fatal breach between them; and she has recorded of her childhood—"My sister and I were allowed dolls, until one tragic day when our father burnt them as he said we were making them into idols; and we never had any more."

Yet he allowed his Mary to go up as a student to Cambridge when such a thing had never been done before. He had been the loving playmate of his children, and who could wish a better education than he devised for them as Mary Marshall recalled it to her mind eighty years later?

I can't remember much about our education till I was nine years old except that Mrs. Markham's History of England was read aloud to us and Geography was learnt from two books "Near Home" and "Far off," and that we played scales on the piano. In 1859 a German governess came and more regular lessons began. History, it is true, was chiefly dates and we learnt them by a Memoria Technica, beginning "Casibelud Boadorp" etc., and Geography was chiefly names of Towns and Rivers. But we were taught French and German pretty thoroughly and the family talked German at meals. Science we learnt from "The Child's Guide to Knowledge" and "Brewer's Guide." All I now remember of these is the date at which black silk stockings came into England and "What to do in a thunder storm at night," the answer being "Draw your bed into the middle of the room, commend your soul to Almighty God and go to sleep." We did a little Latin and even Hebrew with my father and some Euclid. As to story books, we read "The Wide, Wide World," "Holiday House," "Henry and his Bearer," and "Sandford and Merton." On Sundays we learnt the Church catechism, collects, hymns and Cowper's poems, there was a periodical called "Sunday at Home," and we read and re-read the "Pilgrim's Progress" and the "Fairchild Family." This had a prayer and a hymn at the end of each chapter, and some children I knew took all the prayers and hymns at a gulp, so as to get them over and then freely enjoyed that entertaining book. But our chief knowledge of literature came in the evenings when my father read aloud to us. He took us through The Arabian Nights, Gulliver's Travels, the Iliad and Odyssey, translations of the Greek dramatists, Shakespeare's plays and, most beloved of all, Scott's novels. These we acted in the garden and called ourselves by our heroes' names. The evening hour was looked forward to all day long and its memory has followed me through life. One point about this reading has always puzzled me. Though Scott was approved Dickens was forbidden. I was grown up before I read David Copperfield and then it had to be in secret. I suppose that there is a religious tone in Scott which is absent in Dickens.

In 1869 the Cambridge Higher Local Examination for Women over eighteen came into being, and in the warmth of this newly risen sun the country chrysalis prepared to spread her wings. She and her father worked together at Divinity and Mathematics; her French and German were already good; and she went up to London for the examination. "Professor Liveing invigilated and Miss Clough came and comforted me when I was floored by the paper on Conic Sections and was crying over it." As a result of her performance in the examination she was offered a scholarship if she would go to Cambridge with Miss Clough. "My father was proud and pleased and his admiration for Miss Clough overcame his objections to sending his daughter to Cambridge (in those days an outrageous proceeding). My father and she became great friends and in later years when we had dances at Merton Hall I can see them leading off in Sir Roger de Coverley." He cannot have associated her too closely with her free-thinking brother, the poet, Arthur Hugh Clough, Matthew Arnold's Thyrsis. Indeed, her careful ways were more akin to her ancestor, Richard Clough, the famous agent of Sir

Thomas Gresham in the reign of Elizabeth (who, it is curious to remember, was also the ancestor to Mrs. Thrale). Between Mary herself and Anne Clough there was a deep and lasting affection.

Thus in October 1871 Mary Paley was one of the five students who went up to Cambridge to live with Miss Clough at 74 Regent Street (now the Glengarry Hotel), which became the nucleus of Newnham College. In the next year the industrious virgins became twelve and moved to Merton Hall "with its lovely garden where the nightingales kept us awake at nights and with its ancient School of Pythagoras supposed to be haunted, though the only ghosts which visited us were enormous spiders." It was terribly important that there should be no scandal, and the strictest discipline and propriety were enforced by the friends of the new movement of which Henry Sidgwick was the leader. But they were not a dowdy lot, as *Punch* of that day probably assumed. Mary Paley herself had noble features, lovely hair and a brilliant complexion, though she does not record that. And

there was my chum, Mary Kennedy, very beautiful with Irish eyes and a lovely colour. This caused Mr. Sidgwick some anxiety. In after years Mrs. Peile, a devoted friend, amused us by describing how in those early days of the movement he walked up and down her drawing-room wringing his hands and saying "If it were not for their unfortunate appearance." Some of the Cambridge ladies did not approve of women students and kept an eye on our dress. Mr. Sidgwick heard rumours that we wore "tied back" dresses (the then fashion) and he asked Miss Clough what this meant. She consulted us as to what was to be done. Could we untie them?

[This characteristic passage, just as she used to talk of the old days, was written by Mrs. Marshall in about her ninety-third year.]

Three years went by, and then the grand excitement of two women, Mary Paley and Amy Bulley, sitting, as Newnham's first pioneers, for a man's Tripos, the Moral Sciences Tripos of 1874, the only examination at that time of which Political Economy formed a part. It all had to be very informal by agreement with the examiners. I give the story of the last lap in Mary Marshall's own words:

We were examined in the drawing-room of Dr. Kennedy's house in Bateman Street, the Kennedy of the Latin Grammar. He was rather excitable and hot tempered (we called him the purple boy).

The Tripos papers came by "runners," as we called them, who after getting them at the Senate House hurried to Bateman Street: among these runners were Sidgwick, Marshall, Sedley Taylor and Venn. At the Examiners' Meeting there was at that time no chairman to give a casting vote, and as two voted me first class and two second class I was left hanging, as Mr. Sidgwick said, "between heaven and hell" [1] and Dr. Kennedy made the following verses:

> *"Though two with glory would be cramming her*
> *And two with fainter praise be d—— her,*
> *Her mental and her moral stamina*
> *Were certified by each examiner.*
>
> *Were they at sixes and at sevens?—*
> *O Foxwell, Gardiner, Pearson, Jevons!"*

As we were the two first of Miss Clough's students who attempted a Tripos we were made much of. The Miss Kennedys gave us very delicate light lunches, and after it was over they took us to stay with them at Ely until the results were known for fear that the excitement might be too great for us.

All the "runners" were familiar Cambridge figures of my youth. Apart from Marshall, they were all very short, and had long, flowing beards. Though, perhaps, their beards were not as long then as when I knew them twenty-five years later. I see them as the wise, kind dwarfs hurrying with the magical prescriptions which were to awaken the princesses from their intellectual slumbers into the full wakefulness of masculine mankind. As for "her mental and her moral stamina," succeeding generations for another seventy years were going to be able to certify that.

Next year, 1875, Sidgwick invited Mary Paley to come into residence at the Old Hall at Newnham, where Miss Clough had now assembled about twenty students, to take over from Marshall the task of lecturing on Economics to women students. What a galaxy of eminent and remarkable women were assembled at Newnham in those early days! Mrs. Marshall in her notes mentions among these early students "Katherine Bradley, 'the Newnham poetess' (better known along with her niece as Michael Field), Alice Gardner, Mary Martin (Mrs. James Ward), Ellen Crofts (Mrs. Francis Darwin), Miss Merrifield (Mrs. Verrall) and Jane Harrison," not one of them without at least a touch of genius. The mention of Jane Harrison led her to run on:

This was the pre-Raphaelite period, and we papered our rooms with Morris, bought Burne-Jones photographs and dressed accordingly. We played Lawn Tennis and Jane Harrison designed the embroidery for our tennis dresses. Hers was of pomegranates and mine of Virginia Creeper and we sat together in the evenings and worked at them and talked. I had known her as a girl and even then she was called the "cleverest woman in England." Though in the end she read for the Classical Tripos she was nearly persuaded to read Moral Science by Mr. Marshall, and she always afterwards called him "the camel" for she said that she trembled at the sight of him as a horse does at the sight of a camel. She used to declare that she had brought about my engagement to him by stitching clean, white ruffles into my dress on that day.

For in the following year, 1876, Mary Paley and Alfred Marshall became engaged to be married. So far as she was concerned, it had been, I suspect, a case of love at first sight five years before. In her first term in Cambridge at 74 Regent Street she recalls:

My first recollections of Mr. Sidgwick and Mr. Marshall are the evenings when we sat round and sewed the household linen in Miss Clough's sitting-room. This was my first sight of Mr. Marshall. I then thought I had never seen such an attractive face with its delicate outline and brilliant eyes. We sat very silent and rather awed as we listened to them talking to Miss Clough on high subjects.

In her first term she began to go to his lectures—in the coachhouse of Grove Lodge, which had been lent for lectures to women. "Mr. Marshall stood by the blackboard, rather nervous, bending a quill pen which took flight from between his fingers, very earnest and with shining eyes." Mrs. Bateson, wife of the

Master of St. John's, gave a small dance in the Hall of the Lodge. "Seeing that Mr. Marshall seemed rather melancholy, I asked him to dance the Lancers. He looked surprised and said he didn't know how, but he consented, and I guided him through its mazes, though being shocked at my own boldness, I did not speak a word, and I don't think he did either." Next an invitation to tea in his rooms, the highest in the New Court of St. John's, chaperoned by Miss Clough. There is a fascinating account of Marshall's lectures, one extract from which I cannot forgo:

> In these lectures he gave us his views on many practical problems, *e.g.*, dancing, marriage, betting and smuggling. As to marriage. "The ideal of married life is often said to be that husband and wife should live for each other. If this means that they should live for each other's gratification it seems to me intensely immoral. Man and wife should live, not for each other but with each other for some end."

To which Mrs. Marshall added the comment "He was a great preacher."

Meanwhile she had promised Professor Stuart to write a textbook for the Extension lectures. After the engagement he began to help her with it.

> It was published in our joint names in 1879. Alfred insisted on this, though as time went on I realised that it had to be really his book, the latter half being almost entirely his and containing the germs of much that appeared later in the "Principles." He never liked the little book for it offended against his belief that "every dogma that is short and simple is false," and he said about it "you can't afford to tell the truth for half-a-crown."

It was, in fact, an extremely good book; nothing more serviceable for its purpose was produced for many years, if ever. I know that my father always felt that there was something ungenerous in Marshall's distaste for this book, which was originally hers, but was allowed to go out of print without a murmur of complaint from her when there was still a strong demand for it. The book which replaced it in 1892, under a similar title and over his sole name, was of quite a different character, being mainly an abridgement of the *Principles*. The 1879 volume, so great an advance when it came out on what had gone before, is the little book in green covers, not the thicker one in blue Macmillan cloth.

In July of 1877 they were married. But their real honeymoon came, I think, in 1881, when, after four years as Principal of University College, Bristol, Marshall's health broke down and she took him for a long rest cure to Palermo. I fancy that this was the period of most unbroken happiness and perfect contentment in her life. Recalling it sixty years later she wrote:

We were five months at Palermo, on a roof, and whenever I want something pleasant to think about I try to imagine myself on it. It was the roof of a small Italian hotel, the Oliva, flat of course and paved with coloured tiles, and upon it during the day Alfred occupied an American chair over which the cover of the travelling bath was rigged up as an awning, and there he wrote the early chapters of his "Principles." One day he came down from the roof to tell me how he had just discovered the notion of "elasticity of demand."

This is the beginning of a fascinating chapter which describes the Sicilian scene. Marshall, who was suffering from stone in the kidney, was not unduly ill. His powers were at the height of their fertility. There was no controversy, no lectures, no tiresome colleagues, none of the minor irritations to his over-sensitive spirit which Mary was to spend so much of her life soothing away. Nature was kind and lovely. "From the roof we had a view of the *conca d'oro,* the golden shell of orange and lemon groves stretching a few miles inland, and of the mountains which met the sea on either side and formed a semicircle of varied shapes." They looked down upon a little court. "It was a small court but the most was made of it. The trellis work over the pathways was covered with vines loaded with grapes, and there was a lemon tree and an orange tree and plenty of flowers. The houses around had their balconies paved with coloured tiles, which especially near Christmas time were inhabited by turkeys, whilst pigeons lived in holes and corners." She loved the morning visit to the market to buy fruit. All her life, down almost to her latest days, Mary Marshall was a gifted amateur water-colourist, never so happy as when sketching. Whilst Alfred composed the *Principles* on the roof, Mary went out with her brush and colours.

The place I cared for most and in which I spent many hours, trying to make a picture, was the Cappella Palatina. It is small and dimly lighted by slit-like windows so that on entering from the sunlight hardly anything could be seen but a mass of dim golden shadows. Gradually, however, the wonderful beauty of outline and detail emerged. The outlines are Norman, and Saracenic workmen filled in the rich colour and oriental devices. Most beautiful of all was the golden apse, out of which loomed the great Christ's head.

They were months of perfect bliss.

For the next forty years her life was wholly merged in his. This was not a partnership of the Webb kind, as it might have become if the temperaments on both sides had been entirely different. In spite of his early sympathies and what he was gaining all the time from his wife's discernment of mind, Marshall came increasingly to the conclusion that there was nothing useful to be made of women's intellects. When the great trial of strength came in 1896 over the proposal to grant women's degrees he abandoned the friends of a lifetime and took, whatever his wife might think or feel, the other side. But Mary Marshall had been brought up to know, and also to respect and accept what men of "strict principles" were like. This was not the first time that her dolls (which she was in risk of making into idols) had been burnt by one whom she loved.

Yet it was an intellectual partnership just the same, based on profound dependence on the one side (he could not live a day without her), and, on the other, deep devotion and admiration, which was increased and not impaired by extreme discernment. Nothing escaped her clear, penetrating and truthful eye. She faced everything in order that he, sometimes, need not. By a gift of character and her bright mind and, I think one should add, a sort of natural artistry, of which I have never seen the like, she could charm away the petty or the irritating or the unnecessary with an equable, humorous loving-kindness. Neither in Alfred's lifetime nor afterwards did she ever ask, or expect, anything for herself. It was always in the forefront of her thought that she must not be a trouble to anyone.

Thus splendidly equipped, she now merged her life in his. Both at Bristol and at Oxford, where they were soon to go, she lectured on Economics, and when they returned to Cambridge she resumed her lectureship at Newnham, where she was in charge of the students for many years. She kept a watchful eye over the proofs and the index of the early editions of the *Principles,* and there are other ways of influencing the course and progress of a great book than open or direct criticism. The degree of D.Litt. of the University of Bristol was conferred on her. But she never, to the best of my recollection, discoursed on an economic topic with a visitor, or even took part in the ever-lasting economic talks of Balliol Croft. For the serious discussion she would leave the dining-room to the men or the visitor would go upstairs to the study and the most ignorant Miss could not have pretended less than she to academic attainment. Her holiday task was not to debate the theories of the Austrian economists, but to make water-colour sketches of the South Tirol. Indeed, her artistic gift was considerable. She seldom showed her work to her friends, but she exhibited regularly with the Cambridge Drawing Society, and has left to Mr. C.R. Fay, who has deposited them with the Marshall Library, a sub-stantial selection of the scenes, where she sat with her sketching stool and easel whilst the Master, on his " 'throne' with an air cushion and a camp stool which when opened against a pile of stones made a comfortable back to lean against," defined, in a hand less steady than hers, the Representative Firm.

On their return from Palermo there was one more year in Bristol. In 1883 Marshall succeeded Arnold Toynbee at Balliol as lecturer to the Indian students in Oxford. At Oxford he had larger classes than at any other time, since "Greats" men as well as the budding Indian Civilians attended his lectures. She records:

At that time Henry George's "Progress and Poverty" roused much interest. Alfred gave three lectures on it at Bristol which Miss Elliott said reminded her of a boa constrictor which slob-bers its victim before swallowing it. At Oxford he encountered

Henry George in person, York Powell being in the chair and Max Müller on the platform. Shortly after another duel took place with Hyndman, who called forth Arthur Sidgwick's "Devil take the Hyndman." Bimetallism and Home Rule were also raging about that time and were subjects too dangerous to mention at a dinner party.

The short interlude at Balliol, then at its highest point of brilliance and of fame, certainly introduced Alfred Marshall to a larger world than he had known previously. He became one of Jowett's young men. Jowett, who was on the Council of Bristol University, first came across him there, and the time at Oxford confirmed a friendship with both the Marshalls, whom he would afterwards visit at Cambridge. Mrs. Marshall records:

My first sight of the Master was at a dinner party given by the Percivals. He and Henry Smith were on the Council of the College, they came regularly three times a year to its meetings and generally stayed at our house and these visits were a delight. They were such a well-fitting pair and seemed so happy together, for though Jowett was rather shy and silent unless with a congenial companion, he was quite at his ease with Henry Smith who was the most brilliant and humorous talker I have ever met. I used to sit up with them and Alfred till well after midnight. It took me about five years to feel quite at ease with Jowett, for his shyness was a difficulty, but after a while we got on quite well and only talked when we wanted to. I sometimes took walks with him and he would make a remark now and then and fill up the gaps by humming little tunes.

Thus the Marshalls easily took their place in Balliol and Oxford society. Evelyn Abbott, Lewis Nettleship, Andrew Bradley, Strachan Davidson, Albert Dicey and Alfred Milner were Fellows of Balliol.

The Women's Colleges had recently started and I had the great good fortune of getting to know Miss Wordsworth, the first Head of Lady Margaret Hall. She was wise and witty, her bon-mots were proverbial and walks with her were a joy. Then Ruskin was at Oxford giving drawing lessons, lecturing to crowded audiences and inciting undergraduates to make roads. Toynbee Hall was being founded and the Barnetts often came to Balliol to stir up the young men to take an active part. The

Charity Organisation Society had just started. Mr. Phelps was Chairman and Mr. Albert Dicey and Miss Eleanor Smith (accompanied by her dog) regularly attended its meetings. There was also a Society led by Mr. Sidney Ball for the Discussion of Social Questions, so the four terms of our life at Oxford were full of interest and excitement.

And there were Jowett's dinner-parties:

He enjoyed bringing his friends together and almost every week-end during Term he asked people to stay at the Lodge who he thought would like to meet one another or would be likely to help one another. His plan was to have a rather large and carefully arranged party on the Saturday which Arthur Sidgwick used to call a "Noah's Ark" dinner, for so many strange animals walked in in pairs. One amusing pair was Lady Rosebery, a large lady, and the small Prince of Siam. There were the Goschens, the Huxleys, the Matthew Arnolds, Robert Browning, "Dam Theology" Rogers, an Australian Prime Minister, Sir Robert Morier, Cornelia Sorabji and the Alfred Greys among many others. He liked to spend a quiet evening with his friends. He came once to meet Albert Dicey and Eleanor Smith, the sister of Henry Smith, who was as well known for her brusque home-truths as he for his genial humour. Another time he brought Ruskin, who told funny stories and made us laugh with quaint rhymes about little pigs, and Miss Smith who knew him well said she had never seen him merrier. Alfred happened one day to meet Professor Vinogradoff and was so much fascinated that he asked him to dine with us and meet Jowett who had arranged to come that night. There was a little stiffness at first, as Jowett had not met Vinogradoff and as usual was shy with strangers, but as the evening went on talk became more and more free; after dinner we sat out in the little back garden under the birch tree and a full moon and then it became what Jowett called "good," on philosophy and poetry. I never heard him talk as freely as he did that evening and I would give much to be able to recall that conversation. He enjoyed discussing economic questions with Alfred and would bring out his little notebook and take down a remark that specially interested him. He once told me that Alfred's talk was the best he knew. At another time he said "Alfred is the most disinterested man I have ever known." Our faithful old servant "Sarah" interested him and he was the only person to whom she would speak of her religious difficulties. When he stayed with us at Cambridge he would sit with her in the kitchen and talk them over.

The return to Cambridge in 1885 is best described in Mrs. Marshall's own words:

By the end of four Terms we had quite settled in at Oxford. The small house and garden in Woodstock Road suited us well. I taught the women students, Alfred enjoyed teaching his big classes, and though he always felt that Cambridge was his true home, we thought that our future would lie in Oxford. However, in 1884 Fawcett died and Alfred was elected in his place, the only serious competitor being Inglis Palgrave, and in January 1885 we went to Cambridge, hired a house in Chesterton Road for a year and in 1886 Balliol Croft was built and we settled down there for good. In 1885 prices were still low and the contract for the house was £900, though on account of a mistake on the part of the architect it cost £1,100. For several years it was the only house in Madingley Road and we chose the site chiefly for its forest trees. Alfred took immense pains in planning the house and in economising space, especially in the kitchen department. He was anxious to have his study on a higher floor as he thought that in Cambridge it was well to live as far from the ground as possible. However J. J. Stevenson the architect persuaded him to be content with the first floor and a balcony.

It is a commentary on the change in the value of money that after Mrs. Marshall's death, Balliol Croft, with nearly 60 years of its lease expired, was sold to another Professor migrating to Cambridge from Balliol for £2,500. It was part of Mrs. Marshall's small inheritance still preserved from the Archdeacon's large profits as author, from the long Headmastership of Giggleswick in the eighteenth century, from the yeoman farmers of Yorkshire back into the mists of time, which was invested in this house; and has now filtered through to the University of Cambridge for the Marshall Library, the first-fruits of the bequest being the purchase in June 1944 of the original MS. of Malthus's *Political Economy*.

For the next forty years "one year passed much like another." The Marshalls had a very small house and one faithful servant, but were endlessly hospitable not less to the rawest undergraduate than to visitors from the great world. The "one faithful servant" deserves a separate word. For forty-three years Sarah, and after her death Florence. Sarah (Mrs. Marshall wrote) "nearly always gave warning in November, that most trying month, but I paid no attention, for I knew she would not leave." She belonged to the Plymouth Brethren, the gloomiest sect of a gloomy persuasion.

She became an excellent cook and loved having great responsibilities. Though she considered it wrong to "enjoy" herself she used to say that the happiest week in her life was when the British Association met at Cambridge and when there were about twelve at each meal; she ran the whole concern and would lie awake at night considering the menus for the next day. At one time she was troubled by the feeling that she was not being of enough use in the world, but was consoled when she realised that by good cooking she was keeping Alfred in health and was enabling him to write important books.

Mrs. Marshall knew how to win devotion. She recalls how Lady Jebb, who, coming "to England in the 'seventies as a young American widow, took the place by storm, and don after don fell before her," once when the conversation was about servants, said that she believed very much in praise, and ended by "Just think how much praise is required by the Almighty."

In the earliest days of the Labour Movement the Marshalls used to invite the working-class leaders to stay. "Ben Tillett, Tom Mann and Burnet were among our visitors and a specially delightful one was Thomas Burt." Edgeworth would often be there. "We had of course many visits from Economists from U.S.A., Germany, Italy, France and Holland. We were very fond of Professor Pierson and his wife who stayed with us several times and of Professor and Mrs. Taussig." And, of course, we his pupils would be forever lunching there when there were interesting visitors for us to see, or taking tea alone in the study for the good of our souls and minds.

But apart from visitors the Cambridge society of those days formed a remarkable group:

I became a member of a Ladies' Dining Society of ten or twelve who dined at one another's houses once or twice a Term, the husbands either dining at their Colleges or having a solitary meal in their studies. The hostess not only provided a good dinner (though champagne was not allowed) but also a suitable topic for conversation, should one be required, and she was allowed to introduce an outside lady at her dinner; but it was an exclusive society, for one black ball was enough to exclude a proposed new member. Its members were Mrs. Creighton, Mrs. Arthur Verrall, Mrs. Arthur Lyttelton, Mrs. Sidgwick, Mrs. James Ward, Mrs. Francis Darwin, Baroness von Hügel, Lady Horace Darwin, Lady George Darwin, Mrs. Prothero and Lady Jebb.

"There seem," Mrs. Marshall reflected in her extreme old age (and, I fear, with justice) "to be fewer 'characters' now than in by-gone days."

Most of the Long Vacations were spent in South Tirol, especially with Filomena, who kept the small wayside inn at Stern in Abteital.

One year we discovered that in the next village were assembled a large part of the "Austrian school" of economists. The Von Wiesers, the Böhm Bawerks, the Zuckerkandls and several others. We boldly asked the whole company to a tea party in our enormous bedroom, which was the largest and most desirable room in the inn, and we afterwards adjourned to the tent shelter in the field nearby. Filomena was proud of having such distinguished guests and got up at 4 A.M. to make fresh butter and various delicacies for the entertainment. Von Böhm Bawerk was a wiry and agile little man, an ardent mountaineer who climbed a dolomite almost every day. This somewhat exhausted his economic energies and he did not want to discuss the Theory of the Rate of Interest, a subject which I had rather dreaded as he and Alfred had recently been corresponding warmly upon it. Professor Von Wieser was a noble-looking man and a delightful companion with a wife and daughter to match and I much enjoyed the return tea party which the Austrian School gave at the beautiful old peasant's house where they were spending the summer.

In 1920 a last, and rather disastrous, attempt was made to travel abroad. And after that the end of this sweet partnership was not far off.

The next three summers we spent in a lovely and lonely Dorset cove called Arish Mell, where he worked away at his third volume. But after "Industry and Trade" had been finished in 1919 his memory gradually became worse and soon after his doctor told me quietly that "he will not be able to construct any more." And it was so, though fortunately he did not know it. For in the old days he used to come down from his study and say "I have had such a happy time, there is no joy to be compared to constructive work."

Yet after Alfred Marshall's death there were still another twenty years for Mary Marshall of serene beauty and of deeper intimacy with Alfred's old pupils and their wives.

Forty years ago, specialised lending libraries for students, from which they could take books away, were rare. It was an essential part of Marshall's technique of teaching to encourage his pupils to read widely in their subject and to learn the use of a library. To answer a question on price index numbers, a third- or fourth-year student would not be expected just to consult the latest standard authority. He must glance right back at least to Jevons and Giffen, if not to Bishop Fleetwood; he must look at any articles published on the subject in the *Economic Journal* during the last twenty years; and if he is led on to browse over the history of prices since the Middle Ages, or to compare the price of wheat in terms of wages in the times of Solon and of Charles II., no harm will have been done. A favourite pupil would be made to feel unworthy (*i.e.*, of his great mission to be an economist and carry on the tradition of this high clerisy) if his eyes had scanned less than ten to a dozen volumes before his answer was shown up. He had three ways for making this possible. First of all, he established in his lecture-room a library of the more obvious books, small but, of course, much more extensive than any undergraduate's stock. When he resigned from his Professorship he passed this collection on to his successor. I think that I was its first official librarian and prepared its first printed catalogue. Beyond this was his own extensive collection, from which the pupil, after tea at Balliol Croft, would be expected to take away as many volumes as he could carry on the way home along the Madingley Road. Finally, he had long ago adopted a practice of breaking up learned journals, for which purpose he would sometimes acquire an extra set, so as to collect and bind the articles according to subjects. A great number of such volumes now lie in the Marshall Library, and this was a source which, together with its footnotes, could lead the raw student from one reference to another, until, if he persevered, he became, for that week at least, a walking bibliography on the subject. The preparation of these volumes, and subsequently the cataloguing of the items by author and subject in "the brown boxes," had been, for time out of memory, the special task of Mrs. Marshall.

With all this, as a means of education and personal contact and inspiration, Mrs. Marshall had been passionately in sympathy. The book-laden departing visitor would have a word with her downstairs before he left, and she would see him out of the door and along the drive with the deepest satisfaction in her eyes. So when Alfred passed beyond her care, to preserve this tradition and to keep *his* books still living in the hands of the succeeding generations of students became her dearest aim.

First of all, his library passed to the University for the use of students in *statu pupillari,* to be amalgamated with the existing students' library just mentioned, to become *The Marshall Library of Economics.* Next she set up a substantial endowment fund by payments under covenant, which she supplemented by paying into it an annual sum from the royalties of his books, the sale of which for some years after his death, so far from diminishing, increased. (In her will she has left the Library a further £10,000 and all her husband's copyrights.) But above all she decided to become herself in her proper person the tutelary goddess of the books and of the rising generation of students. So in her seventy-fifth year, defying the University Regulations, by which it is now thought proper that we should all be deemed to be deceased at sixty-five, she was appointed Honorary Assistant Librarian of the Marshall Library of Economics; and so she continued for nearly twenty years. Every morning till close of her ninetieth year, when, to her extreme dissatisfaction, her doctor prohibited her (partly at her friends' instigation, but more on account of the dangers of the Cambridge traffic even to the most able-bodied than to any failure of her physical powers), she bicycled the considerable distance from Madingley Road to the Library (which in 1935 was moved to the fine and ample building, formerly the Squire Law Library, adjoining the Geological Museum in Downing Street), wearing, as she always did, the sandals which were a legacy of her pre-Raphaelite period sixty years before. There she spent the morning in charge of the Library, first of all assisted by an undergraduate, afterwards, as the scale of the work grew, by a professional under-librarian, Mr. Missen, from 1933 onwards; thus relieving of routine duties the successive Marshall librarians, Dennis Robertson, Ryle Fay and since 1931 (with an interval) Piero Sraffa. Keeping up "the brown boxes" remained her special and most favourite task. She always spoke of the place as "My Library." Her heart and her head, as was the way with her, were equally engaged, and it became her main contact with the flow of life and the pulse of the Cambridge School of Economists which had begun to beat so strongly in Balliol Croft sixty years ago.

On November 7, 1936,[2] there was a small function in the Library when she presented a copy by William Rothenstein of his portrait of Marshall, which hangs in the hall of St. John's College. Thereafter she sat at the head of the Library at a small central table under the portrait. (There is, fortunately, a most characteristic photograph of her so seated.) In 1941, when she was ninety-one, bronchitis began, for the first time, to make her attendance irregular. In 1942 she was not able to be there, except on November 14, when she was present at the celebration of the centenary of her husband's birth[3] and made a speech in full vigour of mind, telling those present what happiness and delight her husband had drawn from the labours of his study. On March 7, 1944, she died, and her ashes were scattered in the garden of Balliol Croft.

Modest as morn; as Mid-day bright;
Gentle as Ev'ning; cool as Night.

KEY TO PERSONS MENTIONED OTHER-WISE THAN BY THEIR FULL NAMES IN *DR. MELCHIOR* AND *MY EARLY BELIEFS*

Lydia: Lydia Lopokova, Lady Keynes
Maynard: John Maynard Keynes, later Lord Keynes

Lord Robert: Lord Robert Cecil, later Viscount Cecil of Chelwood

Clive: Clive Bell
Roger: Roger Fry

The Provost (Durnford): Sir Walter Durnford, Provost of King's College, Cambridge, 1918-1926
Macaulay: W. H. Macaulay, Vice-Provost of King's College, Cambridge, when Durnford was Provost

Bunny: David Garnett
Bertie: Bertrand Russell (Earl Russell)

Ottoline: Lady Ottoline Morrell
Gertler: Mark Gertler, the painter
Carrington: Dorothy Carrington (Mrs. R. Partridge)

Moore: Professor G. E. Moore
Strachey: Lytton Strachey

Woolf: Leonard Woolf

Sheppard: J. T. Sheppard, now Provost of King's College, Cambridge

Hawtrey: R. G. Hawtrey, C.B., Assistant Secretary, H.M. Treasury

MacCarthy: Desmond MacCarthy

Ainsworth: A. R. Ainsworth, C.B.

Forster: E. M. Forster

McTaggart: J. M. E. McTaggart, the philosopher and Trinity College lecturer in moral sciences from 1897 to 1923

Dickinson: Goldsworthy Lowes Dickinson

Russell: Bertrand Russell (Earl Russell)

Sidgwick: Henry Sidgwick, the philosopher

Bob Trevy: R. C. Trevelyan, the poet

Ludwig: Ludwig Wittgenstein, the philosopher

NOTES

ROBERT MALTHUS

[1] This biographical sketch does not pretend to collect the available material for that definitive biography of Malthus, for which we have long waited vainly from the pen of Dr. Bonar. I have made free use of the common authorities—Bishop Otter's Life prefixed to the second (posthumous) edition of Malthus's *Political Economy* in 1836, W. Empson's review of Otter's edition in the *Edinburgh Review,* January 1837, and Dr. Bonar's *Malthus and his Work* (1st ed., 1885, preceded by the sketch "Parson Malthus" in 1881 and followed by a 2nd ed., with the biographical chapter expanded in 1924, to which edition my subsequent references relate); and I have added such other details as I have come across in miscellaneous reading which has been neither systematic nor exhaustive. Nor have I attempted any complete summary or assessment of Malthus's contributions to Political Economy, which would require a closer acquaintance than I possess with the work of his contemporaries. My object has been to select those items of information which seemed most to contribute to a portrait, and, in particular, to enlarge a little on the intellectual atmosphere in which he grew up, at home and at Cambridge.

[2] For a complete collection relating to records of all persons bearing this family name, *vide* J. O. Paine, *Collections for a History of the Family of Malthus,* 110 copies privately printed, 110, in 1890. Mr. Sraffa possesses Payne's own copy of this book with additional notes and illustrations inserted.

[3] Robert Malthus's mother was a granddaughter of Thomas Graham, apothecary to George I. and George II.

⁴ Sydenham Malthus bought an estate at Little Shelford, near Cambridge, for £2200. His son is recorded as possessing a number of farms in the near neighbourhood of Cambridge—at Hauxton, Newton, and Harston.

⁵ He was the translator of Gerardin's *Essay on Landscape,* published by Dodsley in 1783. T.R.M. wrote to the *Monthly Magazine* of February 19, 1800, indignantly protesting that his father never published translations (*vide* Otter's *Life, op. cit.* p. xxii). I take the above, however, from a note written in a copy of the book in question in Malthus's own library.

⁶ Manning and Bray, *History of Surrey.* (Bray was Daniel Malthus's son-in-law.) A charming pastel picture of a boy in blue, now hanging in Mr. Robert Malthus's house at Albury, is reputed by family tradition to be a portrait of Daniel Malthus.

⁷ Manning and Bray, *op. cit.* In 1768 Daniel Malthus sold The Rookery and the family moved to a less extensive establishment at Albury, not far from Guildford. An early engraving of The Rookery is inserted in Mr. Sraffa's copy of Mr. Payne's book (*vide supra*), and the house is still standing, though with some changes. It was a substantial and expensive essay in Gothicism—another testimony to the contemporary intellectual influences in which Daniel Malthus was interested. Albury House, not to be confused with the Duke of Northumberland's Albury Park nor with either of the two houses in Albury now owned by the Malthus family (Dalton Hill and The Cottage), is no longer standing. An engraving alleged to represent it is inserted in Mr. Sraffa's copy of Mr. Payne's book.

⁸ See Wotton Parish Registers.

⁹ *Vide* Greig, *Letters of David Hume,* vol. ii. p. 24.

¹⁰ See Hume's letters of March 2 and March 27, 1766, Nos. 309 and 315 in Dr. Greig's edition (*op. cit.*). Dr. Bonar reports (*op. cit.* 2nd ed. p. 402) a family tradition, on the authority of the late Colonel Sydenham Malthus, that Daniel Malthus also corresponded with Voltaire, but that "a lady into whose hands the letters came gave them to the flames." The correspondence with Rousseau shows that D. M. was also acquainted with Wilkes, who visited him at The Rookery and from whom he first heard of the story of the quarrel between Rousseau and Hume.

¹¹ An excellent account of the episode is to be found in Courtois' *Le Séjour de Jean-Jacques Rousseau en Angleterre* (1911).

¹² Vide *Diary and Letters of Mme. D'Arblay* (Dobson's edition), vol. v. p. 145. Miss Burney refers to D. M. as "Mr. Malthouse."

¹³ Rousseau writes to Malthus on January 2, 1767: "Je pense souvent avec plaisir à la ferme solitaire que nous avons vue ensemble et à l'avantage d'y être votre voisin; mais ceci sont plutôt des souhaits vagues que des projets d'une prochaine exécution."

[14] Lent by Mr. Richard Davenport. It was here that Rousseau began to write the *Confessions*. One of the refuges almost selected by Rousseau on his visit to Malthus was the other Wotton, Evelyn's Wotton in Surrey, very near to Albury (see Daniel Malthus's letter of March 12, 1766, where he explains that he has been approaching Sir John Evelyn on the matter).

[15] Of course Jean-Jacques was in the wrong. But, all the same, Hume might have shown a serener spirit, taking Adam Smith's advice "not to think of publishing anything to the world." After the superb character sketch of his guest which he wrote to Dr. Blair on March 21, 1766 (Greig, No. 314), showing so deep an understanding, his later letters (as also the *Concise and Genuine Account*, published in 1766, fascinating though it is in itself) are the product, not of a comprehending heart, but of an extreme anxiety to avoid a scandal which his Paris friends might misunderstand.

[16] When Rousseau fails to answer a letter, Daniel Malthus (December 4, 1767) breaks out: "Est-il possible, Monsieur, que vous ayez reçu ma lettre, et que vous me refusiez les deux mots que je vous demandois? Je ne veux pas le croire. Je ne donne pas une fausse importance à mon amitié. Ne me respectez pas mais respectez-vous vous-même. Vous laissez dans le cœur d'un être semblable au votre une idée affligeante que vous pouvez ôter, le cœur qui vous aime si tendrement ne sait pas vous accuser."

[17] Malthus's letters were printed by Courtois, *op. cit.*, and are Nos. 2908, 2915, 2939, 2940, 2941, 2952, 2953 (to Mlle. le Vasseur), 2970, 2979, 3073, 3182, 3440 in the *Correspondance générale de Rousseau*, to which must be added letters of December 14, 1767, and January 24, 1768 [Nos. 3547 and 3578 in vol. 18, 1932]. Rousseau's letter is No. 3211, and is a discovery of M. Courtois, having been wrongly assumed by previous editors to be addressed to another correspondent. It appears that the correspondence was resumed in 1770 and that the two remained in touch. But the later letters were not found by M. Courtois. [The later volumes of the *Correspondance générale* did not disclose anything further. *Ed.*]

[18] *Vide* Courtois, *op. cit.* p. 99.

[19] A niece of Daniel Malthus's mother, referred to by Daniel Malthus in a letter to Rousseau as "la petite cousine qui est botaniste à toute outrance," who evidently shared the botanical tastes of Daniel Malthus and Rousseau, and is recorded as having presented Rousseau with a copy of *Johnson sur Gerard* (presumably Gerarde's *Herball*, 1633) from her own library when Daniel Malthus was unable to get one through the booksellers. (See Daniel Malthus's letter to Rousseau, January 24, 1768, printed by Courtois, *op. cit.* p. 219.) Those who are curious to explore the extensive cousinage of the Malthuses are recommended to consult Mr. Payne's book and preferably Mr. Sraffa's copy of it. They were in the habit,

almost as often as not, of marrying their cousins (T. R. Malthus himself married his cousin), and the result is unusually complicated.

[20] A great-grandson of Sydenham Malthus, the elder brother of T. R. Malthus. The only other living descendants of Daniel Malthus in the male line are, I think, settled in New Zealand. T. R. Malthus, who had three children, has no living descendants. There must, however, be many descendants of Daniel Malthus in the female line. According to Mr. Payne's records (*op. cit.*) Daniel had eight children, and at least nineteen grandchildren, whilst it would seem that his great-grandchildren must have considerably exceeded thirty. I cannot count the present generation of great-great-grandchildren. There would appear, however, to be a safe margin for the operation of the geometrical law! The most distinguished of Daniel's living or recently living descendants are the Brays of Shere near Albury, to which the late Mr. Justice Bray belonged.

[21] This library, still preserved intact at Dalton Hill, is the library of the Reverend Henry Malthus, T. R. Malthus's son. It includes, however, a considerable part of T. R. Malthus's library, as well as a number of books from Daniel's library. Dr. Bonar has had prepared a complete and careful catalogue of the whole collection. It is to him that I am indebted for the opportunity to obtain these particulars.

[22] Perhaps the later volumes of the *Correspondance générale* will throw some light on it. Rousseau, it is true, executed a will during his stay in England, and Malthus may have been mentioned in it. Mr. Sraffa suggests to me that Otter may have been misled by the fact that, shortly before his death, Rousseau entrusted the manuscript of the *Confessions* to Paul Moultou.

[23] Courtois, *op. cit.* p. 221.

[24] *Life of Gilbert Wakefield,* vol. i. p. 344, quoted by Dr. Bonar, *op. cit.* p. 405.

[25] Colonel Sydenham Malthus, the father of the present owner, put them at Dr. Bonar's disposal.

[26] Quoted by Bonar, *op. cit.* p. 408.

[27] I wish I could have included some account of Paley amongst these Essays. For Paley, so little appreciated now, was for a generation or more an intellectual influence on Cambridge only second to Newton. Perhaps, in a sense, *he* was the first of the Cambridge economists. If anyone will take up again Paley's *Principles* he will find, contrary perhaps to his expectations, an immortal book. Or glance through G. W. Meadley's *Memoirs of William Paley* for a fascinating account of the lovable wit and eccentricities of a typical Cambridge don. His great-granddaughter, Mrs. Alfred Marshall, has shown me a little embroidered case containing the Archdeacon's (very businesslike) love letters.

[28] Though Dr. Bonar thinks that Malthus "preferred where he could to draw rather from Tucker than from Paley" (*op. cit.* p. 324). Abraham Tucker, author of the *Light of Nature,* had been for many years a near neighbour of Daniel Malthus at Dorking.

[29] As also on Bentham, a contemporary of Malthus, with whom, however, there is no record of his having been in contact.

[30] "An Effusion on an Autumnal Evening," written by Coleridge "in early youth." It is hard to read without a tear these tender and foreboding lines which end:

> Mine eye the gleam pursues with wistful gaze:
> Sees shades on shades with deeper tint impend,
> Till chill and damp the moonless night descend.

[31] C. W. L. Grice, *Gentleman's Magazine* (1834), quoted by Gray, *Jesus College.*

[32] Coleridge's Unitarian period was under the influence of Frend. Shortly after he went down Coleridge "announced himself to preach in the Unitarian Chapel at Bath as 'The Rev. S. T. Coleridge of Jesus College, Cambridge,' and to mark his severance from the 'gentlemen in black,' so much reprobated in Frend's tract, performed that office in blue coat and white waistcoat" (Gray, *Jesus College,* p. 180).

[33] Coleridge's main criticisms are to be found in manuscript marginal comments on his copy of the second edition of the *Essay on Population* now in the British Museum. See Bonar, *op. cit.* p. 371.

[34] Bonar, *op. cit.* p. 412.

[35] The obituary writer in the *Gentleman's Magazine* (1835, p. 325) records that one (doubtless Otter) "who has known him intimately for nearly fifty years scarcely ever saw him ruffled, *never* angry, never above measure elated or depressed. He had this felicity of mind, almost peculiar to himself, that, being singularly alive to the approbation of the wise and good, and anxious generally for the regard of his fellow creatures, he was impassive to unmerited abuse."

[36] "On the last day of 1792 Tom Paine's effigy was burnt by the mob on the Market Hill at Cambridge" (Gray, *Jesus College,* p. 171). Frend's pamphlet, *Peace and Union recommended to the Associated Bodies of Republicans and Anti-Republicans,* was published two months later. Frend became Secretary and Actuary of the Rock Assurance Company and, dying in 1841, outlived Malthus and all his other contemporaries (Gray, *loc. cit.*).

[37] Two years before he had consulted the head of his College about this, particularly as to whether the defect in his speech would stand in the way. But when he explained that "the utmost of his wishes was a retired living in the country," Dr. Beadon withdrew any objection (*vide* T. R. M.'s letter to Daniel Malthus, April 19, 1786, printed by Dr. Bonar, *op. cit.* p. 409).

[38] I am indebted for this information to Canon Foster of the Lincoln Record Society. The living seems to have been a good one.

[39] Unlike Paley, who sold the first edition of his *Principles* (his first essay in authorship) for £1000.

[40] Cf. G. W. Meadley, *Memoirs of William Paley* (2nd ed.), p. 219.

[41] Cf. Cannan, *History of the Theories of Production and Distribution*.

[42] In January 1800 Daniel Malthus died, aged seventy, and three months later his wife, Robert's mother, followed him, aged sixty-seven. They are both buried in Wotton Churchyard.

[43] His Plato from Patmos is in the Bodleian. The Professor of History wrote:

> I sing of a Tutor renown'd
> Who went roving and raving for knowledge,
> And gathered it all the world round,
> And brought it in boxes to college.

[44] The following from Gunning's *Reminiscences* is well known: "I recollect dining with Outram (the Public Orator) when a packet arrived from Clarke. The first letter began with these words: 'Here I am, eating strawberries within the Arctic Circle.' We were so intent on his dessert that we forgot our own."

[45] See a letter of Malthus's (November 28, 1800), published by Prof Foxwell in the *Economic Journal* (1897), p. 270. Malthus record that Pitt was much impressed, and that in a Report of a Committee of the House of Commons "much of the same kind of reasoning has been adopted."

[46] Not that Malthus neglected this factor. He dealt with it admirably as follows: "To circulate the same, or nearly the same, quantity of commodities through a country, when they bear a much higher price, must require a greater quantity of the medium, whatever that may be. . . . If the quantity of paper, therefore, in circulation has greatly increased during the last year, I should be inclined to consider it rather as the effect than the cause of the high price of provisions. This fulness of circulating medium, however, will be one of the obstacles in the way to returning cheapness."

[47] A scarce pamphlet, which has never, to my knowledge, been reprinted.

[48] In a footnote to *Das Kapital* (vol. i. p. 641, quoted by Dr. Bonar, *op. cit.* p. 291) Marx tells us: "Although Malthus was a clergyman of the Church of England, he had taken the monastic oath of celibacy, for this is one of the conditions of a fellowship at the Protestant University of Cambridge. By this circumstance Malthus is favourably distinguished from the other Protestant clergy, who have cast off the Catholic rule of celibacy." Not being a good Marxist scholar, I was surprised, when in 1925 I lectured before the Commissariat of Finance in Moscow, to find that any mention

by me of the increase of population as being a problem for Russia was taken in ill part. But I should have remembered that Marx, criticising Malthus, had held that over-population was purely the product of a capitalist society and could not occur under Socialism. Marx's reasons for holding this view are by no means without interest, being in fact closely akin to Malthus's own theory that "effective demand" may fail in a capitalist society to keep pace with output.

⁴⁹ The title originally proposed had been "Professor of General History, Politics, Commerce, and Finance."

⁵⁰ Leslie Stephen, who wrote the account of Malthus in the *D.N.B.*, was at that time a young don at Cambridge, chiefly noted for his feats in pedestrianism, and it is recorded that he used to think nothing of a walk from Cambridge to Haileybury to visit his father in the house long occupied by Malthus (vide *Memorials of Old Haileybury College*, p. 196). If only I had an excuse for bringing in "Old Jones"! who occupied this chair for twenty years between Malthus and Stephen, with his famous sermon: "And now, my brethren, let me ask you: which of *you* has not hatched a cockatrice's egg?"

⁵¹ Lists of Malthus's other pamphlets, etc., are given by Otter (*op. cit.* p. xlii) and by Bonar (*op. cit.* p. 421). He also contributed to the *Edinburgh* and *Quarterly Reviews*. His *Definitions of Political Economy*, published in 1827, is a minor work of no great interest (except, perhaps, his attack on Ricardo's definition of *Real Wages*).

⁵² *Memorials of Old Haileybury College*, p. 199.

⁵³ From an obituary notice (by Otter) in the *Athenaeum*, 1835.

⁵⁴ It hangs in the dining-room at Dalton Hill, Albury, with a companion portrait of Mrs. Malthus, also by Linnell, on the other side of the fire-place. Amongst these family pictures there is also to be found a portrait of his son, the Rev. Henry Malthus. There is a copy of the Linnell portrait at Jesus College, Cambridge.

⁵⁵ Mr. J. L. Mallet, in his diary of 1831, mentions that Malthus almost always attended the dinner.

⁵⁶ Before which I read, on April 2, 1924, an earlier version of this essay under the question, "What sort of man was the Reverend Robert Malthus?"

⁵⁷ Mr. Sraffa tells me that this, and not February 1810 as given by Dr. Bonar, is the correct date. Mr. Sraffa's discovery of the Malthus side of the correspondence has enabled him to correct a wrong dating of certain letters ascribed by Dr. Bonar to 1810, but in fact belonging to 1813.

⁵⁸ Malthus speaks in one letter of taking about £5000 in the loan (Aug. 19, 1814).

⁵⁹ *Letters of Ricardo to Malthus*, p. 85.

⁶⁰ One other letter, having been sent by Ricardo to McCulloch and

being with McCulloch's papers in the British Museum, was published by Prof. Hollander in 1895 in his Ricardo-McCulloch correspondence.

[61] [This statement was prophetic. "The present year" is, in fact, 1951. *Ed.*]

[62] For a good illustration of this *vide* Malthus's "Remarks on Mr. Ricardo's Theory of Profits" in his *Principles of Political Economy* (1st ed.) p. 326.

[63] This point is further developed in the "Remarks on Mr. Ricardo's Theory of Profits" referred to in the footnote above.

[64] I refer the reader to the whole of Section IX. as a masterly exposition of the conditions which determine the *optimum* of Saving in the actual economic system in which we live.

[65] *Op. cit.* (1st ed.) p. 495.

[66] *Op. cit.* p. 512.

[67] *Op. cit.* pp. 8, 9.

ALFRED MARSHALL

[1] In the preparation of this Memoir (August 1924) I had great assistance from Mrs. Marshall. I have to thank her for placing at my disposal a number of papers and for writing out some personal notes from which I have quoted freely. Alfred Marshall himself left in writing several autobiographical scraps, of which I have made the best use I could. I prepared in 1924 a complete bibliographical list of the writings of Alfred Marshall, which was printed in the *Economic Journal*, December 1926, and reprinted in *Memorials of Alfred Marshall* (edited by A. C. Pigou, 1925).

[2] By his third wife, Mary Kitson, the first child he christened in his parish, of whom he said in joke that she should be his little wife, as she duly was twenty years later.

[3] This is one of many stories of his prodigious strength which A. M. was fond of telling—how, for example, driving a pony-trap in a narrow Devonshire lane and meeting another vehicle, he took the pony out and lifted the trap clean over the hedge. But we come to something more prognostical of Alfred in a little device of William Marshall's latter days. Being in old age heavy and unwieldy, yet so affected with gout as to be unable to walk up and down stairs, he had a hole made in the ceiling of the room in which he usually sat, through which he was drawn in his chair by pulleys to and from his bedroom above.

[4] Thus Alfred Marshall was third cousin once removed to Ralph Hawtrey, author of *Currency and Credit*. A. M. drew more from the subtle Hawtreys than from the Reverend Hercules.

⁵ "Do you know that you are asking me for £200?" said the Director; but he gave it.

⁶ Mrs. Marshall writes: "As a boy, Alfred suffered severely from headache, for which the only cure was to play chess. His father therefore allowed chess for this purpose; but later on he made A. promise never to play chess. This promise was kept all through his life, though he could never see a chess problem in the newspapers without getting excited. But he said that his father was right to exact this promise, for otherwise he would have been tempted to spend all his time on it." A. M. himself once said: "We are not at liberty to play chess games, or exercise ourselves upon subtleties that lead nowhere. It is well for the young to enjoy the mere pleasure of action, physical or intellectual. But the time presses; the responsibility on us is heavy."

⁷ His chief school friends were H. D. Traill, later Fellow of St. John's College, Oxford, and Sidney Hall, afterwards an artist. Traill's brother gave him a copy of Mill's *Logic,* which Traill and he read with enthusiasm and discussed at meals at the Monitors' table.

⁸ Near the end of his life A. M. wrote the following characteristic sentences about his classical studies: "When at school I was told to take no account of accents in pronouncing Greek words, I concluded that to burden my memory with accents would take up time and energy that might be turned to account; so I did not look out my accents in the dictionary; and received the only very heavy punishment of my life. This suggested to me that classical studies do not induce an appreciation of the value of time; and I turned away from them as far as I could towards mathematics. In later years I have observed that fine students of science are greedy of time: but many classical men seem to value it lightly. I will add that my headmaster was a broad-minded man; and succeeded in making his head form write Latin Essays, thought out in Latin: not thought out in English and translated into Latin. I am more grateful for that than for anything else he did for me."

⁹ He was promoted to a Scholarship in the same year.

¹⁰ There is a letter from Dr. Bateson, Master of St. John's, to Dr. Hessey, Headmaster of Merchant Taylors', dated June 15, 1861, announcing this Exhibition, and giving early evidence of the interest which Dr. Bateson—like Dr. Jowett in later days—always maintained in Alfred Marshall. When A. M. applied for the Bristol appointment in 1877, Dr. Bateson wrote: "I have a great admiration for his character, which is remarkable for its great simplicity, earnestness, and self-sacrificing conscientiousness."

¹¹ One of the famous band of Second Wranglers, which includes Whewell, Clerk Maxwell, Kelvin, and W. K. Clifford.

[12] For Dr. Venn's account of early meetings see *Henry Sidgwick: a Memoir*, p. 134.

[13] Printed in *Henry Sidgwick: a Memoir*, p. 137.

[14] He had decided, in 1861, not to take orders.

[15] Mill's *Essays on Religion*, which gave his final opinions, were not published until 1874, after his death.

[16] For a most interesting summary of Sidgwick's attitude in later life, see his *Memoir*, p. 505. Or see the last paragraph of W. K. Clifford's "Ethics of Religion" (*Lectures and Essays*, ii. 244) for another characteristic reaction of Marshall's generation.

[17] In 1836 Sir William Hamilton, having established his genealogy and made good his claim to a baronetcy, had been appointed to the Chair of Logic and Metaphysics at Edinburgh, and delivered during the next eight years the famous lectures which attempted the dangerous task of superimposing influences drawn from Kant and the German philosophers on the Scottish tradition of common sense.

[18] Stephen, *English Utilitarians*, iii. 382.

[19] *Principles* (1st ed.) pp. 3, 4. [20] *Ibid.* [21] *Ibid.*

[22] Rescued by Mrs. Marshall from the waste-paper basket, whither too great a proportion of the results of his mental toil found their way; like his great-great-uncle, the Reverend Richard Marshall, who is said to have been a good poet and was much pressed to publish his compositions, to which, however, he had so great an objection that lest it be done after his death he burnt all his papers.

[23] He was again in Germany, living in Berlin, in the winter of 1870-71, during the Franco-German War.

[24] In a conversation I had with him a few weeks before his death he dwelt especially on Hegel's *Philosophy of History* and the friendly action of Dr. Bateson as finally determining the course of his life. Since J. B. Mayor, the first "Moral Science lecturer" in Cambridge, had held a similar lectureship at St. John's for some time, while the Rev. J. B. Pearson was also a Johnian and a moral scientist, the appointment of another lecturer in the subject was a somewhat unusual step. Henry Sidgwick had been appointed to a lectureship in Moral Science at Trinity in the previous year, 1867; and Venn had come back to Cambridge as a Moral Science lecturer at Caius in 1862.

[25] Mrs. Marshall remembers how in the early seventies at Newnham, Mary Kennedy (Mrs. R. T. Wright) and she had to write for him "a dialogue between Bentham and an Ascetic."

[26] The occasional articles belonging to this period are included in a Bibliography which I printed in the *Economic Journal*, December 1924.

[27] Clifford, who was three years Marshall's junior, came up to Trinity

in 1863, was elected to a Fellowship in 1868, and resided in Cambridge, where his rooms were "the meeting point of a numerous body of friends" (*vide* Sir F. Pollock's Memoir), until 1871.

²⁸ He used to reckon that his necessary expenditure as a bachelor Fellow amounted to £300 a year, including £60 for vacation travel.

²⁹ Miss Paley was one of the small band of five pioneers who, before the foundation of Newnham College, came into residence under Miss Clough in 1871 at 74 Regent Street, which had been taken and furnished for the purpose by Henry Sidgwick. She and Miss Bulley, taking the Moral Sciences Tripos in 1874 as Students of the "Association for Promoting the Higher Education of Women in Cambridge," were the first of the group to take honours at Cambridge.

³⁰ For a week or two Marshall entertained the idea of becoming a candidate for the Esquire Bedellship at Cambridge, as a help towards keeping himself. But "the more I look at the poker," he finally concluded, "the less I like it." He was actually, for a short time, Steward of St. John's.

³¹ A lecture on "Water as an Element of National Wealth," which has been reprinted, is particularly interesting.

³² In the charming little obituary of Jowett which Marshall contributed to the *Economic Journal* (vol. iii. p. 745), he wrote: "He took part in most of the questions which agitate modern economists; but his own masters were Plato and Ricardo. Everything that they said, and all that rose directly out of what they said, had a special interest for him. . . . In pure economics his favourite subject was the Currency, and he took a keen interest in the recent controversy on it. His views were generally conservative; and he was never converted to bimetallism. But he was ready to follow wherever Ricardo had pointed the way; and in a letter written not long ago he raised the question whether the world would not outgrow the use of gold as its standard of value, and adopt one of those artificial standards which vex the soul of Mr. Griffen."

³³ Jowett always remained very fond of Alfred Marshall, and, after the Marshalls left Oxford, it was with them that he generally stayed on his visits to Cambridge.

³⁴ What a contrast to Marshall's *Principles* the drafting of this famous book presents! Mill's *Political Economy* was commenced in the autumn of 1845 and was ready for the press before the end of 1847. In this period of little more than two years the work was laid aside for six months while Mill was writing articles in the *Morning Chronicle* (sometimes as many as five a week) on the Irish Peasant problem. At the same time Mill was occupied all day in the India Office. (See Mill's *Autobiography*.)

³⁵ Jevons' *Serious Fall in the Value of Gold ascertained, and its Social Effects set forth,* had appeared in 1863 and his *Variation of Prices*

in 1865, from which two papers the modern method of Index Numbers takes its rise. His main papers on the Periodicity of Commercial Crises were later (1875-79).

³⁶ For a complete bibliography of early hints and foreshadowings of mathematical treatment see the appendix of Irving Fisher's edition of Cournot's book. Fleeming Jenkin's brief paper of 1868 was not generally available until 1870, but was certainly known to Marshall about that date (see his review of Jevons in *The Academy*, 1872). Jevons' *Brief Account of a General Mathematical Theory of Political Economy* was presented to the Cambridge Meeting of the British Association in 1862 and published in the *Statistical Journal* in 1866; but this paper does not actually contain any mathematical treatment at all. Its purpose is to adumbrate the idea of "the co-efficient of utility" (*i.e.* final utility), and to claim that this notion will allow the foundations of economics to be worked out as a mathematical extension of the hedonistic calculus.

³⁷ This was the age of Clerk Maxwell and W. K. Clifford, when the children of the Mathematical Tripos were busy trying to apply its apparatus to the experimental sciences. An extension to the moral sciences was becoming obvious. Boole and Leslie Ellis, a little earlier, were an important influence in the same direction. Alfred Marshall, in 1876, trained as he was, an intimate of W. K. Clifford, turning his attention to Ricardo, was *bound* to play about with diagrams and algebra. No other explanations or influences are needed.

³⁸ Particularly §§ 6-8, which were added by Mill to the third edition (1852).

³⁹ This account was contributed by him to a German compilation of Portraits and Short Lives of leading Economists.

⁴⁰ 1867.

⁴¹ Preface to first edition of *Principles of Economics*.

⁴² See, particularly, (1) his footnote relating to his use of the term "marginal" (Preface to *Principles,* 1st ed.), where he implies that the word was suggested to him, as a result of reading von Thünen (though von Thünen does not actually use the word), *before* Jevons' book appeared (in his British Association paper of 1862, published in 1866, Jevons uses the term "coefficient of utility"), that, after its appearance, he temporarily deferred to Jevons and adopted his word "final" (*e.g.* in the first *Economics of Industry*), and that later on he reverted to his original phrase as being the better (it is also an almost literal equivalent of Menger's word "Grenznutzen"); and (2) his footnote to bk. iii. chap. vi. § 3 on Consumers' Rent (or Surplus), where he writes (my italics): "The notion of an exact measurement of Consumers' Rent was published by Dupuit in 1844. But his work was forgotten; and the first to publish a clear analysis of the relation of total to marginal (or

final) utility in the English language was Jevons in 1871, when he had not read Dupuit. The notion of Consumers' Rent was suggested *to the present writer* by a study of the mathematical aspects of demand and utility under the influence of Cournot, von Thünen, and Bentham."

[43] I believe that Marshall only wrote two reviews in the whole of his life—this review of Jevons in 1872, and a review of Edgeworth's *Mathematical Psychics* in 1881.

[44] The main interest of the review, which is, so far as I am aware, A. M.'s first appearance in print (at thirty years of age), is, perhaps, the many respects in which it foreshadows his permanent attitude to his subject.

[45] P. 166 (3rd ed.).

[46] In the *Note on Ricardo's Theory of Value*, which is, in the main, a reply to Jevons.

[47] How disappointing are the fruits, now that we have them, of the bright idea of reducing Economics to a mathematical application of the hedonistic calculus of Bentham!

[48] The last proposition of *Foreign Trade* (which comes first) is Prop. XIII.; the first of *Domestic Values* is Prop. XVII.

[49] "Chiefly between 1869 and 1873"—see *Money, Credit and Commerce*, p. 330.

[50] See the Preface to the first edition of the *Principles*. Jevons refers to them in the second edition of his *Theory,* published in 1879; and Pantaleoni reproduced much of them in his *Principii di Economia Pura* (1889).

[51] The London School of Economics published a facsimile reprint of these two papers in 1930 as No. 1 in their series of *Reprints of Scarce Tracts in Economic and Political Science.*

[52] Mathematical economics often exercise an excessive fascination and influence over students who approach the subject without much previous training in technical mathematics. They are so easy as to be within the grasp of almost anyone, yet do introduce the student, on a small scale, to the delights of perceiving constructions of pure form, and place toy bricks in his hands that he can manipulate for himself, which gives a new thrill to those who have had no glimpse of the sky-scraping architecture and minutely embellished monuments of modern mathematics.

[53] Professor Planck, of Berlin, the famous originator of the Quantum Theory, once remarked to me that in early life he had thought of studying economics, but had found it too difficult! Professor Planck could easily master the whole corpus of mathematical economics in a few days. He did not mean that! But the amalgam of logic and intuition and the wide knowledge of facts, most of which are not precise, which is required for economic interpretation in its highest form is, quite truly, overwhelmingly difficult for those

whose gift mainly consists in the power to imagine and pursue to their furthest points the implications and prior conditions of comparatively simple facts which are known with a high degree of precision.

⁵⁴ "The argument in the text is never dependent on them; and they may be omitted; but experience seems to show that they give a firmer grasp of many important principles than can be got without their aid; and that there are many problems of pure theory, which no one who has once learnt to use diagrams will willingly handle in any other way."

⁵⁵ "The chief use of pure mathematics in economic questions seems to be in helping a person to write down quickly, shortly and exactly, some of his thoughts for his own use. . . . It seems doubtful whether anyone spends his time well in reading lengthy translations of economic doctrines into mathematics, that have not been made by himself."

⁵⁶ Marshall himself always used them freely in his lectures.

⁵⁷ Two former pupils of Marshall's, Sir Henry Cunynghame and Mr. A. W. Flux, have done something to supply the want. But we still, after fifty years, lack the ideal text-book for this purpose. Professor Bowley's lately published *Mathematical Groundwork of Economics* runs somewhat counter to Marshall's precepts by preferring, on the whole, algebraical to diagrammatic methods.

⁵⁸ Indeed, it is not very clear why he abandoned the publication of this book. Certainly up to the middle of 1877 he still intended to publish it. My father noted in his diary on February 8, 1877: "Marshall has brought me part of the MS. of a book on foreign trade that he is writing, for me to look over." Both Sidgwick and Jevons had also read it in manuscript, and had formed a high opinion of it, as appears from their testimonials written in June 1877, when Marshall was applying for the Bristol appointment. Sidgwick wrote: "I doubt not that his forthcoming work, of which the greater part is already completed, will give him at once a high position among living English economists." And Jevons: "Your forthcoming work on the theory of Foreign Trade is looked forward to with much interest by those acquainted with its contents, and will place you among the most original writers on the science."

⁵⁹ His unsystematic method of lecturing prevented the average, and even the superior, student from getting down in his notes anything very consecutive or complete.

⁶⁰ Professor Irving Fisher has been the first, in several instances, to publish in book-form ideas analogous to those which had been worked out by Marshall at much earlier dates.

⁶¹ The *Economics of Industry* (1879) was not intended to cover this part of the subject and contains only a brief reference to it. The references to the Trade Cycle in this book are, however, important.

[62] I can speak on this matter from personal recollection, since it was only a little later than this (in 1906) that I attended his lectures on Money.

[63] In expounding his "Symmetallism" to the Commissioners he said (Q.9837): "I have a bimetallic hobby of my own. . . . I have had it by me now for more than 10 years"—which brings this particular train of thought back to before 1878.

[64] When I attended his lectures in 1906 he used to illustrate this theory with some very elegant diagrams.

[65] This extract, as well as that given above, is from the manuscript of 1871.

[66] This is Marshall's phrase for what I have called "real balances."

[67] In repeating the substance of this Note to the Indian Currency Committee (1899) he refers in generous terms to the then recent elaboration of the idea in Professor Irving Fisher's *Appreciation and Interest* (1896). See also for some analogous ideas Marshall's first *Economics of Industry* (1879), bk. iii. chap. i. §§ 5, 6.

[68] Entitled *Memorandum as to the Effects which Differences between the Currencies of different Nations have on International Trade*. His illustrations are in terms of English gold and Russian paper roubles; and alternatively of English gold and Indian silver. He argues that a prolonged departure from purchasing power parity (he does not use this term) is not likely except when there is "a general distrust of Russia's economic future, which makes investors desire to withdraw their capital from Russia"—a remarkable prevision of recent events. A portion of this Memorandum was reproduced as the first part of Appendix G of *Money, Credit and Commerce*.

[69] See also, *Money, Credit and Commerce*, pp. 64-67.

[70] Entitled "How far do remediable causes influence prejudicially (a) the continuity of employment, (b) the rates of wages?"

[71] It would almost be better to read the footnotes and appendices of Marshall's big volumes and omit the text, rather than *vice versa*.

[72] The last part of this sentence presumes the adoption of Symmetallism. The second plan is akin to Prof. Irving Fisher's "Compensated Dollar."

[73] In December 1923, after I had sent him my *Tract on Monetary Reform*, he wrote to me: "As years go on it seems to become ever clearer that there ought to be an international currency; and that the—in itself foolish—superstition that gold is the 'natural' representative of value has done excellent service. I have appointed myself amateur currency-mediciner; but I cannot give myself even a tolerably good testimonial in that capacity. And I am soon to go away; but, if I have opportunity, I shall ask newcomers to the celestial regions whether you have succeeded in finding a remedy for currency-maladies." As regards the choice between the advan-

tages of a national and of an international currency I think that
what he wrote in 1887 was the truer word, and that a constant-
value currency must be, in the first instance at least, a national
currency.

[74] *The Present Position of Economics*, 1885.

[75] This is a portmanteau quotation—I have run together non-
consecutive passages. Parts of this lecture were transcribed almost
verbatim in the *Principles*, bk. i. chap. iv.

[76] How Jevons hated Mill, just because he had been compelled to
lecture on Mill's *Political Economy* as a Gospel Text-book!

[77] So far, however, from being out of sympathy with the ideals underlying the Extension Movement (or its modern variant the
W.E.A.), Marshall had been connected with it from the beginning,
and had himself given Extension Courses at Bristol for five years.

[78] So much did the public like it that 15,000 copies had been sold
before it was suppressed.

[79] Its preface mentioned a forthcoming companion volume on the
"Economics of Trade and Finance," which was never written.

[80] Mrs. Marshall writes: "Book III. on Demand was largely thought
out and written on the roof at Palermo, Nov. 1881-Feb. 1882."

[81] It appears in outline in an article written in about two days in
the summer of 1884, when he was staying at Rocquami Bay,
Guernsey. This was published in the *Co-operative Annual* for 1885
under the title "Theories and Facts about Wages," and was reprinted in the same year as an appendix to his paper read before
the Industrial Remuneration Conference.

[82] The following extracts are from some notes he put together sum-
marising his work from 1885 to 1889.

[83] Also, "Work during the summer a good deal interrupted by
making plans for my new house in Madingley Road."

[84] After the first edition this Book was incorporated in Book V. So
that *Value* again became Book VI.

[85] "Rarely in modern times," said the *Scotsman*, "has a man achieved
such a high reputation as an authority on such a slender basis of
published work."

[86] This was the first book in England to be published at a *net* price,
which gives it an important place in the history of the publishing
trade. (See Sir F. Macmillan's *The Net Book Agreement*, 1899, pp.
14-16.) It has been a remarkable example of sustained circulation.
In the first thirty years of its life 27,000 copies were sold, being
throughout at an almost steady rate of 1000 copies a year, exclud-
ing the war. During the next ten years 20,000 copies were sold,
i.e. at the rate of 2000 copies a year. The total number printed up
to the present time (end of 1932) is 57,000.

[87] The suffix Vol. I. was not dropped until the sixth edition in 1910.

[88] Not that Old P. E. was really thus, but this was the journalists'

way of expressing the effect which Marshall's outlook made on them.

[89] Including hints and anticipations in earlier writings; as Professor Edgeworth wrote, reviewing the first edition of the *Principles* (*The Academy*, August 30, 1890): "Some of Professor Marshall's leading ideas have been more or less fully expressed in his earlier book (the little *Economics of Industry*), and in certain papers which, though unpublished, have not been unknown. The light of dawn was diffused before the orb of day appeared above the horizon."

[90] Already in 1872, in his review of Jevons, Marshall was in possession of the idea of the mutually dependent positions of the economic factors. "Just as the motion of every body in the solar system," he there wrote, "affects and is affected by the motion of every other, so it is with the elements of the problem of political economy."

[91] *Principles,* bk. vi. chap. xi. § 5.

[92] *Principles,* bk. vi. chap. xi. § 1.

[93] The vital importance of this distinction to a correct theory of Equilibrium under conditions of increasing return is, of course, now obvious. But it was not so before the *Principles*.

[94] Nevertheless, Professor Edgeworth points out, even "before the publication of the *Principles* Marshall quite understood—what the critics of the doctrine in question have not generally understood, and even some of the defenders have not adequately emphasised—that the said measurement applies accurately only to transactions which are on such a scale as not to disturb the marginal value of money."

[95] *Industry and Trade,* however, is partly devoted to illustrating it. "The present volume," he says in the Preface to that book, "is in the main occupied with the influences which still make for sectional and class selfishness: with the limited tendencies of self-interest to direct each individual's action on those lines, in which it will be most beneficial to others; and with the still surviving tendencies of associated action by capitalists and other business men, as well as by employees, to regulate output, and action generally, by a desire for sectional rather than national advantage."

[96] *Quarterly Journal of Economics,* 1896, vol. xi. p. 129.

[97] Supplemented by the mathematical note in the Appendix.

[98] Strictly, the earliest reference to "elasticity" is to be found in Marshall's contribution "On the Graphic Method of Statistics" to the Jubilee Volume of the *Royal Statistical Society* (1885), p. 260. But it is introduced there only in a brief concluding note, and mainly with the object of showing that a simple diagrammatic measure of elasticity is furnished by the ratio between the two sections into which that part of the tangent to the demand curve which lies between the axes is divided by the point of contact. Mrs.

Marshall tells me that he hit on the notion of elasticity as he sat on the roof at Palermo shaded by the bath-cover in 1881, and was highly delighted with it.

[99] Mill quotes Tooke's *History of Prices* in this connection.

[100] Professor Edgeworth in his article on "Elasticity" in Palgrave's *Dictionary* refers particularly to Mill's *Political Economy*, bk. iii. chap. ii. § 4, and chap. viii. § 2, as representative of the pre-Marshall treatment of the matter. The first of these passages points out the varying proportions in which demand may respond to variations of price; the second treats (in effect) of the unitary elasticity of the demand for money. Professor Edgeworth now adds a reference to bk. iii. chap. xviii. § 5, where Mill deals in substance with the effect of elasticity on the Equation of International Demand. Elsewhere in this chapter Mill speaks of a demand being "more extensible by cheapness" (§ 4) and of the "extensibility of their [foreign countries'] demand for its [the home country's] commodities" (§ 8).

[101] Marshall himself wrote (in his reply to Dr. Cunningham, *Economic Journal,* vol. ii. p. 507): "I once proposed to write a treatise on economic history, and for many years I collected materials for it. Afterwards I selected such part of these as helped to explain why many of the present conditions and problems of industry are only of recent date, and worked it into the chapters in question. But they took up much more space than could be spared for them. So I recast and compressed them; and in the process they lost, no doubt, some sharpness of outline and particularly of statement."

[102] Dr. Clapham writes: "In reading the Appendices to *Industry and Trade* I was very much impressed with Marshall's knowledge of economic history since the seventeenth century, as it was known thirty years ago, *i.e.* at the time of the controversy. I feel sure that at that time he understood the seventeenth to nineteenth centuries better than Cunningham, and he had—naturally—a feeling for their quantitative treatment to which Cunningham never attained."

[103] As one intelligent reviewer remarked (*The Guardian,* October 15, 1890): "This book has two aspects. On the one hand, it is an honest and obstinate endeavour to find out the truth; on the other hand, it is an ingenious attempt to disclaim any credit for discovering it, on the ground that it was all implicitly contained in the works of earlier writers, especially Ricardo." But most of them were taken in. The following is typical (*Daily Chronicle,* July 24, 1890): "Mr. Marshall makes no affectation of new discoveries or new departures; he professes merely to give a modern version of the old doctrines adjusted to the results of more recent investigation."

[104] Marshall carried this rather too far. But it was an essential truth

to which he held firmly, that those individuals who are endowed with a special genius for the subject and have a powerful economic intuition will often be more right in their conclusions and implicit presumptions than in their explanations and explicit statements. That is to say, their intuitions will be in advance of their analysis and their terminology. Great respect, therefore, is due to their general scheme of thought, and it is a poor thing to pester their memories with criticism which is really verbal. Marshall's own economic intuition was extraordinary, and lenience towards the apparent errors of great predecessors is treatment to which in future times he will himself have an exceptional claim.

[105] Fashions change! When, nearly thirty years later, *Industry and Trade* appeared, one reviewer wrote (*Athenaeum*, October 31, 1919): "Perhaps its least satisfactory feature is its moral tone. Not because that tone is low—quite the contrary; but because, in a scientific treatise, a moral tone, however elevated, seems altogether out of place."

[106] She lived with them for more than forty years on terms almost of intimacy. Marshall would often extol her judgement and wisdom. He himself designed the small kitchen, like a ship's cabin, in which she dwelt at Balliol Croft. Here Jowett, when he was staying with the Marshalls, visited Sarah to discuss her religious difficulties. Marshall was much loved by his servants and College gyps. He treated them like human beings and talked to them about the things in which he was interested himself.

[107] In the Preface to *Industry and Trade* he wrote: "For more than a decade, I remained under the conviction that the suggestions, which are associated with the word 'socialism,' were the most important subject of study, if not in the world, yet at all events for me. But the writings of socialists generally repelled me, almost as much as they attracted me; because they seemed far out of touch with realities: and, partly for that reason, I decided to say little on the matter, till I had thought much longer. Now, when old age indicates that my time for thought and speech is nearly ended, I see on all sides marvellous developments of working-class faculty: and, partly in consequence, a broader and firmer foundation for socialistic schemes than when Mill wrote. But no socialistic scheme, yet advanced, seems to make adequate provision for the maintenance of high enterprise and individual strength of character; nor to promise a sufficiently rapid increase in the business plant and other material implements of production. . . . It has seemed to me that those have made most real progress towards the distant goal of ideally perfect social organisation, who have concentrated their energies on some particular difficulties in the way, and not spent strength on endeavouring to rush past them."

[108] I have papers which I wrote for him on which his red-ink com-

ments and criticisms occupy almost as much space as my answers.
[100] This book has been frequently reprinted, and revised editions were prepared in 1896 and 1899. 108,000 copies of it have been printed up to date (end of 1932). The book has sold at a steady rate of about 2500 copies a year since it first came out, and after a life of forty years is still maintaining the same rate. In conjunction with the sale of the *Principles* (*vide* p. 181, above), this is a measure of the overwhelming influence which Marshall has exercised over economic education for nearly half a century.

[110] The concluding chapter on "Trade Unions" goes outside the field of the *Principles* and incorporates some material from the earlier *Economics of Industry*.

[111] He had many devoted Indian (and also Japanese) pupils.

[112] They were stolen by a local post-mistress in the Tyrol for the sake of the stamps on the envelope.

[113] Marshall signed, I think, primarily in his capacity as President of the Economics Section of the British Association for 1890, at that year's meeting of which the need for the establishment of an Economic journal had been strongly urged.

[114] The chief difference of opinion, discovered at the outset, regarding the Society's scope, was indicated as follows: "Almost the only question on which a difference of opinion has so far shown itself is whether or not the Association should be open to all those who are sufficiently interested in Economics to be willing to subscribe to its funds. . . . There are some who think that the general lines to be followed should be those of an English 'learned Society,' while others would prefer those of the American Economic Association, which holds meetings only at rare intervals, and the membership of which does not profess to confer any sort of diploma." At the meeting a resolution was carried unanimously, proposed by Mr. Courtney and supported by Professor Sidgwick and Professor Edgeworth, "that any person who desires to further the aims of the Association, and is approved by the Council, be admitted to membership." The wording of the Society's constitution shows some traces of compromise between the two ideas, but in practice the precedent of the American Economic Association has always been followed.

[115] Mr. Bernard Shaw read a paper before the Economics Section of the British Association in 1888, remarking, as Mr. L. L. Price (who was then secretary) relates, that his promotion from the street corner to read a paper to a learned body was a sign of the times. It was of this occasion that Sidgwick wrote: "The Committee had invited a live Socialist, red-hot 'from the streets,' as he told us, who sketched in a really brilliant address the rapid series of steps by which modern society is to pass peacefully into social democracy. There was a peroration rhetorically effective as well as

daring. Altogether a noteworthy performance—the man's name is Bernard Shaw. Myers says he has written books worth reading." (*Henry Sidgwick: a Memoir*, p. 497).

116 At Marshall's lectures in the late eighties, apart from students from other departments and B.A.'s who might be attracted out of curiosity about the subject, there would be a dozen or less Moral Science students and two dozen or less History students.

117 Marshall summarised the history of the matter as follows in his *Plea for the Creation of a Curriculum in Economics* (1902): "In foreign countries economics has always been closely associated with history or law, or political science, or some combination of these studies. The first (Cambridge) Moral Sciences Examination (1851-1860) included ethics, law, history, and economics; but not mental science or logic. In 1860, however, philosophy and logic were introduced and associated with ethics; while history and political philosophy, jurisprudence and political economy formed an alternative group. In 1867 provision was made elsewhere for law and history; and mental science and logic have since then struck the keynote of the Moral Sciences Tripos."

118 For his contentions with Sidgwick about this (and for a characteristic specimen of Sidgwick's delightful and half-humorous reaction to criticism) see *Henry Sidgwick: a Memoir*, p. 394.

119 From his article "The Old Generation of Economists and the New," *Quarterly Journal of Economics*, January 1897.

120 Sidgwick had been finally converted to the idea in 1900, shortly before his death. Marshall's ideals of economic education are set forth in his "Plea for the Creation of a Curriculum in Economics" and his "Introduction to the Tripos in Economics. . . ."

121 "The Economic Movement in England," *Quarterly Journal of Economics*, vol. ii. p. 92.

122 Dr. Jowett took strong exception to this phrase.

123 All his many services to the State were, of course, entirely unpaid.

124 In 1913 he transferred to the University a sufficient capital sum to provide an equivalent income in perpetuity.

125 He always insisted on charging a lower price for his books than was usual for works of a similar size and character. He was a reckless proof-corrector, and he kept matter in type for years before publication. Some portions of *Industry and Trade*, which he had by him in proof for fifteen years before publication, are said to constitute a "record." He never regarded books as income-producing objects, except by accident.

126 He still continued, up to the time of the war, to see students in the afternoons—though perhaps former pupils (by that time young dons) more than newcomers.

127 "Those," he wrote to *The Times* on August 22, 1914, "who know and love Germany, even while revolted at the hectoring militarism

which is more common there than here, should insist that we have no cause to scorn them, though we have good cause to fight them. . . . As a people I believe them to be exceptionally conscientious and upright, sensitive to the calls of duty, tender in their family affections, true and trusty in friendship. Therefore they are strong and to be feared, but not to be vilified."

[128] Cf. the remarkable footnote to p. 101 of *Money, Credit and Commerce.*

[129] 5000 copies were sold immediately, and 9000 had been printed altogether by the end of 1932.

FRANCIS YSIDRO EDGEWORTH

[1] *Memoirs of Richard Lovell Edgeworth,* vol. i. p. 15, where many entertaining stories may be found of Edgeworth's forbears. This Francis has to-day no representatives in the male line in the Old World.

[2] His last wife, F. Y. Edgeworth's grandmother, under whose roof at Edgeworthstown he lived for the first twenty years of his life, survived until 1865, a hundred and twenty-one years after her husband's birth and her own ninety-sixth year.

[3] The eldest son of Richard Lovell, after being educated on Rousseau principles in early youth, emigrated to America and predeceased his father, who cut his American grandsons out of the estates. I am told that there are Edgeworths in the United States to-day who claim descent from this son.

[4] He was ashamed, and not proud, of his years, and enjoined on me most seriously to make no reference in the *Economic Journal,* as I had desired to do, to his eightieth birthday, on the ground that he did not like to be connected with suggestions of senility and incapacity. His was:

> An age that melts in unperceiv'd decay
> And glides in modest innocence away.

[5] Edgeworth's father Frank was, in fact, the hero of several of Maria's tales. But (according to T. Mozley, *Reminiscences,* vol. i. p. 41) "Maria Edgeworth cared for the actual Frank as much as he cared for her, which was so little that it was better not to mention her." F. Y. E. remembered his Aunt Maria as "a very plain old lady with a delightful face" (*Black Book of Edgeworthstown,* p. 244). He was four years old when she died.

[6] T. Mozley's account of him (*Reminiscences,* p. 41) is as follows: "He was a little fair-haired, blue-eyed, pale-faced fellow, ready and smooth of utterance, always with something in his head and on his tongue, and very much loved in a small circle at Charter-

house. With a fertile imagination and with infinite good-nature he would fall in with any idea for the time and help you on with it. . . . At school he was on Perpetual Motion, so often the first round in the ladder that leads nowhere."

[7] *Reminiscences,* vol. i. p. 52.

[8] Hare's *Sterling,* p. lxxiv.

[9] Carlyle, *loc. cit.*

[10] His great-grandfather was Daniel Augustus Beaufort, the son of a French Huguenot refugee. A genealogical record of the Beaufort family and of the Edgeworths connected with them will be found in *The Family of the Beaufort in France, Holland, Germany, and England,* by W. M. Beaufort, printed for private circulation in 1886.

[11] Mrs. A. G. Butler and her daughter, Miss C. V. Butler, to whom I am much indebted for some of the foregoing particulars.

[12] Like his grandfather before him, as Maria Edgeworth records.

[13] A list of twenty-five books and papers, published between 1877 and 1887, is to be found in an Appendix to his *Metretike.* I have re-corded twenty-nine items, which bear on the Theory of Probability, ranging between 1883 and 1921 and partly overlapping with the above, in the bibliographical appendix to my *Treatise on Probability.* Thirty-four papers on Economics and seventy-five reviews are reprinted in his *Papers relating to Political Economy.* The Royal Statistical Society has published a Memoir by Prof. A. L. Bowley on *Edgeworth's Contributions to Mathematical Statistics* at the end of which there is an annotated bibliography covering seventy-four papers and nine reviews.

[14] A paper entitled "Hedonical Calculus," which is reprinted in *Mathematical Psychics,* had appeared meanwhile in *Mind,* 1879.

[15] In 1932 a facsimile reprint of this book was issued in the London School of Economics Series of *Reprints of Scarce Tracts.*

[16] *Mathematical Psychics,* p. 78.

[17] In his early adherence to Utilitarianism Edgeworth reacted back again from his father's reaction against Maria Edgeworth's philos-ophy in these matters. Mozley (*op. cit.*) records of Frank Edgeworth that "he showed an early and strong revolt against the hollowness, callousness, and deadness of utilitarianism."

[18] I refer to Edgeworth's first contribution to the *Statistical Journal* (1883), "The Method of ascertaining a Change in the Value of Gold." This was followed by the well-meaning memoranda pre-sented to the British Association in 1887, 1888, and 1889, and a long series of articles thereafter, several of which are reprinted in his *Collected Papers,* vol. i.

[19] *On the Relations of Political Economy to War, The Cost of War, Currency and Finance in Time of War,* and *A Levy on Capital.* None of these is amongst his best work.

[20] The difficulty of his articles was often enhanced by the fact that they were packed with misprints, especially in the symbolic parts.

[21] He invented and attached much importance to what he termed a law of diminishing returns in the remuneration of articles, by which the rate falls after ten pages have been exceeded and sinks to zero after twenty pages.

F. P. RAMSEY

[1] *The Foundations of Mathematics.* By F. P. Ramsey. Kegan Paul. 1931.

[2] Published by Messrs. Kegan Paul in 1931 under the editorship of Mr. R. B. Braithwaite. I am indebted to the publishers and the editor for permission to reproduce here the passages which follow.

[3] *The Foundations of Mathematics,* pp. 263, 264. In these quotations there are small omissions here and there which I have not in every case indicated. I hope readers will be led on to consult the full text of the original.

[4] *Op. cit.* pp. 267-69.

[5] "What I believe."

WILLIAM STANLEY JEVONS

[1] I have, of course, drawn freely on the main source for Jevons's life —his *Letters and Journal* edited by his wife. I am also much indebted for information to his son, H. S. Jevons, who is a member of our Council to-day.

[2] "With Step so majestic the *Snail* did advance,
And promis'd the Gazers a Minuet to dance.
But they all laugh'd so loud that he pulled in his Head,
And went in his own little Chamber to bed."

Written to amuse his own children, it was published in 1807, sold 40,000 copies in the first year and was popular for at least three-quarters of a century after that.

[3] *The Coal Question,* p. xviii.

[4] The influence of his scientific training on his approach to economics, statistics and logic was recognized by his election (in 1872) as a Fellow of the Royal Society—the first economist so elected, I think, since Sir William Petty, and followed only by Giffen and Palgrave.

[5] *Letters and Journal,* p. 23.

[6] *The Coal Question,* p. 149.

[7] *Op. cit.,* p. 150.

[8] *Op. cit.,* p. 149.

9 *Op. cit.,* pp. 150, 151, slightly abridged.

10 *Op. cit.,* p. 154.

11 *A Serious Fall in the Value of Gold ascertained, and its Social effects set forth, with two Diagrams.*

12 Fawcett quoted it in an address to the British Association, and Cairnes wrote to *The Times* about it. Jevons records that the *Economist* (*semper idem*) "has been induced to notice the subject in a cautious manner, and, though attributing to me some exaggeration of the matter, comes over to my conclusion substantially." *Letters and Journal,* p. 191.

13 "I have just received the bill for my pamphlet on Gold, the total cost of printing, advertising, etc., is £43, and the offset by sales only £10; only seventy-four copies seem to have been sold as yet, which is a singularly small number." (Letter of July 24, 1863, *Letters and Journal,* p. 188.)

14 *Letters and Journal,* p. 181.

15 *The Coal Question* was published (as were nearly all his subsequent books) by Macmillan, whose treatment of the young and unknown author should serve as a model of promptness to all succeeding generations of publishers. Jevons's entry in his notebook is as follows: "First attention given to the subject in 1861 or 1862. Inquiry commenced in January 1864. Chiefly carried out at Museum Library, June and July 1864. Writing completed before Christmas. Transmitted to Mr. Macmillan about 28th December. Accepted 6th January, 1865. Published during the week 24th and 30th April, 1865." *Letters and Journal,* p. 203.

16 *Loc. cit.,* p. 215.

17 *Loc. cit.,* p. 219.

18 *Loc. cit.,* p. 226.

19 *Loc. cit.,* p. 222.

20 *The Coal Question,* p. 179.

21 Prof. Gregory has lately recorded the similar propensity of Edwin Cannan.

22 Reprinted in *Investigations in Currency and Finance.*

23 The *Charts of Trade,* mentioned by Jevons in the passage quoted in the footnote to p. 272 below, was doubtless Playfair's *Commercial and Political Atlas,* published in 1786.

24 He had published in Waugh's *Australian Almanac* for 1859, "Some Data concerning the Climate of Australia and New Zealand," a paper over fifty pages in length, which is best described by his closing words: "My object has been to present in an available form such accurate numerical data as are attainable, and secondly, to group together general information as to the winds, rains, rivers, floods, the geographical features of the country, and the meteorological circumstances of this part of the globe, so as to show what

remarkable problems have to be solved, and what interesting connections of cause and effect may ultimately be traced and proved."
(*Letters and Journal,* p. 112.)

[25] *Op. cit.,* p. 4.

[26] *Investigations,* p. 16.

[27] As was habitual with Jevons, he took great interest in discovering and recording the work of his precursors.

[28] *Op. cit.,* p. 17.

[29] *Investigations in Currency and Finance,* p. 96.

[30] Jevons's own italics.

[31] *Op. cit.,* p. 28.

[32] This parenthesis had been originally a part of the *Statistical Atlas* which he had been working at in 1861. In a letter to his brother (April 7, 1861) he wrote: "The chief interest of the work will be in the light thrown upon the commercial storms of 1793, 1815, 1826, 1839, 1847, 1857, etc., the causes of which will be rendered more or less apparent. I find that the number of Acts of Parliament, the number of patents, and the number of bricks manufactured, are the best indications of an approaching panic, which arises generally from a large investment of labour in works not immediately profitable, as machinery, canals, railways, etc. It is truly curious how well the curve of *bricks produced* shows this, bricks and mortar being the most enduring form of product. Most of the statistics, of course, are generally known, but have never been so fully combined or exhibited *graphically.* The statistics of patents, and some concerning literature, will be quite new. The mode of exhibiting numbers by curves and lines has, of course, been practised more or less any time on this side the Deluge. At the end of last century, indeed, I find that a book of *Charts of Trade* was published, exactly resembling mine in principle; but in statistics the method, never much used, has fallen almost entirely into disuse. It ought, I consider, to be almost as much used as *maps* are used in geography." (*Letters and Journal,* pp. 157, 158.)

[33] *Letters and Journal,* p. 199.

[34] In addition to what I have recorded, his *Pure Logic, or the Logic of Quality apart from Quantity, with Remarks on System and on the Relation of Logic and Mathematics* was published in 1863.

[35] His paper *On Condition of the Gold Coinage of the United Kingdom, with reference to the question of International Currency,* read before the Statistical Society in 1868, is of secondary importance, though ingenious and laborious.

[36] *Investigations,* p. 206.

[37] *Op. cit.,* p. 195.

[38] *Op. cit.,* p. 195.

[39] *Op. cit.,* p. 204.

[40] *Op. cit.*, p. 207. The paper was reprinted posthumously in the *Investigations in Currency and Finance.*

[41] Mr. J. C. Ollerenshaw had explained in a communication to the Manchester Statistical Society in 1869 "that the secret of good trade in Lancashire is the low price of rice and other grain in India" (*op. cit.*, p. 236).

[42] *Op. cit.*, p. 235.

[43] Already in 1869 (in his Inaugural Address to the Manchester Statistical Society) Jevons had adopted Mills's theory of the trade cycle.

[44] *Op. cit.*, pp. 203-4.

[45] *Op. cit.*, p. 226.

[46] *Op. cit.*, pp. 239-40.

[47] Whilst this is now believed to be the *average* interval, it is not a uniform one; and over the limited period which Jevons had particularly examined the average interval actually was, as he believed, about 10.45 years.

[48] *The Sun's Heat and Trade Activity,* supplemented by his paper on "The Causes of Fluctuations of Industrial Activity and the Price-level," *Statistical Journal* (1933), vol. XCVI, pp. 545-605.

[49] Published in articles in the *Economic Journal* in 1920 and 1921 and in the *Statistical Journal* in 1922. In the discussion at the Statistical Society serious objections were raised by Mr. Yule and others to the further analysis of the (apparent) 15.2-years period.

[50] In December 1862 he wrote in his Journal: "I thought what I did very clever then (*i.e.* in Sydney), but it seems foolishness to me now and my first efforts at a theory of economy look strange beside the theory which has gradually opened before me."

[51] *Letters and Journal,* p. 151.

[52] *Loc. cit.*, p. 169.

[53] Reprinted (as an appendix) in the fourth edition of Jevons's *Theory of Political Economy,* edited by H. S. Jevons in 1911.

[54] *Statistical Journal* (1866), vol. XXIX, pp. 283, 284.

[55] *Loc. cit.*, p. 286.

[56] *Loc. cit.*, p. 287.

[57] In editing the fourth edition of *The Theory,* p. lvii.

[58] This note (as nearly as I can decipher it—written, as usual, on the back of an old envelope) runs as follows:—

"In regard to this & certain other essays of Professor Fleeming Jenkin, it seems desirable that I should make the following explanation, to prevent misapprehension. My theory was originally read at the Brit. Assoc. in 1862, & printed in the Stat Journal in 1867 (*sic*). In March 1868 Prof Jenkin wrote an article for the Br. Quarterly Review (*sic*) in which he restated (?) . . . the law of supply & demand in math language. He courteously sent a copy to me and requested my opinion thereon; in replying I sent a copy of the paper mentioned above, & a correspondence ensued concerning the correctness of the theory, in the course of which curves were used in illustrations by both parties.

In 1870 appeared Prof. Jenkin's 'Graphic Illustration (sic)' in which no reference is made to my previous (?).

Partly in consequence of this I was led to write & publish the Theory in 1871.

In 1872 Prof. Fleeming Jenkin published in the Proceedings of the Roy Soc Edin (?)."

[59] *Theory of Political Economy,* p. 164.

[60] *Theory of Political Economy* (4th ed.) p. 223.

[61] Seven years passed before it had sold 1,000 copies.

[62] *Memorials of Alfred Marshall,* p. 94.

[63] *Loc. cit.,* p. 95.

[64] *Loc. cit.,* p. 99.

[65] *Letters and Journal,* p. 309.

[66] *Loc. cit.,* p. 311 (in the same letter as that from which the immediately preceding quotation is taken).

[67] *Vide* pp. 154-5 in the present volume.

[68] When *The Economics of Industry,* by Alfred and Mary Marshall, was published in 1879, the authors sent Jevons a copy, which is now in the possession of his son. At the beginning and at the end Jevons has pasted in letters from Marshall. In the first of these, printed in *Memorials of Alfred Marshall,* p. 371, Marshall speaks of "the results of abstract quantitative reasoning in Economics of which I recognize in you the chief author." The second responds to Jevons's acknowledgment of the book and begins: "My dear Jevons, My wife and I have often wondered what you would think of our book; we were more anxious for your good opinion of it than for anyone else's. . . ." When Marshall applied for an appointment at Bristol (1877), Jevons furnished him with a testimonial (*vide* p. 161 above).

[69] *Letters and Journal,* p. 331.

[70] *Loc. cit.,* p. 408.

[71] Apparently written in 1897.

[72] *Memorials of Alfred Marshall,* p. 99. To this may be added Marshall's tribute to Jevons printed by Professor Foxwell in his introduction (p. xliii) to the *Investigations in Currency and Finance,* to the effect that the great body of Jevons's work "will probably be found to have more constructive force than any save that of Ricardo, that has been done during the last hundred years," and that "the pure honesty of Mr. Jevons's mind, combined with his special intellectual fitness for the work, have made them models for all time."

[73] *Letters and Journals*, p. 344.

[74] *Theory of Political Economy* (2nd ed.) p. lvii.

[75] *Letters and Journal*, p. 329.

[76] Cf. the letter to his brother written at this time from which I have quoted above, p. 280.

[77] *Letters and Journal*, p. 154.

[78] This and other information relating to the teaching of Economics at University College has been very kindly supplied to me by Miss C. E. Collet (who was examined by Jevons in 1880 in the philosophical subjects for the London B.A.). She tells me that the sessional examination was confined to the work done during the year under the Professor (Jacob Waley, who was more of a lawyer than an economist), and gave little scope for showing superiority outside this course, whereas the scholarship examination was wider and brought in an external examiner (R. H. Hutton in 1860, Bagehot having been the external examiner in the previous year). The actual papers set are to be found in the U.C.L. Calendars for 1860-1 and 1861-2.

[79] In explaining his methods of teaching at Owens College (*Letters and Journal*, p. 284) he writes: "I have generally followed somewhat the order of subjects in Mill's Pol. Econ. in perfect independence, however, of his views and methods when desirable. In the subject of currency I have always abandoned his book altogether." But this fell far short, I believe, of his venturing to teach the marginal principle and other characteristic doctrines of his own *Theory;* whilst on currency his own outlook did not differ significantly from Mill's. *Cf.* also *Letters and Journals*, p. 409, where many years later (1879) he defended his recommendation of Mill's *Political Economy* for the Bankers' Institute examinations on the ground that "it is one thing to put forward views for rational judgment of competent readers, it is another thing to force these views on young men by means of examinations." Miss Collet tells me that, since Political Economy was a subject only for the London M.A. degree and not for the London B.A., those of Jevons's pupils at Owens College who sat for the London examinations in Political Economy were very few indeed as compared with those who sat in Logic for the B.A. examination, and she argues that Jevons's irritation against Mill was concerned more with his Logic than with his Political Economy. But there can, I think, be little doubt as to the strength of Jevons's hostility to Mill's *Political Economy,* at least equally with his Logic.

[80] Some qualification to the above is suggested by the following note appended by Jevons in his list of his mathematico-economic books: "From about the year 1863 I regularly employed intersecting curves to illustrate the determination of the market price in my lectures

at Owens College." The lecture notes referred to above do, indeed, include a sketch of a demand curve, but the accompanying text contains no reference to the marginal principle.

[81] There are many passages which show Jevons's own awareness of the complex qualities required by an economist. Vide *Letters and Journal*, p. 101 (also pp. 116-18): "*Economy*, scientifically speaking, is a very contracted science; it is in fact a sort of vague mathematics which calculates the causes and effects of man's industry, and shows how it may best be applied. There are a multitude of allied branches of knowledge connected with man's condition; the relation of these to political economy is analogous to the connection of mechanics, astronomy, optics, sound, heat, and every other branch more or less of physical science, with pure mathematics. . . . There are plenty of people engaged with physical science, and practical science and arts may be left to look after themselves, but thoroughly to understand the principles of society appears to me now the most cogent business."

[82] "Why," said Jevons to Foxwell one day, "don't you walk sometimes down Great Portland Street" (then a centre of the secondhand booksellers, especially where it joins the Euston Road, as it is to-day of secondhand cars), "there are few days I don't find something there." And that, Prof. Foxwell tells me, was the beginning. In 1881 he wrote to Prof. Foxwell: "I hear of you at the booksellers' occasionally, and fancy you must be getting a good collection of economic books," a remark which has remained *à propos* any day in the fifty-five years since then.

[83] *Letters and Journal*, p. 397.

[84] *Ibid.*, p. 436.

[85] *Ibid.*, p. 428.

[86] *Op. cit.*, p. 421.

[87] Reprinted in *Methods of Social Reform*, p. 99.

[88] Reprinted in *Methods of Social Reform*.

[89] His essay on *The Use and Abuse of Museums*, reprinted in *Methods of Social Reform*, deserves to be read to-day.

[90] Reprinted in *Methods of Social Reform*.

[91] Kindly supplied to me by Messrs. Macmillan.

[92] The last three of these were published posthumously.

[93] Miss Collet writes to me: "It was (I believe) through Mill's own views that Political Economy was never even an optional subject in the University examinations until after graduation in Arts or Science. From 1835 (when McCulloch retired) to 1853, when Jacob Waley began to lecture, the subject was dropped at University College. Waley lectured until 1866, when Cairnes succeeded him [until 1872; then Leonard Courtney 1872-1875; Jevons 1875-1880; Foxwell 1881-1928]."

[94] *Letters and Journal*, pp. 12, 13 (see also p. 85).

[95] *Ibid.,* p. 96.

[96] *Letters and Journal,* pp. 213-14.

[97] Jevons was an enthusiastic concert-goer who never missed a chance of hearing classical music, an early Wagnerite, an admirer of Berlioz. He had a small organ built into his house at Hampstead.

[98] *Op. cit.,* p. 451.

[99] *Op. cit.,* p. 421.

[100] Also (Miss Collet adds) with Philip Wicksteed. Jevons may have played a significant part in drawing both Wicksteed and Edgeworth to economics. Both had been educated in classics. Edgeworth began his academic work by lecturing on English Language and Literature at Bedford College and on Logic at King's College, and I have no evidence that his interest in economics antedated his contact with Jevons. Wicksteed, Edgeworth and Foxwell may be considered Jevons's offspring, but his contact with all three came some time after they had taken their degrees. The memoir of Jevons in Palgrave's *Dictionary* is by Wicksteed, *q.v.* for W.'s impression of his conversation.

[101] [Reproduced with this essay in the *Journal of the Royal Statistical Society,* vol. XCIX, part III, 1936, facing p. 516.]

[102] At least, there are no extracts from it in the *Letters and Journal* after this date.

[103] *Letters and Journal,* p. 219.

WINSTON CHURCHILL

[1] *The World Crisis, 1916-1918.*

[2] *The World Crisis: the Aftermath.*

[3] I recorded my impressions of this episode soon after the event, but the time to consign them to print is not yet. [They are printed in this edition as "Dr. Melchior: A Defeated Enemy."]

MR. BONAR LAW

[1] This note was written during Bonar's lifetime, on the occasion of his final retirement from office in May, 1923.

DR. MELCHIOR

[1] *Dr. Melchior* was certainly read before January 1932, and probably in the summer of 1931. D. G.

[2] The General Weygand was a dark, suave, pleasant-looking, well-mannered, adroit, efficient, articulate little man of about forty-

five, who seemed a sort of principal private secretary to the Marshal. I do not think I ever saw the Marshal without him. His duties
were multifarious, but he seemed to attend to all of them and was
never flustered. At first I thought he was the Marshal's intellect;
but this was a mistake. He was, however, his mouthpiece; and
supplied his minor deficiencies. I take him to be a Catholic, Jesuit
bred, like his master.

[3] A Sussex farm-house, the home of Clive and Vanessa Bell, near
Lord Keynes's farm-house, Tilton. D. G.

[4] In the manuscript this paragraph was lightly struck out in pencil.
D. G.

MY EARLY BELIEFS

[1] Professor G. E. Moore tells me that he sat next Lawrence in Hall
that night and found nothing to say to him, but that afterwards
Lawrence was introduced to Professor Hardy, the mathematician,
with whom he had a long and friendly discussion. From the moment of Lawrence's introduction to Hardy, the evening was a success. D. G.

THE COUNCIL OF FOUR, PARIS, 1919

[1] He alone amongst the Four could speak and understand both
languages, Orlando knowing only French and the Prime Minister
and the President only English; and it is of historical importance
that Orlando and the President had no direct means of communication.

[2] For the details of this piece of work *vide* the author's *A Revision
of the Treaty*, chap. v.

TROTSKY ON ENGLAND

[1] L. Trotsky, *Where is Britain Going?*

NEWTON, THE MAN

[1] Read by Mr. Geoffrey Keynes at the Newton Tercentenary Celebra-
tions at Trinity College, Cambridge, on 17 July 1946, and therefore
not revised by the author who had written it some years earlier.

THE GREAT VILLIERS CONNECTION

[1] W. T. J. Gun, *Studies in Hereditary Ability*.
[2] 21 April, 1938.

MARY PALEY MARSHALL

[1] This is literally borne out by the parchment certificate of the Tripos results which has been found amongst Mrs. Marshall's papers. It actually records that two examiners placed her in the first class and two in the second, and leaves it at that!
[2] See *Economic Journal*, December 1936, p. 771.
[a] *Ibid.*, December 1942, p. 289.

MERIDIAN BOOKS